VICTORIA'S CROSS

South Africa: A Travel Guide

The Doughboys:
America and the Great War

The Good Soldier:
The Biography of Douglas Haig

VICTORIA'S CROSS

THE UNTOLD STORY OF BRITAIN'S
HIGHEST AWARD FOR BRAVERY

GARY MEAD

Atlantic Books

LONDON

First published in Great Britain in 2015 by Atlantic Books,
an imprint of Atlantic Books Ltd.

Copyright © Gary Mead, 2015

1 2 3 4 5 6 7 8 9

A CIP catalogue record for this book is available from the British Library.

Hardback ISBN: 978 1 843 54269 8
Paperback ISBN: 978 1 843 54270 4
EBook ISBN: 978 1 782 39638 3

Text design by Richard Marston
Printed in Great Britain by TJ International Ltd.

Atlantic Books
An Imprint of Atlantic Books Ltd
Ormond House
26–27 Boswell Street
London
WC1N 3JZ

www.atlantic-books.co.uk

To Freya, Theodora and Odette

Contents

Acknowledgements   ix
List of illustrations   xi
Preface   xiii

1   The Price of Courage   3

2   A Most Grand, Gratifying Day   31

3   Small Wars   66

4   Big War   114

5   Go Home and Sit Still   149

6   Bigger War   184

7   The Integrity of the System   214

Current Military Decorations   249
Select Bibliography   251
Notes   255
Index   305

Acknowledgements

Many people have helped steer this book safely into harbour after a long journey. I wish to thank the staff of the London Library; the National Archives; and the Royal Archives. I particularly thank James Nightingale of Atlantic, who edited it; Angus MacKinnon, formerly of Atlantic, who commissioned it and courageously defended it to his own superiors; Christopher Sinclair-Stevenson, my indefatigable agent and, if I may presume, friend; and finally my family.

Illustrations

1. First presentation of the Victoria Cross by Queen Victoria, in Hyde Park, 26 June, 1856. Original watercolour signed by Orlando Norie, 1832–1901 (*Courtesy of the Anne S. K. Brown Military Collection, Brown University Library*)
2. Prince Albert, after George Baxter, 1804–67 (*Yale Center for British Art, Paul Mellon Collection*)
3. Captain William Cecil George Pechell (*standing, third from right*) and men of the 77th Regiment in their winter dress in the Ukraine, during the Crimean War, *c.* 1855 (*Roger Fenton/Hulton Archive/Getty Images*)
4. Thomas Henry Kavanagh being disguised during the Indian Mutiny, 1857 (*Hulton Archive/Getty Images*)
5. Ethel Grimwood, from *My Three Years in Manipur*, 1891
6. Winston Churchill (*right*) with other captured prisoners of war during the Boer War (*Time Life Pictures/Mansell/The LIFE Picture Collection/Getty Images*)
7. Lord Kitchener, depicted on a poster in 1915
8. Poster showing a flag-draped portrait of Frederick Roberts, 1st Earl Roberts, 1916
9. John 'Jack' Travers Cornwell (© *Imperial War Museum/Robert Hunt Library/Mary Evans*)

10. William Avery Bishop (© *Photo Researchers/Mary Evans*)
11. Women politicians at the House of Commons, London,
    5 December, 1935 (*Central Press/Hulton Archive/Getty Images*)
12. Violette Szabo with her husband Etienne Szabo, *c.* 1940
    (*Popperfoto/Getty Images*)
13. Winston Churchill shakes hands with Wing Commander Johnny
    Johnson during an inspection of French airfields, 30 July, 1944
    (© *Bettman/Corbis*)
14. Dame Margot Evelyn Marguerite Turner by Hay Wrightson
    (© *National Portrait Gallery, London*)
15. Lance Corporal Johnson Beharry poses for photographs at
    the unveiling of a new portrait of him by Emma Wesley at the
    National Portrait Gallery, London, 21 February, 2007 (*Leon Neal/
    AFP/Getty Images*)

Preface

*I may be accused of animus toward the recipients of the Victoria Cross,
to whom I have referred. To this I have only to say that they are one and all
personally unknown to me, and that I believe they are as much deserving of
the honour as a great many men who have not obtained it, while, on the other
hand, it is an unquestionable fact that there are hundreds of officers who have
not got the order, who are much more entitled to it than those who have it.*[1]

LIEUTENANT-GENERAL H. J. STANNUS

Hundreds of books have been published about the Victoria Cross,
most a mélange of train-spotting and hero worship, compendiums
of deeds of derring-do about one or other of the 1,357 (to date) VC
holders.[2] Others focus on particular battles, branches of the armed
services, regiments, or the VCs of individual Commonwealth nations.
There is also clearly an appetite for arcane minutiae regarding the
Cross; but is it really any longer of significance – was it ever? – that
the metal used to produce a VC comes from Russian, as opposed to
Chinese, cannons captured in the Crimean War?[3] To some extent all
these books rely upon the official citations of individual VCs as published in the *London Gazette*. These citations are a splendid assortment
of painstaking description and creative invention, some quite lengthy

and others very brief. All are carefully crafted, with a suitable veneer of authoritative objectivity, a smoothed-out uniform tone that adopts a lofty indifference to perhaps the most pertinent question: 'Did it really happen like that?' A degree of scepticism is called for when reading these official accounts.

The military is well accustomed to this scepticism. In an effort to demarcate between someone who has done something remarkably brave and someone who 'merely' fulfilled their duty, they have long had their own informal distinction between a 'good' VC and a lesser one in order to winnow out the authentic hero. But what is an authentic hero? Is it someone who calculates the risks and nevertheless stifles their fears; or someone who is so angered that they lose all self-regard? Is it someone who merely does their duty? Or someone who did not act very courageously at all, but to whom granting a VC was a personal or political gesture? The annals of the Victoria Cross have a fair sprinkling of all three types.

There has always existed a written royal warrant, which sets out the terms on which VCs are to be awarded – the rules. But, in a very British fashion, rules are one thing, behaviour often quite different. In the nineteenth century the VC rules were regularly adjusted to accommodate recipients that some establishment figure believed should be recognized by the award of a VC, but who, strictly speaking, were ineligible. Equally important was the need for that figure to possess the clout to push home a revision to the warrant. Senior military officers pushed through some extremely dubious VCs, motivated by personal or political reasons. In the twentieth century this trend for ignoring the terms of the royal warrant, and implementing informal rules of eligibility, was carried even further and given more systematic force, not through a conspiracy but instead by that very British tendency, the following of custom-and-practice. This served to warp still further the definition of exceptional courage, bending it to serve a broad political purpose: that of boosting national morale and encouraging others to emulate the selected act, while simultaneously tightening distribution of the VC significantly, and in ways that utterly diverged from what was laid down in the royal warrant. This book asks how it is that, over more than a century and a half, the VC has mutated from its no doubt flawed but remarkably open and democratic origins, to become the tightly controlled, rather secretive, and undemocratic honour it has become today.

The kind of behaviour that is necessary to gain a VC today is not so much courage as madness; how else to describe a situation where those put forward for a VC are required to have risked a 90 per cent chance of death? When it was first created, the VC went to (usually) brave men. Today it still goes to brave men, but men who are carefully scrutinized for how their story will be judged by the media, assessed to determine if they are the 'right' character, and who are generally investigated far beyond their deeds in battle. Today, men are never chosen for a VC nomination by their fellows, even though they still have the right to do so. Women and civilians are also excluded, even though their eligibility is clearly stipulated in the most recent (1961) royal warrant. This book explores the anomalies, contradictions, injustices and absurdities that infuse the history of this deeply important symbol of British courage, national stoicism and patriotic pride. Ultimately, the distribution of the Victoria Cross is shaped by subjective decisions that intrude all along the route between the act of courage and the final pinning of the honour to a tunic. Courage possibly was never enough; it certainly is not today.

That the VC has deep symbolic meaning for British society cannot be doubted. Not only has the VC played a bit part in thousands of memoirs, novels, plays and poems, featured on postage stamps, in a nineteenth-century board game, in musical compositions, and even on railway engines.[4] It is also, arguably, one of the two most instantly associative icons in the British mind that is attached to war – this cheap little cross represents ultimate courage, as the poppy stands for ultimate sacrifice. The VC, as with the poppy, has thoroughly embedded itself in the psyche, not just of Britain but also that of Commonwealth nations.

To win a VC today is an astonishing rarity which, given we have just been engaged in a war of considerable ferocity lasting thirteen years, is remarkable. You need first of all to be 'lucky' enough to find yourself in a situation where extreme courage is required, and prove yourself capable of demonstrating that degree of courage. Then you need to have the good fortune that your courageous act is noticed by a superior – even better, two superiors. After that, you must hope that your superiors are capable of writing up your brave deed in compelling prose – neither too simple nor too flowery, as the first will attract indifference and the second suspicion. It gets more difficult beyond that stage. You then need to be lucky enough that the write-up of your action gets passed upwards, and is not rejected by one or other higher officers through a chain of ever-more stringent oversight. If you are *exceptionally* lucky, your recommendation for a VC will reach the highest pinnacle, a special committee of very senior armed forces officers. They will then proceed to judge not just your action, your courage, your heroism, but also whether you are the right sort of person to be given a VC, whether the campaign in which you fought was significant enough, whether the quota of operational (battle) decorations justifies a VC in this case, and much else besides. Bravery – even exceptional bravery – is not enough.

Greater transparency is needed regarding the way that VCs are decided. In this day and age, when much is being made of the 'Military Covenant',[5] the 'assertion of an unbreakable bond of identity between soldier, Army and nation', in which armed forces' personnel are being treated with a greater maturity, it is no longer acceptable that the distribution of such a prestigious decoration – the foremost in the land – is arranged by a cabal of faceless uniformed men meeting in secret. A wholesale revision of the intricate system of military decorations and awards is also needed, drastically reducing their number simply because it attempts the impossible – the over-fine gradation of levels of courage. More VCs need to start being awarded, giving them where they are truly merited, and not restricting the numbers artificially, according to some pre-determined quota system that is poorly understood, even by the military. Distributing the VC according to rationing rather than purely on merit was not Queen Victoria's intention and was never done in Victoria's time. They were once freely given out to the brave; today they are as rare as rain in the Sahara, the supply artificially constricted by informal 'rules' of recent invention and unsanctioned by royal warrant. This is an absurd situation for our highest national decoration. For it is a certainty that Britain's armed forces will, one day, again fight a war.

VICTORIA'S
CROSS

1

The Price of Courage

'*Courage is the stuff of good stories.*'
WILLIAM MILLER[1]

'*The award of decorations, even Victoria Crosses, is an arbitrary business.*'
SIR MAX HASTINGS[2]

The Victoria Cross has gripped the public imagination in Britain and
the Commonwealth unlike any other military or civil honour. It is an
emotionally charged emblem, one that reverberates far beyond the
ranks of the armed forces. In today's Britain, with public esteem for
many institutions at an all-time low, Britain's armed forces are a pillar
of national pride, the pinnacle of which is the Victoria Cross.[3] To be a
'hero' today is not what it was, thanks to reckless overuse of the word
in the mass media:

> contemporary gender, sexual, and ethnic politics argues that all
> are entitled to their stories of courage... the modern movement
> has gone farther to 'dephysicalize' courage... by using it loosely to
> congratulate anyone who by his own estimation undertakes some
> struggle for self-realization... Merely being all you can be need hardly

involve courage; more likely it is a less glorious matter of plain hard work.[4]

Yet there remains one national symbol that is untarnished, one universally admired honour that has not been debauched by being lavished on all and sundry: the Victoria Cross. But the VC's survival beyond its current status as an almost impossible aspiration for a gallant person is under threat; the paradox is that, in the effort to preserve its status, the extremely high standard now required to win a VC threatens to turn it into an exclusive graveyard. In the latter half of the nineteenth century, the civil servants responsible for the VC in the War Office occasionally worried that it had been distributed with a degree of abandon by senior military officers and was being given away too freely. Since the Second World War, Britain's senior military figures have consistently tried to prevent the VC from becoming devalued by giving it away too easily. That admirable desire, however, ignores a core principle of one of the VC's originators, Prince Albert, who specified that he wanted the Cross to be 'unlimited in number'. This tension – give the VC away too freely and risk devaluing it, or restrict it too tightly and make it almost impossible to win – remains at the heart of the decoration. Prince Albert's thoroughly democratic view of the Cross, with a clear process of adjudication, has been lost; instead, the VC has become a remote symbol, entangled in bureaucracy and subject to all manner of political considerations, none of which are ever made explicit.

On the contemporary battlefield, where death is often by remote control, and hand-to-hand combat increasingly rare, the likelihood is that very few VCs will be won in the future, for the simple reason that individual combatants will have a diminishing chance of demonstrating astonishing gallantry. The understandable concern to preserve the status of Britain's most prestigious decoration has led to an inexorable rise in the human price of winning the Cross; for years there has been an informal stipulation that, to be eligible for a VC, a candidate must have incurred a 90 per cent risk of death. This is the first of several puzzles that will crop up in this book. The 1856 royal warrant which established the VC made no reference to the level of risk that needed to be incurred; nor is there anything about the level of personal risk in the most recent revision to the warrant, that of 1961. Only custom and practice – both notoriously amorphous – dictates the 90 per cent risk-of-death requirement. Moreover, there is no objective means of assessing this percentage; nor could there be. It comes down to a subjective rule of thumb – did so-and-so *almost* die? How close to death is 'almost'? If we place the VC within a broad historical context, it becomes clear that the pendulum has swung too far in one direction. Over more than 150 years, the VC has mutated from being available for a brave but relatively innocuous act, to a position where it is almost synonymous with death.

In 1856 the VC statutes were thought to have been set in stone, but the granite turned out to be jelly. A flurry of adjustments and amendments were made to those statutes in the years following 1856, making room for cases that were strictly ineligible. Some of the changes were not even formally embodied in statute until long after they were implemented, perhaps the most profound being in 1907, when Edward VII, under private, military and media pressure, abruptly changed his mind and ruled that the VC could, after all, be awarded posthumously. At the stroke of a pen he granted permission for the relatives of six dead soldiers to receive the Cross, even though he feared this would open the floodgates and encourage lobbying by families anxiously seeking a Cross for a dead relative. The entire First World War was fought in a state of uncertainty as to whether VCs could be bestowed posthumously; many were, but only because there was nothing precise in the statutes preventing it. In 1920 posthumous VCs were formally accepted in a thoroughgoing revision of the VC statutes.[5]

This kind of muddle recurs throughout the VC's history. Confusion concerning the rules and regulations of the VC is one thing, injustice another. Families who believe that justice has not been done for courageous but long-dead relatives have in some cases pursued the VC for many years. This kind of pressure usually meets with stiff resistance from government and military. There is great institutional reluctance to reopen cases where a VC might have been justified, but was not awarded; the VC's statutes are silent on retrospective posthumous VC awards. The authorities understandably fear opening up old cases, as incontrovertibly convincing evidence of exceptional courage may be lacking after the passage of time, and setting a precedent is always a concern. Yet the number of obvious cases of exceptional gallantry that, for whatever reason, were not considered for a VC at the time are very few, and to reconsider them today would not usher in a rush of similar claims. There are very few outstanding cases where a retrospective VC might be considered not only reasonable, but an instance of justice delayed.[6]

There is, in any case, a good precedent for the retrospective recognition of military courage: the belated granting of battle honours to British regiments that can be displayed on their colours, drums and other regimental regalia. Such honours, which have considerable symbolic significance, are proudly displayed by regiments. Yet, like the VC, their distribution has always had a somewhat random quality, depending largely on the persuasive powers of the regimental commanding officer. Some battle honours commemorate ignoble defeats while others record memorable victories. By 1880 some regiments with more than a century of good and loyal service still lacked a battle honour, an indignity that offended their regimental colonels. In 1882 the government set up a committee, chaired by Major General Sir Archibald Alison, to investigate anomalies in the distribution of battle honours. As a result of its recommendations, battle honours were retrospectively awarded to regiments that had fought as far back as the Battles of Dettingen in 1743 and Quebec in 1759. A subsequent committee of 1909 looked into the same matter and went back to the seventeenth century, exhuming battles thought worth commemorating on regimental colours.[7] The Alison committee and its successor are today largely forgotten, but it's clear that the authorities were once prepared to make retrospective judgements regarding courage and honour – and in 1882 saw no problem in setting a precedent.

The clearest deserving cases for retrospective posthumous VC awards concern the men and women of Special Operations Executive (SOE) who fought and died, often in hideous circumstances while displaying the utmost courage, during the Second World War. It is often argued that female SOE agents were ineligible for VC recommendations as they were not 'really' soldiers: their military commissions were only temporary or honorary. It is surprising that this canard has gained such wide currency as, under the terms of the 1920 VC warrant, women and civilians, if under military command at the time of their deed, were (and remain) entitled to be considered for the VC. Moreover, five civilians were awarded the VC in the nineteenth century – against the wishes of some War Office civil servants, establishing a precedent that ought not to have been neglected. No civilian – or woman – has been considered for a VC in the twentieth century, or in the twenty-first, as yet. The VC's statutes were last adjusted in 1961; they need revisiting in the twenty-first century. If to win a VC marks a person as being truly exceptional, how bitter is it be to be denied one, how long a struggle can be waged by families, friends or communities angry at an alleged Victoria Cross injustice. For as many tales as there are of remarkable courage that actually succeeded in winning a Victoria Cross, there are just as many concerning equally deserving candidates, which were overlooked at the time and remain blocked today.

Ordinary Seaman Teddy Sheean enlisted in the Royal Australian Naval Reserve in April 1941. In November 1942 Sheean was with HMAS *Armidale*, a corvette on active duty, steaming close to Timor, north of Australia. On 1 December 1942 *Armidale* was attacked by Japanese aircraft and hit by two torpedoes and a bomb. As *Armidale* started listing, the order to abandon ship was sounded. Panicking men clambered into lifeboats or jumped into the water, while Japanese aircraft returned to machine-gun them. Several eyewitnesses saw Sheean try to free a lifeboat from its fixings, as the planes swooped down yet again, injuring Sheean. Despite his wounds, he was observed scrambling across the tilted deck and strapping himself into the seat of an anti-aircraft gun, which he began firing at the attacking Japanese aircraft, shooting one down. Sheean remained at his post, firing his gun as the ship and he slipped beneath the waves; a more inspirational example of supreme self-sacrifice is difficult to imagine. Sheean was Mentioned in Despatches (MiD), then the lowliest of all military honours in the British and Commonwealth forces. Apart from the VC, MiD was at that time the only available posthumous decoration. The pressure to obtain a retrospective posthumous VC for Sheean has, over the years since his death, been fairly consistent, but has always run into strong resistance from the authorities. His case is not helped by the fact that on 15 January 1991 Australia gained the right to award its own VC; in 1942 Sheean would technically have been eligible for an 'Imperial' VC, i.e. a VC handed out from London, as Australia was at that time a dominion. An opportunity to show magnanimity towards Sheean was declined in February 2013, when a two-year, taxpayer-funded public tribunal in Australia rejected his claim (along with twelve others) for a retrospective VC.[8] The tribunal refused to grant retrospective VCs, not because the claims were suspect, but because that would undermine the 'integrity of the system'. In its summary, the tribunal resorted to legal technicalities to avoid granting retrospective VCs:

The VC for Australia, created by letters Patent, replaces the Imperial VC in the Australian system and has the same eligibility requirements. The VC for Australia is intended to be held in the same standing and value as the Imperial VC. It is no longer possible for the Australian government to recommend honours and awards in the Imperial honours and awards system. Specifically, the government cannot recommend to the Queen the award of an Imperial VC.[9]

The report quoted Professor Bill Gammage, historian at the Australian National University, who made the following comment on all disputed cases, not just Sheean's: 'The award of the VC has always been imperfect. The requirement to have officers or more than one independent witness makes chance a factor, as does reliance on written recommendations.'

The correction of possible past injustice is always fraught, and usually there are good arguments on both sides. Yet retrospective posthumous pardons for wrongly convicted murderers, exonerations for those convicted of criminal acts that society no longer regards as crimes, or apologies for things that were not previously regarded as unjust but which are today, such as slavery, are now a regular occurrence. The VC should be no different. Arguments based on floodgates, integrity of the system and so forth are weak; individual cases could be assessed by a standing committee of retired military officers, military historians and experts in military honours. Formally denying the VC to individuals such as Sheean will continue to court controversy. That it was difficult to create rules covering all possible cases that might be considered or recommended for the VC naturally did not trouble Queen Victoria or Prince Albert, the creators of the Cross. As it transpired, civilian administrators of the VC's statutes in its early days did their best to interpret the wording of the original 1856 warrant and to apply strict rulings, but senior field officers flouted those rules with scant regard for what the VC warrant actually said.

Teddy Sheean probably merited a VC; but the overall action, the context in which he displayed his courage, was relatively insignificant and no one in authority took a special interest. Had a senior officer written-up Sheean's case with greater flair, or pushed for the Cross, he may well have joined the illustrious ranks of VC holders. Medal citations are official accounts, as Spencer Fitz-Gibbon correctly puts it: 'If the army tells a story in a citation, that story is what we are intended to believe happened during that part of the battle.'[10] A polished and scrupulously worded VC citation, as it finally appears in the *London Gazette*, often conceals months of agonizing in the upper echelons of the armed forces and Whitehall; it is carefully authored by committee and designed to tell a good 'story'. The original recommendation that so-and-so ought to be considered for a VC may be very rough and is just the starting point, stemming as it usually does from a field officer who may lack the kind of eloquence looked for in a VC citation. By the time the initial recommendation has gone up through several layers of officialdom, the original rough edges will have been smoothed. With luck, the caterpillar recommendation might metamorphose into a butterfly citation.

Many VC holders performed astonishingly courageous actions, beyond not just the call of duty but far beyond what most of us believe possible of ourselves, or others. A VC winner joins a relatively small, select band of brothers, all linked by an intangible romantic aura as they are dubbed an unquestionable 'hero'. Almost immediately on its first appearance, the Cross and those who won it were endowed with chivalric qualities, for the snatching of lost regimental colours or the rescue of fallen comrades from certain death, interwoven into a tapestry of unalloyed endeavour. While the rest of us look on VC holders as rare creatures, they usually see themselves as quite ordinary – people who just did their duty. The heraldic landscape that flourished around the VC is populated with tales of inspirational men who did astonishing things against the enemy, be they the stereotypes of nineteenth-century 'Fuzzy-Wuzzies' or twentieth-century Nazis. A staple of the stirring tales told in the Religious Tract Society's *Boy's Own Paper*, the VC frames our sense of what it means to be superlatively courageous in battle. This genre of hero worship made it perfectly reasonable for an 1878 book about the VC to state, without any irony:

> This book is written for Boys... Boys – worthy to be called boys – are naturally brave... a man who has done battle, who has been thrown in the lists, who has been ready to mount and splinter lance again, who in the gaining of experience hast lost nothing of the Boy's boldness – such a man is brave.

This book's avowed purpose was to encourage boys-become-men to risk their lives in battle:

> 'The young fellows,' said an old soldier to the writer, 'are always pushing forward in a battle charge – they are in a mighty hurry to smell powder – *the veterans fall into the rear!*'... But is it better than the Boy's eagerness to be foremost? – is it not – answer, brave hearts – better to die planting the colours on the wall, than to share the spoil which others have won?
>
> This is the leading thought in this book about Soldiers – it is meant to keep alive the bravery of youth in the experience of manhood.[11]

Hero-worshipping of courageous individuals endured well into the twentieth century. In 1959 Macdonald Hastings, father of military historian Sir Max Hastings, told Second World War VC yarns in his book *Men of Glory*.[12] The only difference between the *Boy's Own Paper* and Hastings senior's pulp fiction was that khaki had been substituted for red coats; otherwise the texts are indistinguishable. Neither text speaks of war's underlying reality of brutal, bloody, individual despair.

Early reception of the VC was almost entirely adulatory, as the Victorian press unquestioningly adopted it as a contemporary version of medieval heraldry; a symbol without monetary value, but nevertheless priceless:

> Its intrinsic value! But who can tell the price a soldier puts upon it? He had rather have that piece of bronze on his breast than be made a Knight of the Garter... The Victoria Cross is as much to a soldier as the *gage d'amour* the knight errant in days of chivalry received from his lady love, and swore never to part with... When our soldiers come to value their crosses at threepence each, the price they will fetch at a marine store, we shall not long survive as a nation. There are things – God be thanked – which we *do* love and value more than life itself – things which gold can *not* purchase. The Victoria Cross is one of them.[13]

Patriotism, the encouragement of self-sacrifice and the reinforcement of morale: all were and indeed are served by the VC. As with all mythologies, however, there are realities that sit uneasily alongside the myth. That the VC was born out of a military shambles – one so embarrassing to the civilian and military authorities that old rigidities could no longer be sustained – tends to be overlooked. One of the most remarkable aspects of the VC is how it symbolized a revolution in attitudes towards the British soldier and sailor; the idea that only officers could demonstrate gallantry died under the Russian cannons at Sevastopol in the Crimean War. The hitherto undifferentiated other ranks became individualized, personalized, recognized and feted as national heroes in the British press.

Statistics cannot tell a complete story but they provide some objectivity; they reveal that the distribution of the VC has been extraordinarily erratic. Between 1856 and 1913, the period in which Britain's armed forces were largely engaged in punitive policing expeditions to preserve the empire, 533 VCs were distributed – more than 39 per cent of all VCs. Around 20 per cent of those – 111 – went to actions during the Crimean War, when some 83,000 men formed the British contingent and fought for seventeen months; approximately one Cross per 747 men. In 1857, during the Indian Mutiny, when some 40,000 British regular troops and East India Company soldiers fought rebellious Indian sepoys for around fourteen months, 182 VCs were given out; one Cross for every 219 men. In the First World War around 9 million British and Commonwealth troops were in combat for almost fifty-two months, during which 634 VCs were awarded, or around one Cross per 14,000 men. During the Second World War, when some 8 million British and Commonwealth military personnel served for seventy-two months, 182 VCs were distributed; one Cross for approximately every 44,000 men. Had the same ratio of men to VC been applied in the First and Second World Wars as was seen during the Indian Mutiny, each conflict would have resulted in around 36,500 VCs. This seems a huge number, especially when it is compared to the 1,357 VCs that have been handed out so far; but it is a very small number if compared to the medal distribution of other similarly sized countries. Since 1945, when British armed forces have been involved in several lengthy and large-scale actions, from Korea to Afghanistan, there have been just fourteen VCs; the stream has dried up almost totally. Obviously, it was considerably easier to win a VC in the nineteenth century than in the twentieth. Why?

One explanation is that more medals of a lesser status were created early on in the First World War, giving the military hierarchy more options when it came to recognizing gallantry. But that merely begs the question: why was it thought necessary to invent the Military Cross (1914) and the Military Medal (1916), when perfectly good gallantry decorations already existed in the form of the VC, the Distinguished

Service Order (for officers) and, for other ranks, the Distinguished Conduct Medal? The invention of new awards was justified by a supposed desire to avoid cheapening the VC, as the mechanized mass slaughter of the First World War overwhelmed the authorities with thousands of examples of VC-style heroism. But no one at the time decried the quantities of VCs given for service in the Crimea, or indeed during the Indian Mutiny.

Queen Victoria and Prince Albert tried to adopt an Olympian approach, accepting that senior officers would pluck out examples of individual courage that merited the new Cross wherever they might be, only to have that initial, generous impulse steadily distorted by later monarchs, military officers and politicians, who in varying ways and from different motives sought to bend the rules of the original VC warrant, or more finely grade the definition of courage. The consequence of these subsequent tinkerings with the VC is that for much of its existence the process of adjudicating who does and does not merit the Cross has been extremely muddled; there are numerous examples not just of people such as Sheean being overlooked, but of string-pulling, of Crosses going to individuals who scarcely merited it, and of Crosses being denied to those who obviously deserved them. For General Sir Horace Smith-Dorrien, a fine professional officer who probably should have been in command of the BEF in 1914, having performed a courageous action was not sufficient to gain the Cross; as he wrote in his memoirs, 'Friends at Court' – influential people who could pull strings – were necessary.

The haphazard way in which a VC may or may not be granted has been remarked on many times, and most armed forces personnel understand and accept that the luck of the draw plays a huge part in any VC; but from another perspective – that of protecting the status of one of the few nationally esteemed honours that has not been debauched (such as the Order of the British Empire) or tainted by scandal – such as the Peerage – it leaves a sour taste. The fluctuations in the VC's distribution obviously do not reflect a rise or fall in the courage of the armed forces, but are directly related to an evolving social and political view of what the VC is for and how its distribution should be *managed*. Victoria's desire was that men should be rewarded for exceptional courage; she did not, could not, contemplate a situation in which this process required 'managing'. The current situation is alarming, as the Cross has increasingly been managed almost to death. The more prized the VC has become, the more difficult it has become to win one – and in turn, the more prized it becomes. In 2002 the military historian Sir John Keegan drew the inescapable conclusion from this unfortunate yet avoidable spiral:

> there is concern that Britain's highest award for bravery, the Victoria Cross, will die out. Some of those who wish to see the Victoria Cross survive believe that the medal is becoming ever harder to win, and that to do so requires exposure to almost certain death. Although no such criterion is laid down it is generally believed that a winner must have undergone a 90 per cent risk of death. It is also generally held that the man… must by his action have materially affected the outcome of the engagement.[14]

The 90 per cent death risk has been an informal criterion since at least the 1970s.[15] A Ministry of Defence paper, *Examination of the Standards of Australian Citations for the Award of the Victoria Cross*, considered in the 1970s whether the VC eligibility standard had 'been lowered in recent years' following the award of four VCs – two posthumous – to members of the Australian Army Training Team in Vietnam. The onerous eligibility conditions for a VC were made explicit:

(1) For the most conspicuous gallantry of the highest order in the presence of the enemy. (A guide as to the standard required may be

taken as a 90 per cent possibility of being killed in performing the deed.)

(2) Each recommendation should be accompanied by signed statements of three independent witnesses. A joint signed statement is not permitted.

(3) Posthumous awards may be made.[16]

Keegan was right about the threat to the VC's survival. Since he wrote, just three British VCs have been awarded: two posthumously, to Corporal Bryan Budd in 2006 and Lance Corporal James Ashworth in 2013; the third to Private Johnson Beharry in 2005. Beharry was so badly injured that he was not expected to survive.

Other nations do things differently, although exact comparisons are difficult and invidious and clearly reveal the risks in widely distributing gallantry awards. Germany handed out more than 6 million Iron Crosses during the First World War, and France millions of Médailles Militaires and Croix de Guerre.[17] Arguably, these decorations were highly prized only by the individual who gained them – and sometimes not even then. The USSR exercised much more restraint; between 1934 and 1991 various categories of the Hero of the Soviet Union, the highest military medal of the USSR, were awarded more than 12,700 times. A fairly tight grip has been exercised by the US over the distribution of its foremost military decoration, the Medal of Honor, established in 1862, six years after the VC. Even here, however, more than twice as many Medals of Honor have been distributed than VCs, almost half of those during the American Civil War. Germany and France certainly cheapened their military decorations, while the VC has retained its prestige by being so exceptionally difficult to win. Yet there must be a balance between flinging medals around like confetti and withholding them so tightly that to win them it is necessary to sacrifice life itself.

At the heart of the VC is the paradox that it is both worthless and priceless. Since the 1960s the monetary value of a VC on the secondary market has soared: we have moved a long way from impoverished First War soldiers returning from Flanders, unable to find a job and selling their Crosses to pawnbrokers for almost nothing.[18] In 1856 no one could have anticipated that the VC would become so scarce that it had resale value; it was assumed that the winner, or his family, would keep it as a treasured heirloom. Even in the handful of cases where it was forfeited following a criminal conviction, the main punishment – apart from losing the £10 pension attached to it[19] – was to lose the honour of being included in the VC Register, the roll-call of names of VC winners. What once was heinous is no longer; the names erased from the VC Register to prevent sullying the royalty were restored.[20]

As the potential fatal cost of VC eligibility has risen, so too has the VC's other price, its monetary value, drawing the attention of thieves and counterfeiters, the latter's task made slightly easier by the fact that a sprinkling of duplicate VCs have officially been issued to replace lost or stolen original Crosses. VCs have disappeared in fires and burglaries, they have been left on trains and, on occasion, buried with their owner; at least twenty-five original VCs are thought to have been destroyed, or are missing. The record price (as of July 2013) is 1 million Australian dollars – approximately £410,000 at the prevailing exchange rate – in Sydney on 24 July 2006, paid for medals formerly belonging to Captain Alfred John Shout, including one of nine VCs awarded to Australians who fought at Gallipoli in 1915.[21] Shout was awarded a posthumous VC for hand-to-hand combat at the Lone Pine trenches.[22] His was the last Lone Pike VC still in private hands, and the purchaser, the Australian billionaire Kerry Stokes, donated Shout's VC to the Australian War Memorial in Canberra, where it joined the other eight.

If risk of death is a requirement of gaining a VC on contemporary battlefields, deep pockets are necessary to buy one off the battlefield. While it is admirable that philanthropists donate VCs to national museums, it is disquieting that the most highly prized military honour, awarded to someone who has performed a noble self-sacrifice, has become the subject of extreme self-interest. The 1856 VC statutes were silent on ownership but many today believe that such a national treasure needs to be owned by the nation of the person who gained it. The person awarded the Cross, or their surviving family, should be designated the holder of the VC until such time as they decide to place it either in the museum of the unit to which it belongs or some other place of safety, accessible to public viewing. The current situation, with second-hand VCs sold to the highest bidder, is antipathetic to the spirit of the VC.

And the price keeps going up. In 1955 a set of medals belonging to Edmund Barron Hartley, including the VC he gained for rescuing injured men in Basutoland on 5 June 1879, was sold at Sotheby's for what was then a record price, £300, and is now on display at the Army Medical Services Museum in Mytchett, Surrey. In January 1969 a fresh record of £1,700 was achieved, for the medal set of William Rennie, who fought at Lucknow during the Indian Mutiny; his VC is now at the Cameronians Regimental Museum at Hamilton, in Lanarkshire. By the first decade of the twenty-first century such prices seemed paltry. In April 2004 the VC awarded in 1944 to Sergeant Norman Jackson of the RAF Volunteer Reserve was sold at auction for £235,250 to Lord Ashcroft, a keen enthusiast for everything related to the VC.[23] Jackson gained his VC for crawling onto the wing of his Lancaster bomber to extinguish a fire in one of its engines. He was thrown off the wing and dragged behind the aircraft, clinging to his burning parachute.

The price history of the VC awarded to Leading Seaman James

Magennis, a naval diver, illustrates the inflation. Magennis gained his VC for attaching limpet mines to the hull of the Japanese cruiser *Takao* on 31 July 1945. He was Northern Ireland's only VC winner in the Second World War, and when he returned to Belfast its citizens raised for him more than £3,000 in public donations. By 1952 Magennis was struggling financially and sold his VC for £75. Lord Ashcroft bought his first VC, that of Magennis, at auction in 1986 for £29,000, plus fees. Ashcroft's VC collection – more than 160 at the last count – is now displayed at the Lord Ashcroft Gallery in the Imperial War Museum in London. As the gallery's website states, the VC was 'deliberately intended to have little actual value... Its value lies in what it stands for and what people do to earn it.' In *Victoria Cross Heroes*, his book about the VC, Lord Ashcroft wrote: 'The trustees of the medals know that I wish to see the collection preserved long after my death, and I am glad that the trust's rules prevent it from selling any of the medals.'[24] Today the question on everyone's mind (but which few dare ask, like the unspoken rule of the BBC's *Antiques Roadshow*) is how much a particular VC might be worth.

Some inheritors of VCs resist the temptation to cash in on the bravery of their ancestor, instead donating the medal to the relevant regimental museum; but the high auction prices seduce others. When a replacement VC was sought in 1978 by the surviving family of Private Thomas Byrne of the 21st Lancers, who won his original for the last great cavalry charge, at Omdurman on 2 September 1898, the approval of Queen Elizabeth II had first to be obtained.[25] The duplicate was soon after put up for sale and went at auction for £700. The Queen apparently took a decidedly dim view. Sir Angus Ogilvy, husband of Princess Alexandra of Kent, first cousin to the Queen, reported the Queen as saying: 'If this is what people are going to do, I will never grant another replacement Victoria Cross.'[26] In the US it is a federal offence to sell or trade a Medal of Honor, but venality is enterprising.

Selling the box containing the Medal of Honor or the certificate that accompanies it is not illegal – and the medal itself can then be passed on as a 'gift'.[27]

Because of its prestige, the VC has also been, on occasion, a natural peg for commerce. In a letter to The Times in 1895, a reader asked if anyone else had 'ever met with a case in which this coveted and most honourable distinction has been used for purposes of trade or business?'[28] The letter reported that a pub, the Durweston Arms, displayed 'in large letters' the name of the publican, F. Hitch, VC, in its window. The illiterate Hitch won his VC, one of eleven granted on 22 January 1879, for the defence of Rorke's Drift against massed Zulu warriors.[29] As with other VC winners from humble backgrounds, Hitch was sometimes desperately short of money, and may have sold his VC to raise funds. It is known that he applied for and received a duplicate, now in the possession of the Regimental Museum of the Royal Welsh; the whereabouts of Hitch's original VC is a mystery.

More recently, officials have sought to preserve the dignity of the VC by unsuccessfully trying to prevent its commercial use. On 28 February 1968, William Brown complained to the MP Edward Taylor about the use of the VC design in the letterhead of a medal dealer, J. B. Hayward, of Piccadilly, London: 'I think that it is sacrilege that any commercial enterprise should use the emblem of this high honour on a correspondence note paper... [Is] there any right or authority for a commercial company using such an honour on their letter-head?' Whitehall deliberated for months, with the Treasury solicitor commenting on 29 March 1968 that

> The use by Haywards of the picture of a VC does not in our opinion contravene Section 197 of the Army Act 1955 and we do not know of any regulation or law which would prevent a firm using a picture of

a decoration or medal on their notepaper... There is no copyright or other property in the design of the Victoria Cross and a person commits no offence merely by using the design, so that there are no means by which the dealer can be prevented from continuing the use of it.

Squadron Leader K.J. Appelboom – one of many officials asked to comment in the following months – wrote on 17 May: 'Brigadier Sir John Smyth, President of the V.C. Association... took the view that "the less said, the better", though I do not think we should quote him.' In the National Archives' file there is a handwritten note from a Treasury official: 'The Treasury do come across this kind of thing from time to time and they usually find that a fairly "stuffy" letter does the trick.'[30] Stuffy letters are all that can be done to prevent anyone from using the VC design to advertise anything from fish and chips to microchips. Untidiness is a besetting sin of Britain's arrangements for military gallantry awards: while private commercial use of the VC for any purpose appears to be perfectly legal and may only elicit a 'stuffy letter' from Whitehall, perversely there is a strict legal ban against any commercial use of the George Cross without prior approval of the prime minister.[31]

When the VC's statutes were last revised in 1961, the standard of courage required for eligibility was stated as 'only... for the most conspicuous bravery, or some daring or pre-eminent act of valour or self-sacrifice or extreme devotion to duty in the presence of the enemy'. The question of the scale of distribution was, regrettably, left aside. Outside military circles the assumption is that operational gallantry awards, including the VC, are made purely on merit. This is incorrect. A quota system for gallantry awards, covering all ranks in a particular operation, has been applied to operational decorations for many years. It is not only that some potential VC winners fall by the wayside by mistake; it is that many potential VC-winning acts are, thanks to the quota system, likely to be ruled out before they are even considered.

Questions of ownership, distribution, eligibility – these topics are rarely aired, but are important given the inexorable shrinking of the pool of surviving VC holders. An opportunity for a sensible public debate about the VC was missed in 1993, when Prime Minister John Major announced a sweeping reform of the honours system. In the House of Commons on 4 March that year Major announced:

> Acts of courage, lives of sacrifice, inventiveness, generosity and commitment to others are formally recognized and acknowledged... To retain its valued role in our national life, the honours system must, from time to time, be reviewed and renewed.[32]

The prime minister's inspired decision was to try to fully democratize the honours system, distributing honours purely on merit and not by quota. One repercussion of Major's reformist drive was that the distinction between officers and other ranks in military operational gallantry awards was largely eliminated. Prior to 1993 there had been a long-standing tradition that 'officers get crosses while other ranks get medals'. This 'class' distinction was partially eradicated by Major's reforms. The Military Medal was abolished and the Military Cross (MC), hitherto for commissioned officers only, was extended to all ranks.[33] The Conspicuous Gallantry Cross (CGC) was, peculiarly, created and inserted immediately after the VC and before the MC in terms of ranking.[34] It was unfortunate that senior ranks of Britain's armed forces, perpetually anxious to preserve hierarchies, resisted Major's reformist impulse. The Distinguished Service Order (DSO) survived as an officers-only decoration, no longer granted for bravery but henceforth for 'leadership'. But perhaps the greatest failure of the 1993 review was the continuation of the quota system of operational gallantry awards, despite Major's insistence that quotas should no longer exist for civil awards.

Pressure to end the quota system for gallantry awards is long-standing, as this view from 1969 by Major R. Clark shows:

> The rationing of operational awards is a bad policy and should cease. Awards should be given to cover deserving acts of gallantry, regardless of numbers. To help eradicate past inadequacies, an Awards Board should be established to investigate any recommendations which were lost or not approved due to their exceeding the ration. A similar board has been established in the USA where today awards are being made for deserving acts in World War I which had been missed for various reasons.[35]

Removing quotas and rewarding all courageous acts, perhaps graded according to degrees of bravery, would certainly mean many more medals given out; but this need not entail the kind of cheapening seen with the Iron Cross or the Croix de Guerre. Unfortunately, the British armed forces continue to support quotas for operational decorations, the end result being that, as John Wilkinson, MP for Ruislip-Northwood, baldly stated during the same Commons debate: 'Anyone with military experience knows that the heroism of the bravest and the best usually goes unrecognized.' Switching from a quota to a merit system for operational military decorations might ruffle feathers but would be eminently sensible for all such awards, and particularly for the VC. Senior officers want to preserve a quota system for operational decorations as they regard this as the only certain defence against a slide towards ever-cheapening of prestigious awards, which they privately believe has been the case with civilian honours. But it is questionable policy to try to preserve the spiritual value of the VC by raising the VC standard such that the bodily sacrifice of the VC candidate is necessary. It ought to be a matter of national regret that Britain's foremost battle honour has mutated into an emotively supercharged symbol, something never intended by Victoria and Albert.

Courage, like love, is incorrigibly subjective. Debate over both all too easily falls into circularity – 'we know it when we see it'. Yet just as we yearn to formalize definitions of love – to demonstrate that it has an objective reality, through some form of externalized institution, such as marriage – so we long to objectively recognize courage, most obviously through the ceremonial process of giving a medal. If only it were so simple.

We lack a clear, universally agreed objective definition of courage; this is a bedevilling problem when it comes to awarding military honours. The higher up the scale we go, with the VC at the very top, the more intractable it becomes. The VC plucks out an individual who has done something remarkable. But the intrinsic subjectivity associated with making a VC award inevitably opens up space for accusations of inconsistency and anomaly; the history of the VC is littered with both. As there are no VC 'grades', all VC winners are considered equal, even though they are not. There is an understandable yearning to discern some quality, some human capacity that all VC holders have in common; the easiest, if laziest, course of action is to label them all 'heroic'. This circular definition really tells us nothing. Tommy Atkins won a VC and therefore is a hero. What is a hero? Someone like Tommy Atkins, who won the VC. The VC does not simply rank men morally, it also ranks them socially and politically. As William I. Miller, who has written extensively on courage, writes, the courageous

> are not only objects of admiration and awe; they are also objects of gratitude... Prizes, praises, and medals breed envy among those eligible and not-so-eligible who are passed over... Disgruntlement, anger, distrust, and cynicism over the award of medals and honors is a commonplace of military memoirs.[36]

Indeed it is. Frank Richards wryly concluded his 1933 First War memoir, *Old Soldiers Never Die*, by observing how time flattens the heights separating the brave from the rest, until all dwell in a valley of ordinariness:

> It is Armistice day today and the ex-Service men are on parade wearing their War medals. The men who served at the Bases and a hundred miles behind the front line are wearing their medals more proudly than the men who served in the firing line. There is no distinction between the War medals.[37]

Time blurs many things, including what we once regarded as courageous or the merely mundane. This can be brought into sharper focus by comparing two essentially similar acts by members of Britain's armed forces, one taken from the Crimean War, the other an example from Afghanistan in 2009. On 8 September 1855, an assistant surgeon serving with the 23rd Regiment left the safety of his trench and, under heavy enemy fire, ran to the aid of a wounded lieutenant. In so doing the surgeon exposed himself to Russian gunfire, but escaped uninjured. The second incident happened on 12 March 2009, when a detachment of the 1st Battalion, The Rifles, found itself in a gun battle with Taliban forces in Helmand Province, Afghanistan. An able seaman, a trained medic attached to The Rifles, dashed seventy yards forward through a hail of enemy gunfire to assist a lance corporal who had been shot in the face and severely injured.

These two acts of courage are in essence identical: the medical helpers demonstrated complete indifference to their personal safety while going to the aid of a wounded comrade. But there the similarities end. The (male) Crimean assistant surgeon was Henry Thomas Sylvester, the last Crimean War VC holder to die. He certainly tried his best, but his wounded lieutenant unfortunately died on the battlefield. The (female) able seaman was Kate Nesbitt, and her lance corporal survived. For his deed Sylvester gained the VC.[38] Nesbitt was honoured in November 2009 with the Military Cross (MC). This was a remarkable step – Nesbitt was only the second woman to receive the MC (and the first female from the Royal Navy), the first being Michelle Norris, of the Royal Army Medical Corps, who gained her MC for a similar action in Iraq in 2006.[39] What Sylvester may have thought about his deed is not recorded, but we know Nesbitt's modest reaction: 'I just did what I'm sure everyone else would have done for me.'[40] Sylvester would probably have said very much the same, because modesty and self-deprecation are intrinsic to our understanding of what it means to show gallantry. Nesbitt's citation read (in part): 'Under fire and under pressure her commitment and courage were inspirational and made the difference between life and death.' The Prince of Wales, who pinned the MC on Nesbitt at Buckingham Palace on 27 November 2009, described her act as an example of 'extraordinary' heroism.[41]

While the Military Cross is unquestionably highly esteemed, it ranks third – a kind of bronze medal – in the hierarchy of military decorations, after the Conspicuous Gallantry Cross (silver) and the Victoria Cross (gold). Why was it thought that Nesbitt deserved the MC rather than the CGC, or even the VC? Why will Sylvester's name be forever up there with the 'bravest of the brave', whereas Nesbitt's will eventually be lost on a list of tens of thousands? What separates Sylvester and Nesbitt, apart from 154 years? Objectively their deeds were no different in terms of what they did, the courage it took, and the (minimal) consequences for the overall campaign in which they participated. While women are nominally eligible to be considered for a VC, any chance they might have of winning one has actually been reduced almost to zero, partly because newly-created gallantry awards have served to push the VC almost beyond male, never mind female, attainment.

Lord Ashcroft, in an interview in 2010, dismissed the issue of inconsistencies in the awarding of the VC when he opened his eponymous gallery at the Imperial War Museum:

> Even in my own House of Lords there are some that should be there and some who shouldn't. We shouldn't get side-tracked by saying maybe X shouldn't have received it and Y should. Such debates should not detract from the aggregate bravery of this group of people.[42]

There are a number of reasons why Lord Ashcroft would say this; he would not want his gallery's showpieces to be in any way diminished, and no doubt he genuinely feels that discrimination of this kind is unhelpful, although he himself has publicly called for a VC to be awarded in one case where a lesser decoration was granted. Yet it is possible to rationally demur from his opinion, and call for a public debate about the criteria for VC eligibility; a need to open up for discussion past cases of those who failed to receive a VC and why; and a need to remove the suspicion that the bestowal of a VC, while not entirely arbitrary, is, thanks in part to the quota system, a matter of chance. This would not detract from the 'aggregate bravery' (if such a thing exists) of the group of VC winners as a whole.

In the contrast between the cases of Sylvester and Nesbitt lie 154 years of the British establishment grappling with the intractable problem of how to maintain military morale in the context of a tarnished honours system, an aggressive media with a rapacious appetite for heroes, and a general public that, in recent years at least, seems bewitched by celebrity culture. The VCs awarded to the gallant defenders of Rorke's Drift in January 1879 and that granted to Private Johnson Beharry in 2005 in Iraq share something other than courage. In the first instance, the pride of the British army had previously been smashed by a black African army at Isandlwana; the second was one of the most unpopular wars Britain has ever engaged in. The award of their VCs was not simply a matter of personal heroism, but also of wider political purpose, to rally the nation at a time of crisis.

The way to preserve the VC as a respected living symbol is, paradoxically, to return to its historic origins and permit wider and more generous distribution. This would be easier to achieve if some of the other decorations were eliminated. If the process of judging who deserves a VC was more transparent, then there would be a greater chance of avoiding future anomalies. Fears that the VC would be cheapened if more were given out are overdone; if a dozen VCs were distributed tomorrow for good work in Afghanistan, the medal would still remain exceptionally rare. This suggestion – to relax the astonishingly stringent rules that have been applied for the past fifty years or more – might evoke protest, yet all it would do is to return us to past practice, when battlefield courage was not so scarce as it apparently is today.

A further useful reform would be to reiterate and promote the 'elective peer principle', whereby officers and men can choose from their own number individuals to be recommended for a VC. The election system was first used in the 1859 Indian Mutiny, when twenty-nine such 'balloted' VCs were awarded. Clause 13 of the 1856 warrant provided for the election of one VC per officer, one per NCO, and two for privates, for each regiment involved in an action. Eight regiments in the sieges of Delhi and Lucknow (and for the later relief of Lucknow) elected VCs from their ranks, but only two adhered to the strict regulations; three regiments submitted (and had accepted) five recommendations, while three others submitted fewer names than authorized.[43] This election by officers and men actually involved in a military operation of candidates to be recommended for the VC has unfortunately been neglected for far too long, having fallen into abeyance since the First World War. This dormant procedure injects a healthy dose of something that was inherent in the original VC statute: democracy. The elective principle has continued to be part of successive warrants. It stipulates that if a 'gallant and daring act' was performed by a unit, and the commanding officer deemed that all were 'equally brave and distinguished' and was unable to single out any one person, he 'may direct' officers to nominate one, and the other ranks two, of their own number, to be recommended for the VC. In the 1961 warrant this principle endures as clause 9, which addresses the case in which a ship or flotilla, a regiment or other 'detached body of soldiers', a squadron 'or other body of airmen' (the categories were deliberately broadly drawn) has 'distinguished itself collectively by the performance of an act of heroic gallantry or daring in the presence of the enemy in such a way that the Flag, General, Air or other Officer in Command of the Force to which such a unit belongs' cannot choose a specific individual; in such a case, 'one or more of the personnel comprising the unit shall be selected to be recommended' for the VC by a secret ballot of the whole unit. Of the total number of VCs, just forty-six have been allocated by self-selection, more than half of these – twenty-nine – during a single and fairly brief campaign, that of the Indian Mutiny in 1857. This is only 2 per cent of the total VCs. Yet surely this is a more equitable method of initial selection than a write-up by a senior or commanding officer? Let the personnel serving in the field themselves choose who is worthy to be considered for a VC. There might be mistakes, which happen in any case; but there would also be a strong dose of raw honesty, beyond the opaque adjudication of desk officers in Whitehall who may never have heard a shot fired in anger.

Early views of the VC's significance emphasized its democratic nature:

Every Colonel in the army will be eager for the new distinction, and we are sure will not consider it plebeian because it is not the Order of the Bath but the Cross of Victoria. Every soldier who wins it will prize it highly, not only because it is the gift of his Queen, but because it will be the common mark distinguishing the bravest men in the army. Every officer will prize it, and none the less because it will be worn by the men; because there is nothing brave men recognise more cordially than bravery in others.[44]

This democratic promise has been lost sight of in the determination to avoid cheapening the VC.

2

A Most Grand, Gratifying Day

'There is nothing so stupid as a gallant officer.'
DUKE OF WELLINGTON[1]

*'We have moved a step. Valour in Private Jones is to be alike
distinguished with valour in Major Mayfair... This is something.'*
LLOYD'S WEEKLY[2]

London, Friday, 26 June 1857: a blazing sunny day. Thousands of hot
and excitable people, slaking their thirst with slugs of porter and gin-
ger beer, flocked to Hyde Park from the early hours of the morning. All
were anxious to catch a glimpse of the first investiture of a new medal,
one that had tantalized public interest by being widely and – mostly
– favourably reported by the newspapers. No one knows how many
were actually in the throng that day, but there was room for several
thousand of the most eminent – courtiers, MPs, judges, senior clergy
and the like – to take their places in a ticket-holders-only grandstand,
from where they could observe the ceremony without being forced to
rub shoulders with their social inferiors. These privileged individuals
tightly clasped their red passes for the enclosure, where they were able
to have an elevated view of proceedings; a dubious pleasure, it turned

out, since the stand was merely a sloping set of planks, forcing the illustrious guests to perch painfully at an angle, craning for a view as they sweltered. One anonymous MP sarcastically informed The Times, it was 'slow torture... two or three benches ... would have been far more comfortable... than the awkward structure standing upon which for some hours last Friday morning 7,000 ladies and gentlemen did not see the distribution of the Victoria cross by her gracious Majesty'.[3] Many thousands more lined the nearby streets and jostled to enter the park, eagerly craning their necks to glimpse the sixty-two soldiers, sailors and marines, judged the bravest of the brave, who were about to receive their Victoria Crosses from the Queen's hand.

On display that day was the ritualized pomp of a great power, one that had only recently narrowly avoided complete humiliation in a calamitous war 2,000 miles distant. The splendour of the uniforms, the glittering military bands, the crashing thunder of the twenty-one-gun salute – all reasserted the ritualistic bonds between Crown and subjects, and affirmed the majesty not just of queen but country too. They also imparted a sense of planning that helped disguise the fact that the final details of the ceremony had been hastily arranged. The final list of VC recipients was not delivered to Lord Panmure, Secretary of State for War, until 19 June, just a week before the investiture; Hancocks, the London jewellers who had the contract to produce and engrave the Crosses (and retain it to this day), were only handed the final list of names on 22 June.

Riding her horse Sunset and wearing a military-style scarlet jacket above a dark-blue skirt, with a gold-embroidered sash and a gold-banded black riding hat with red and white plumes, Victoria entered the park at 10 a.m., whereupon the guns of the Royal Horse Artillery unleashed a royal salute. Victoria had breakfasted 'early' at 9.15, full of 'agitation for the coming great event of the day, viz: the distribution of the "Victoria Cross"'.[4] At her side rode Albert, Prince Consort and

Victoria's fellow architect of the VC, decked in the uniform of a British field marshal, followed by a train of dazzlingly attired family members. As Victoria rode through the glittering ranks of dragoons, life guards, hussars, highlanders, engineers, marines and sailors – almost 600 representatives from each branch of the services and Crimea veterans – the horrors of the recent war were put aside, as the crowd revelled in the haughty demeanour of their thirty-five-year-old monarch. Britain's pride had been pricked by events in the Crimea; this day was to be devoted to the restoration of self-esteem. *The Times*, with customary hyperbole, wrote: 'everybody went who could; everybody suffered considerable discomfort in doing so; and everybody was nevertheless much delighted with the smallest share in the day's work.'[5]

On behalf of the War Office, Lord Panmure, gouty and intellectually ponderous, handed Victoria the eponymous Crosses, one by one. She remained mounted as twelve sailors, two marines, and forty-eight soldiers smartly marched up to have their queen pin the medal to their breast; crimson ribbons for the army, blue for the navy and marines. Never again would so many VCs be handed out on a single occasion. It is said that Victoria inadvertently stabbed the flesh of Commander Henry James Raby as she pinned his VC to his left breast, while he maintained a stoical silence. It might be true; after all, his rank placed Raby first in line to receive the VC, and perhaps the Queen needed a little practice to get it right. But the same was said of other personal investitures of the VC by Victoria; it is the stuff of VC legends, of which there are many. Raby had gained his Cross at Sebastopol on 18 June 1855, when he had been second-in-command of a scaling party. Together with John Taylor, who held a rank equivalent to petty officer, and Henry Curtis, a boatswain's mate, Raby spotted at seventy yards' distance a soldier of the 57th Regiment sitting up and calling for help; he was immobilized, having been wounded in both legs. Raby, Taylor and Curtis left the shelter of their battery and, reportedly under heavy fire, ran to retrieve the wounded man. For this they each received the VC, a show of generosity that was not unusual at the time.

The crowd cheered as each of the recipients marched forward for his Cross, the hurrahs rising to a crescendo for Sergeant George Walters, late of the 49th (Royal Berkshire Regiment) and now dressed in the uniform of his new profession, a policeman. The official government journal, the London Gazette, published on 24 February 1857 the names of the III inaugural VC winners, ninety-six of them from the army; of the sixty-two distributed by Queen Victoria on 26 June 1857, more than a third – twenty-four – went to officers.[6] The first Victoria Cross in the list was that of Lieutenant Cecil William Buckley, for his actions in the Sea of Azov on 28 May 1855; the earliest action to gain the VC was that of the Irish-born Charles David Lucas, a twenty-year-old lieutenant serving on the HMS Hecla, who, on 21 June 1854, threw overboard a fizzing live shell which had landed on his ship, which was on service in the Baltic, far from the Crimea.[7] The investiture was over in a few minutes. The troops then marched past the Queen, the bands of the Coldstream Guards and the Fusilier Guards playing 'See the Conquering Hero'.

One of those soldiers not present to receive his VC in person was Private William Stanlack of the Coldstream Guards, a Devonshire lad who, at the Battle of Inkerman, had crawled to within a few yards of the Russian lines and brought back some useful information; such was the relative ease with which the first VCs might be gained. Shortly before the Hyde Park investiture, Stanlack had been summarily punished by his CO for theft from a fellow soldier; he would have entirely forfeited the right to be included on the VC Register, the list of names of the honoured, had he been found guilty in a court of law. Instead he was deprived of receiving his VC from the hand of the Queen.[8] This moral dimension – the monarchy could not be embarrassed by association with a criminal – was covered by the fifteenth clause of the founding statues of the VC, the 1856 warrant,[9] which permitted the removal from the Register of the Cross of those convicted of 'treason, cowardice, felony or of any infamous crime' – a clause that was removed in the 1919 revisions of the warrant.[10] Another absentee was Mrs Elizabeth Taylor, wife of John Taylor, one of Commander Raby's two helpers. John Taylor died of his wounds on 24 February 1857, the very day the VCs were gazetted. Mrs Taylor asked the War Office if she might attend the Hyde Park ceremony to receive her husband's Cross. She was politely informed that that would not be necessary; the Cross was forwarded to her.[11]

Victoria herself wrote in her journal later that day: 'I never saw finer troops, nor better marching. The heat was very great, but I felt it less than I had expected. It was indeed a most grand, gratifying day.' It was less gratifying for those relatives of dead soldiers and sailors who thought their sons deserved a Cross, but were denied. In early 1856 Mr John Godfrey importuned the War Office on behalf of his dead son, killed in action in the Crimea, and so first raised the issue of posthumous awards, on which the warrant was silent. Lord Panmure regarded the VC as an 'Order' rather than a medal, analogous to the Order of the Bath; to qualify for an Order, one had to be alive. He decreed in April 1856 that posthumous awards of the VC were impermissible and authorized a reply to Mr Godfrey: 'Inform Mr G that in this Order, as in the Bath, the friends of deceased Officers cannot have any claim for it as in the case of medals. It is an order for the living.'[12]

This was not Victoria's first public medals' investiture. By November 1854 the War Office had agreed to Victoria's wish that there should be a Crimean campaign medal, with clasps for various battles such as Alma and Inkerman. As Victoria said: '*Sebastopol*, should it fall, or any other name of a battle which Providence may permit our brave troops to gain, can be inscribed on other clasps hereafter to be added...The Queen is sure that nothing will gratify and encourage our noble troops more than the knowledge that this is to be done.'[13] Victoria personally distributed some of these campaign medals to Crimean survivors, some terribly injured, at Horse Guards Parade in London on 18 May 1855. Victoria wrote of her emotions that day to King Leopold I of Belgium, himself a British field marshal and the widower of Prince Charlotte of Wales, George IV's only legitimate offspring:

> From the highest Prince of the Blood to the lowest Private, all received the same distinction for the bravest conduct in the severest actions, and the rough hand of the brave and honest private soldier came for the first time in contact with that of their Sovereign and their Queen! Noble fellows! I own I feel as if they were *my own children*; my heart beats for *them* as for my *nearest and dearest*. They were so touched, so pleased; many, I hear, cried – and they won't hear of giving up their Medals, to have their names engraved upon them, for fear they should *not* receive the *identical one* put into *their hands by me*, which is quite touching.[14]

This ceremony had a profound impact on Victoria and on those who received the medals, the spectators, and the newspaper editors who guided much of what the rest of the country thought. Victoria and the men assembled before her that day saw each other differently – humanly. This personal contact between ruler and ruled helped cement Victoria's sense, perhaps illusory, that she had a special place in the hearts and minds of individual soldiers and sailors, and that she in turn had a special duty of care over them. At first, Victoria monitored all VC recommendations, normally accepting all, but we know that she denied it to a private.[15] Her first cousin, the Duke of Cambridge, who took over as commander of the Crimean army in July 1856 and later became commander-in-chief of the army, reminded the troops on every possible occasion that they were all 'Soldiers of the Queen'.

Some were more 'of the Queen' than others. Social divisions between officers and men in the mid-nineteenth century were deep and rigid;

officers usually purchased their commissions, often for thousands of pounds, while the rank and file lived on a shilling a day, with deductions for food and clothing.[16] The Crimean debacle fatally undermined the purchase system, lodestone of the British officer class. As one anonymous writer put it in 1860: 'Indeed, we ascertained, in 1854–5, to the indignation of Belgravia, no doubt, that ancient lineage and military genius were by no means synonymous; nay, that a heavy purse and a heavy head were now and then owned by the same person.'[17] But the immediate crisis in 1855 was how to bring the Crimean War to a successful end without further damage being done to the army – or to the reputation of the Crown.

Thus the grand spectacle in Hyde Park on 26 June 1857 was the culmination of two fraught years, during which the monarchy agonized over the obvious failures of Britain's armed forces and the widespread public condemnation of the country's political and military leadership, and, by extension, of the Crown itself. The Victoria Cross, created in part in an effort to regain public support for the monarchy, is the greatest legacy of that war. The creation of the VC was mutually beneficial to Crown and the rank-and-file soldier. The latter finally found some individual recognition and public acclamation from those for whom he risked his life, while the Crown used the VC to brighten its tarnished image. The VC strengthened the ligaments that bound citizens and Crown, ensuring the continued 'reverence of the population' for the monarchy, as the contemporary journalist Walter Bagehot put it.

Bagehot believed that Britain's constitutional monarchy owed its continued success to the imaginative weakness of the masses, what he called the 'vacant many'. In that sense the Victoria Cross was a profound and enduring success; here at last was a mechanism by which heroes could be identified, individualized and rewarded. These same heroes, individually endorsed by Victoria herself, were often one of the vacant many; that they had been granted the Cross named for the monarch

37

was a sign of the monarch's undying affection. The invention of the VC was therefore a timely stroke of public relations genius, one that was sparked by a vigorous and independent-minded press, without which the British public would never have become aware of the suffering, the stoicism, and – on occasion – the individual courage of the soldiers stuck in the Crimea. Carefully preserved over succeeding years, the VC has evolved into a fetish of remarkable talismanic power.

The VC owes its existence to many factors: deepened public sympathy for the common soldier, born out of greater awareness of his miseries; a monarchy anxious to retain what authority it still had over the army; and the democratizing example set by Britain's allies during the Crimean War. In 1852, in France, the emperor Napoleon III, desperate to burnish his poor popular image, created the Médaille militaire, an individual decoration to be awarded to privates and non-commissioned officers who had particularly distinguished themselves in battle. The British press noted the distribution of the Médaille Militaire in the Crimea, and asked why Britain had no such decoration; did the country want for courageous men? By the time the war ended, more than 500 Médailles militaires and 700 Légions d'honneur had been sprinkled across the French contingent in the Crimea, and also over the armed forces of France's allies, Britain included.[18] Traditionally, Britain gave relatively fewer orders, decorations or medals than other comparable powers. King Edward VII was to prove considerably more generous than his mother, Victoria, but by comparison with other monarchs even he was tight-fisted. Frederick Ponsonby, an Assistant Private Secretary to both Victoria and Edward, who was closely involved in royal decisions about orders and decorations, said: 'Whereas in Germany they gave yearly thirty thousand, in England the most that were ever given at that time was about eight hundred, and therefore a British decoration was far more difficult to get... British decorations became like a rare stamp or rare egg, and were much sought after.'[19] The lack of something British to pin on the breast of valiant marines, soldiers and seamen who had served in the Crimea – the campaign medal, and clasps for particular battles during the campaign, gave no recognition to individual courage – became a public embarrassment, giving rise to questions in the House of Commons, angry letters and leader columns in the press – and invidious comparisons with the French way of doing things.

Prior to the advent of the Victoria Cross, there were three possible ways to recognize and reward individual bravery: the Order of the Bath; a brevet (temporary) promotion; or a Mention in Despatches. The first was for senior officers only, majors and above, while the second two were normally granted to junior officers. CBs – Companion, the lowest category of the Bath – had in any case been distributed so lavishly among senior officers of the military that a CB had come to be a sign not so much of meritorious but lengthy service. The example set by the French led to the creation of two medals for other ranks early in the Crimean War: the Distinguished Conduct Medal in 1854 (for the army) and the Conspicuous Gallantry Medal in 1855 (for the Royal Navy and marines). The CGM and the DCM, which carried a £20 annuity, broke the mould in that they were awarded for individual acts of gallantry, and thus can be seen as necessary precursors to the VC.[20] But they failed to capture the public imagination, not least because they perpetuated the existing division within the armed forces between officers and men. The real revolution, one that generated intense public interest, came with the creation of the Victoria Cross. For one thing, it was personally identified with the monarch – it was Victoria's Cross. For another, it appeared to be a truly democratic award, indifferent to rank or status; suddenly a cook could be the equal of a colonel, an able seaman take precedence (in one way at least) over an admiral. For an armed forces steeped in the traditional divide between officers and men, this was a remarkably radical step. For the other ranks who gained the VC, there was a £10 pension, from which officers were initially excluded.[21] This was no mean sum; in 1857 £10 was more than a third of the annual wage of an agricultural labourer.

The first public call for some new military decoration that might be available to all ranks for individual courage came on 19 December 1854, when a former naval officer, Captain George Treweeke Scobell, Liberal MP for Bath, raised in the House of Commons the idea of the creation of an 'Order of Merit'. In Scobell's view, such an award would be 'for distinguished and prominent personal gallantry during the present war, and to which every grade and individual, from the highest to the lowest, in the United Services, may be admissible'. He pointed out that the Order of the Bath was 'entirely confined to the upper ranks of the Army and Navy, for no one under the rank of Major in the Army, or Captain in the Navy, could partake of the distinctions of that Order', and, because a campaign medal made no reference to individual bravery, 'some change was imperatively required'.

Scobell withdrew his motion for his Order after Lord John Russell, foreign minister in the Aberdeen administration, assured the House that the matter was being considered by the government. Russell's response was, in all likelihood, an attempt to bat aside Scobell's argument; but Scobell gained the valuable support of the Duke of Richmond in the House of Lords on 23 January 1855:

> My Lords, formerly, in the late war [against Bonaparte], Parliament and the country were satisfied if they gave ribands and stars to the commanding officers of regiments, and to commanding officers of the Army; but, I am happy to say, that system is entirely exploded now... What is the use to a private soldier of a Vote of Thanks of Parliament?[22]

The appearance and regulations of the VC were largely Prince Albert's handiwork. He led the royal household's discussions with government representatives about the VC, with Victoria contributing ideas about its design and making alterations to the warrant. Victoria and Albert were united in their wish that the new medal should be plain, simple and unglamorous. On 20 January 1855 the Duke of Newcastle, then Secretary of War, wrote to Prince Albert about the new and as yet unnamed decoration:

> I confess it does not seem right or politic that such deeds of heroism as this War has produced should go unrewarded by any distinction outward of honours because they are done by Privates or by Officers below the rank of Major, – and it is impossible to believe that Her Majesty's Troops fighting side by side with those of France do not draw an invidious contrast between the rewards bestowed upon themselves and their Allies.
>
> The value attributed by soldiers to a little bit of ribbon is such as to render any danger insignificant and any privation light if it can be attained, and I believe that great indeed would be the stimulus and dearly-prized the reward of a Cross of Military Merit.
>
> There are some Orders which even Crowned Heads cannot wear, and it would be a Military reward of high estimation if this Cross would be so bestowed as to be within the reach of every Private Soldier and get to be coveted by any General at the head of an Army. Such a reward would have more effect in the Army than the grant of Commissions, – and the sight of one of these Crosses on the breast of a Soldier returned home invalided would bring more Recruits than any of the measures we can now adopt.
>
> Of course, great care would be required to prevent abuse, – but I am sure Your Royal Highness will not consider the dangers of abuse a sufficient reason to reject this proposal if there appears sufficient good in it to justify its adoption.[23]

On 22 January 1855 Prince Albert outlined in a memorandum to the Duke of Newcastle his own view as to the parameters of the new decoration:

> It is now proposed to establish a mode of reward, neither reserved for the few nor bestowed upon all, which is to distinguish on a liberal scale individual merit in the Officers of the lower Ranks, in Sergeants & in Privates...
>
> 1./ That a small cross of Merit for *personal deeds of valour* be established.
>
> 2./ That it be open to all Ranks.
>
> 3./ That it be unlimited in Number.
>
> 4./ That an annuity (say of £5) be attached to each cross.
>
> 5./ That it be *claimable* by an individual on establishing before a Jury of his Peers, subject to confirmation at home, his right to the distinction.
>
> 6./ That in cases of general actions it be given in certain quantities to particular Regmts, so many to the Officers, so many to the sergeants, so many to the men (of the last say 1 per Company) & that their distribution be left to a Jury of the same rank as the persons to be rewarded. By this means alone could you ensure the perfect fairness of distribution & save the Officers in command from the invidious task of making a selection from those under their orders, which they now shrink from in the case of the Bath. – The limitation of the Number to be given to a Regmt at one time, inforces [sic] the necessity of a selection & diminishes the pain to those who cannot be included.[24]

A week later, Newcastle felt sufficiently confident that the new decoration was going to happen that he could inform the House of Lords:

> Her Majesty has been advised to institute a Cross of Merit, which shall be applicable to all ranks of the Army in future. It is not intended,

my Lords, that this new Order shall in any way affect the present Order of the Bath, but that a separate and distinct Cross of Military Merit shall be given, which shall be open to all ranks of the Army, and which, I hope, will be an object of ambition to every individual in the service, from the General who commands down to the privates in the ranks... the Order will be somewhat analogous to those existing in some countries of the Continent... while I may also state generally that its distribution will be so arranged as to obviate the invidious task of selecting the individuals upon whom it is to be conferred from devolving upon officers; for in all cases the principle will be adopted of adjudicating the distinction according to the verdict of a jury of the peers of the individual who is to be distinguished; that verdict, however, will have to be confirmed by the decision of the home authorities.[25]

But a day later Newcastle was out of office, the result of the fall of the Aberdeen administration, toppled by public outrage over the mishandling of the war – a turn of events that would briefly delay the establishment of the VC.

Albert's memorandum is notable for the emphasis he gave to two points – no limit on numbers of the Cross and the 'elective peer principle' – that have since been lost sight of. From the outset, the Crown wanted men and officers on the ground to be able to choose individuals from their own number to be rewarded and recognized. Yet this principle – though embodied in all the warrants pertaining to the VC, including the current one – has not been invoked since the Zeebrugge naval raid on 22–23 April 1918, and was only used on eight occasions prior to that. It is regrettable that this method of VC selection has become dormant, both because it seems, prima facie, a more equitable and immediately just method of VC selection, and also because it would mean that more VCs would be distributed. As the

Liverpool Mercury commented when the VC first appeared, the suggestion that officers and men should choose VC winners from their own ranks was sensible: 'an admirable provision, which at once precludes all possible jealousies, and leaves a difficult question to be decided by a tribunal which may safely be regarded as next to infallible'.[26] There is no obvious reason why the elective peer principle has been so little used, but the suspicion must be that ceding control over such a potent symbol has become increasingly distasteful to both military and civilian authorities.

By the end of 1855 the proposed new decoration had taken definitive shape.[27] In the Royal Archives at Windsor Castle there is a document from December 1855, entitled 'Copy Memorandum on Proposed Victoria Cross'.[28] It is peppered with revisions, crossings out and suggestions by Victoria and Albert.[29] From this it is clear that alternative names were considered. 'The Military Order of Victoria' was deleted, while 'The Victoria Cross? The Reward of Valour? The Reward of Bravery? For Bravery?' were suggested. On 5 January 1856 Victoria wrote to Lord Panmure, who had been appointed Secretary of State for War in the new government formed by Lord Palmerston, marking with a cross the design sketch she preferred, a cross pattée. She added an eminently sensible point: '[The] Motto would be better "For Valour" than "For the Brave" as this would lead to the inference that only those are deemed brave who have got the Cross.'[30] Every soldier was expected to be brave; to be valorous was to be exceptional.

On 5 February 1856 Victoria wrote again to Panmure, revealing the minute interest she took in an early mock-up of the Cross:

> the metal is ugly, it is copper & not bronze & as such looks very heavy on a red coat with the Crimson Ribbon. Bronze is properly speaking gun metal, this has a rich colour & is very hard; copper would wear very ill & soon look like an old penny. Ld Panmure should have one

prepared in real bronze & the Queen is inclined to think that it ought to have a greenish varnish to protect it.[31]

By 26 February 1857 *The Times* was able to report the names of the first recipients, noting that 'this decoration shall be given only for courage displayed in the presence of the enemy. Skill or conduct does not entitle a man to the distinction, nor can the soldier earn it by extinguishing a fire in a powder magazine at home, nor the sailor by gallantry in saving his vessel in a storm at sea.'[32] This bar against being able to earn the VC by a brave deed carried out not in the 'presence of the enemy' was to be overturned in later years – only to be reasserted even later. The newspaper also welcomed the award's classlessness: 'It is a happy thing that in a country with such disparities of rank and fortune the display of great qualities is able to unite the noble and the low-born, the rich and the poor, in a common honour.'[33]

The ceremonials in Hyde Park that June day in 1857 were therefore the culmination of a remarkably profound revolution in British social attitudes. Up to that point few questioned the fiction that officers were natural gentlemen, born to lead, while the other ranks were brutes in need of regular flogging to punish drunkenness and generally maintain discipline. Under the pressure of widespread public anger, fed by detailed newspaper reporting of events in the Crimea, this fiction was rent apart. In the Crimea, Britain's political and military leaders had revealed themselves to be incompetent and, on occasion, selfishly callous, while those whom they led endured unnecessary hardships and sometimes demonstrated remarkable individual bravery. Of course, this had long been true; there was qualitatively little difference between the rank and file of Waterloo and their successors at Balaclava. What had changed was that newspapers sent to the Crimea skilled professional reporters, such as *The Times*'s William Howard Russell, whose colourful writing brought home starkly the appalling conditions endured

45

by officers and men. It became impossible for the monarchy and Parliament to remain in ignorance, and, in turn, it became politically useful to elevate some of the rank and file to hero status. The lasting importance of the VC is that henceforth individuals from the 'brute' class could claim a place alongside the most elevated peer of the realm, as decreed by the highest rank of all, the monarchy, driven by political pressure, exercised beyond the ballot box through newspapers.[34]

Yet although Victoria felt genuine sympathy for the men who stood before her that day (and the thousands more, alive and dead, who could not), this deliberately public gesture also helped shore up the crumbling edifice of the royal prerogative – the 'residue of discretionary or arbitrary authority', according to the constitutional theorist A. V. Dicey, 'which at any given time is legally left in the hands of the Crown',[35] in this case authority over Britain's military forces.[36] Over the course of Victoria's reign, the royal prerogative gradually shrank in significance, while Victoria fought every step of the way to defend against Parliamentary encroaches her vestigial control over the army. For her, the creation of the VC was primarily a deeply conservative step, a reassertion of her dwindling personal authority in military matters; that it paradoxically also represented a radical departure from tradition by dissolving the 'them and us' officers-and-men distinction was welcomed by her as enlarging her status as the *people's* monarch.

The warrant establishing the Victoria Cross was promulgated on 29 January 1856. The War Office then instructed Horse Guards, the army's headquarters in London, to circulate a letter to all Crimean war commanders, asking for nominations of suitable candidates for the new medal. The response was extremely varied. Some commanding officers returned lengthy lists of names, with colourful descriptions of events, while others listed a few names and brief accounts. Still others asserted that their subordinates required no medal to encourage them to do their duty. Indeed, the COs of the 42nd, 50th, 56th, 62nd, 71st and 79th regiments, most of which had seen action in the Crimea,[37] declined to nominate anyone, which meant their officers and men missed the chance of a possible VC. Some COs were astonishingly importunate on their own behalf. Lieutenant Colonel Daubeney of the 55th Foot nominated himself, staking his claim over six densely written pages and obtaining endorsements from six privates and one sergeant. His ink was wasted; he failed to get the VC he so obviously coveted.[38]

The first 111 Victoria Cross winners were therefore doubly fortunate: they had survived – no posthumous VCs were permitted – and their commanding officer had bothered to write a recommendation. In fact, they were *trebly* fortunate: in the Crimea, as in all wars, certainty of what actually happened amid the shot and shell, the smoky confusion, the cacophony of voices struggling to be heard above dying men and horses, was shaky to say the least. A contemporary account from a British officer reveals the kind of confusing disinformation that was standard on the Crimea's battlefields:

> [I]t is almost impossible to get at the truth of things that take place out here. We hear one day that 'A. behaved very well in the Sortie last night'. Next day it appears that 'A. couldn't be found on that occasion' & that B. was the man, & perhaps next day we find that B. was not there at all! Just conceive of the difficulty of 'an authority' getting at the truth of anything. I could give you 50 illustrations of this... To this day I don't know, & cannot find out, who was the Officer of Artillery who at 'Inkerman' brought up two large guns that helped materially to gain the day. I ought to know for they fired away within 20 yards of me for some hours, & I positively cannot say who it was. 4 or 5 Officers all claim the honour of it. Where is the truth there?[39]

The genesis of the Crimean War was little understood even at the time, steeped in the treacherous waters that always swirled around the Sublime Porte, as the Ottoman Empire was usually described in contemporary diplomatic language. In Britain, the Crimean War's enduring legacies are a national reverence for Florence Nightingale, feted as the saviour of forlorn British wounded, and the Victoria Cross.[40] The events of October 1853 to February 1856 in which Britain, France, Turkey and Sardinia were victorious in their struggle to contain, temporarily, the political and territorial ambitions of Russia, saw the VC blossom from the corpse heaps at Sebastopol, Alma and Inkerman. For Britain the political and military humiliations were grievous, the death toll unnecessarily high.

Prior to actual hostilities Britain was engulfed by war fever and anti-Russian sentiment, stoked by newspaper depictions of Russia as an uncivilized despotism opposed to liberty and free trade. Russian troops invaded the Turkish-ruled principalities of Wallachia and Moldavia; Turkey declared war on Russia on 23 October 1853. Britain and France followed suit at the end of March 1854, after Russia initially ignored an ultimatum to withdraw its troops, although it eventually did so in July 1854. The immediate *casus belli* had therefore disappeared; but resentment against Russia in Paris and London had reached such a pitch that neither capital was in a mood for compromise. In Britain Lord Lyndhurst made an inflammatory anti-Russian speech in the House of Lords on 19 June 1854:

> If this semi-barbarous people with a Government of the same character, disguised under the thin cover of a showy but spurious refinement... a despotism the most coarse and degrading that ever afflicted mankind – if this Power with such attributes should ever establish itself in the heart of Europe (which Heaven in its mercy avert!) it would be the heaviest and most fatal calamity that could fall on a civilized world.[41]

Lyndhurst wanted to see Sebastopol, the Russian Black Sea port on the Crimean peninsula, 'razed to the ground'. Queen Victoria enthusiastically endorsed the war, as did many others with radically different views, including Marx and Engels; unlike them, Victoria frequently stood on the balcony of Buckingham Palace to wave farewell to her troops. At the start of the war the British monarch's only regret was that none of her four sons was old enough to fight. The chauvinist British public had its hatred of Russia fed by an intoxicated press that was just becoming aware of its power to influence public opinion. The Queen, the press, public opinion – all pushed the irresolute and instinctively non-interventionist prime minister Lord Aberdeen into declaring war, even as he informed Victoria that he had 'such a terrible repugnance for it, in all its forms'. To which she retorted: 'This will never do.'[42]

On 24 February 1854, a month before war was declared, Victoria wrote to Aberdeen that 'we are going to make war upon Russia!' and that 'the country is eager for War at this moment, and ready to grant men and money'.[43] If Victoria was ready for war, her army was not. It embarked with no maps of the Crimea, instead relying on outdated travellers' memoirs. The assumption was that the war would be short, so no winter clothing or hut-building equipment was shipped out. Army commanders had no idea how many Russian troops were stationed on the peninsula, nor where they were situated. General Sir Ian Hamilton, a professional soldier who in 1921 reviewed the British army's history, considered that the men who went to the Crimea were impressive:

England has never sent forth a more splendid body of troops than those she embarked for the Crimea... but its indomitable spirit had been broken... Not the skill of Todleben, not the fighting qualities of the Russian soldiers, not General January or February, not pestilence, not superior armament, but just the good old British national Generalissimo, Sir Muddle T. Somehow, K.G, O.M, G.C.B, marched our poor fellows off by battalions into another and, let us hope, better organised world.[44]

Cholera, scurvy and dysentery swept through the army's ranks in the first few months. As early as mid-November 1854, two-thirds of the British army's pack animals were dead, mostly through starvation or disease. George Frederick Dallas, a lieutenant with the 46th Regiment, wrote on 11 December 1854: 'The horses have all been so starving that they have eaten each other's tails! & it is a fact that not one horse in ten of the Artillery has any hair at all left on that ornamental part of their persons, which adds considerably to their ghastly appearance.'[45] The casualty rate was astonishingly high. Out of the total British contingent of almost 83,000, around 19,000 died, mostly from disease, and a further 11,374 were disabled. The Commissariat Department in London was responsible for supplying the army, but was controlled by the Treasury and rapidly became a byword for corruption and mismanagement. Among its achievements was the shipping of left and right boots for the army on different vessels, one of which sank in a severe gale off the shore of Balaclava on 14 November 1854. On 14 January 1855, at the height of a bitterly cold Crimean winter and less than a month after Captain Scobell stood up in the House of Commons to call for a new Order of Merit for the British armed forces, Lieutenant Dallas gave his family joyful news – boots had arrived:

> We got up at last about 20 pairs of boots per company [around 100 men], a great want as the men were all in a wretched state. Would you believe that they are all too small! & except for a very few men useless!... With endless wealth, great popular enthusiasm, numberless ships, the best material for Soldiers in the World, we are certainly the worst clad, worst fed, worst housed Army that ever was read of.[46]

Eleven days later The Times scathingly denounced those responsible for the unfolding disaster: 'If Government... choose to sell themselves to the aristocracy, and through the aristocracy to their enemies, it is their own affair; we wipe our hands of the national suicide.'[47]

Abortive efforts were made to investigate the origin of the Crimean shambles and to allocate responsibility. Two commissioners, Colonel Alex Tulloch and Sir John McNeill, were sent by Parliament to the Crimea in February 1855. Tulloch knew the army's ways intimately, having spent twenty years at the War Office; McNeill was a Scottish surgeon and Poor Law commissioner. Their report was devastating:

> Out of about 10,000 men who died during these seven months [the winter of 1854–5], belonging to the Crimean Army, only 1,200 were cut off by that epidemic [cholera], the remainder perished by no foeman's hand – no blast of pestilence, but from the slow, though sure, operation of disease, produced by causes, most of which appeared capable at least of mitigation.[48]

To Queen Victoria's consternation, their report was presented to Parliament in January 1856.[49] For the army's senior ranks, the report was an affront to their authority and their dignity. Victoria admonished Palmerston, then prime minister, that if 'military officers of the Queen's Army are to be judged as to the manner in which they have discharged their military duties before an enemy by a Committee of the House of Commons, the command of the Army is at once transferred from the Crown to that Assembly'.

The government responded by announcing on 17 February 1856 a Commission of Inquiry consisting of seven senior military officers, none of whom had either served in or visited the Crimea; this commission exonerated all the officers censured by Tulloch and McNeill. Detailed daily newspaper reports presented the British breakfast table with a grotesque contrast between the valiant struggle of the rank and file and the appalling conditions in which they lived and died, and the managerial blunders of the Commissariat in London and the ineptitude of the military commanders. Readers of *The Times* enjoying their morning coffee discovered that even this small luxury was beyond the troops:

> The cruellest farce now performing in the Crimea is that of giving the soldiers their coffee in the berry. One has hardly patience to read the detail of its preparation – it has to be roasted over a few twigs in the lid of a can, and then pounded between stones!... I would ask if the authorities have yet sent out ground coffee packed in tin, or – which might be as convenient – coffee in the berry already roasted, and to grind it some thousand or two of coffee-mills, which may be readily purchased at about 3s each? Our bigwigs are certainly contemptible blunderers.[50]

Lord Raglan, the commander of the British expeditionary force, despite his complete lack of experience of commanding troops in the field, finally caught up with the coffee chaos, complaining in a letter to Queen Victoria on 20 January 1855 about the Commissariat's delivery of unroasted coffee beans to the front.[51]

To the chagrin of Raglan, target of much of the newspapers' bile, British reporters were allowed to roam the battlefield freely, reporting what they saw without official interference. According to *Lloyd's Weekly Newspaper*, 'everybody knows that Lord Raglan commands in the Crimea because he is the son of a duke', a malicious quip that nevertheless rang true for many readers.[52] Raglan was sixty-five years old, tired and frequently ill; had he the stamina of someone half his age, he would still have struggled with the muddle he faced. On 28 November 1854 Raglan sent an urgent request to London for 3,000 tents, 100 hospital marquees, 6,000 nosebags, and large numbers of spades, shovels, pickaxes and other essential items. At the end of April 1855 no ship had been allotted to carry these stores. On 5 May 1854, *The Times* referred to the Crimean conflict as 'the people's war', signalling a slightly alarming drift in the direction of republicanism. The Times's chief of foreign affairs, Henry Reeve, applauded the fact that the press was no longer the servant of lords and masters but had become instead 'the instrument by means of which the aggregate intelligence of the nation criticises and controls them all'.[53] Even Punch, always lagging behind the zeitgeist, published in April 1855 a Leech cartoon showing the Queen confronting a medicine bottle, representing the army medical service, with the inscription 'ought to be well shaken'; an empty larder, representing the Commissariat; and a pig, intended to depict the military bureaucracy. The caption, an ironic reference to Victoria's hospital visits to the injured, ran: 'The Queen Visiting the Imbeciles of the Crimea.'[54]

Such forthright press hostility made life in Whitehall, Horse Guards and Buckingham Palace deeply uncomfortable. Inevitably, the establishment saw the accusers as the villains and shrugged aside responsibility. Lord Clarendon, the British foreign secretary, wrote to the British ambassador at Constantinople in September 1854: 'The press and the telegraph are enemies we had not taken into account but as they are invincible there is no use complaining to them.'[55] Sympathy for the men who defended the realm was easily evoked; in previous times, when the other ranks had been largely absent from public attention, it had been relatively simple to dismiss them as 'brutes', but now, under such intense scrutiny, the ordinary soldier and sailor became recognizable as fellow human beings. As the historian Orlando Figes writes: 'If the British military hero had previously been a gentleman all "plumed and laced", now he was a trooper, the "Private Smith" or "Tommy" ("Tommy Atkins") of folklore, who fought courageously and won Britain's wars in spite of the blunders of his generals.'[56] Without the British press, the VC might not have come into being – and the British press has feasted on the VC ever since.[57] But the British press did not simply reveal the scandals;

it also delighted in identifying heroic acts. As the *Aberdeen Journal* commented:

> We have heard many complaints of the evils of the presence of newspaper correspondents at the seat of war, but we humbly think that this at least is one advantage which they have conferred on the army, for it is not to any chance of system, but to the fact that every gallant action was chronicled and known at home, that the army owes this acknowledgement of individual services.[58]

All army officers owed their appointments and allegiance to the monarch. The failure to bring the conflict to a swift, smooth and satisfactory conclusion therefore reflected poorly on the monarchy.[59] The revelation that senior officers were not just inept on the battlefield – the ambiguity of the order leading to the hopeless but magnificent charge of the Light Brigade was just one example – but also careless of the men's welfare away from the battlefield, threatened to damn the aristocratic regime that governed the military, including Victoria's husband. Much of the British press openly loathed Prince Albert; that he was born in the Duchy of Saxe-Coburg-Saalfeld gave rise to xenophobic suspicions.[60] At the height of the Crimean conflict, the monarchy seemed unable to repair its broken public reputation, instead lending its name to a series of blunders. In his memoir of the war, Douglas Reid, assistant surgeon with the 90th Light Infantry, found it particularly galling that, in the name of the Queen, a nationwide day of 'solemn fast, humiliation and prayer' was declared for 21 March 1855. He quoted *The Examiner* of 18 March 1855: 'We have starved the army – therefore let us fast; we have found our vaunted system worthless – therefore, let us humble ourselves; we have taken all measures to ensure disaster, disaster has attended our efforts – therefore let us pray!'[61] Victoria felt betrayed, and felt her army had been betrayed too. She began to insist that every message from Lord Raglan to Lord Panmure, Secretary of State for

War, and every instruction of any significance sent by Panmure to Raglan, should be shown to her – 'if possible *before* they are sent.'[62]

Threats to the monarchy's assumed right to control the army; appalling examples of maladministration in the army's supply; terrible battlefield and front-line conditions for the troops; plentiful examples of individual courage daily served up by an eager national press; generous distribution of individual medals by the French – all these factors called for a dramatic response by Britain's governing class and, more particularly, the Crown. That response was the creation of the VC.

Just how radical a step this was has been rather lost sight of today. The common soldiery prior to the Crimean War had little incentive to exceed their duties. What military honours that existed were *ad hoc* affairs, dependent on the whimsicalities of political influence, and usually (the Bath, for example) for officers only. Campaign medals, such as the Military General Service Medal (MGSM), which was distributed retroactively to all officers and men who fought in the Napoleonic Wars, were notable precisely because they were so unusual. The MGSM was indiscriminate; all that was required was merely to have been present on one of the battlefields.[63] After the final victory over Bonaparte at the Battle of Waterloo in 1815, the Prince Regent, the future George IV, had struck a silver medal in celebration. From the humblest drummer boy to the Duke of Wellington, all were eligible for the first medal since 1650 to be authorized by the government for general distribution.[64] Wellington considered the Prince Regent 'the worst man he ever fell in with his whole life, the most selfish, the most false, the most ill-natured, the most entirely without one redeeming quality' and suffered the royal hijacking of his glory.[65] The prince, safely tucked up in London during Waterloo, commanded that the medal's entire obverse should be occupied by his own profile; the reverse grudgingly acknowledged the true victor with a single word – 'Wellington' – above the seated figure of Victory.

Such indiscriminate medal distributions rankled, as *The Times* pointed out when the VC was first mooted:

> Many men who never heard the pealing of the artillery at Waterloo... received the Waterloo medal, in common with the bleeding survivors of the diminished squares. The same principle has been observed in the Crimea. Medals and clasps have been given for particular actions to men who took no further part in those actions than the troops now encamped at Aldershott.[66]

Away from the battlefield, the typical redcoat was assumed to be drunk, debauched, dirty and disreputable; during combat his only duty was to stand his ground and unquestioningly obey orders. Nor was this image a vast distortion: 'In the British army... a staggering 5,546 men (roughly one in eight of the entire army in the field) behaved so badly that they were court-martialled for various acts of drunkenness during the Crimean War.'[67] While the rank and file could expect no individual recognition for any act of exceptional courage, officers might hope for a CB, KCB or even a GCB, the Knight Grand Cross. In 1815 the Prince Regent decided that the Order of the Bath, hitherto a purely civilian title, should also have a military version, for officers only.

But in general, money, not medals, was what the victorious British soldier or sailor looked for. This might come through private enterprise – corpse-robbing[68] – or state-distributed prize money.[69] Two years after Waterloo, Parliament sanctioned a financial grant to all surviving veterans, which was paid on a sliding scale. The Duke of Wellington received £61,000 (almost £4 million in 2014, using the retail price index, and more than £60 million if we consider it on the basis of economic status);[70] lesser generals more than £1,274[71] (more than £81,000 or £1,322,000 respectively). Corporals, drummers and privates were awarded £2 11s 4d (£164 or £2,665). A silver medal was better than nothing – but for the majority, no doubt, cash was better still.[72]

By the time the eighteen-year-old Victoria became queen in 1837, it was a largely unquestioned assumption that, constitutionally, the army was subject to a system of 'dual control': raising the money to finance the army was a matter for Parliament, while its command, the way in which that money was spent, was in the hands of the Crown. This division was blurry, not least because Parliament provided a home for many senior officers on half-pay, all of them regarding their allegiance as being first and foremost to the monarchy that had appointed them: between 1790 and 1820 almost 20 per cent of MPs had spent time in the regular army.[73] Nevertheless, there was an accepted division of control between monarchy and Parliament, consolidated by a royal warrant of 1812, which stipulated that while the Secretary at War – a civilian minister – was responsible to Parliament for the financial control of army expenditures, the commander-in-chief was answerable to the Crown for discipline and army administration. This was thought to ensure that the tendency of monarchs to use military power for their own ends would be counterbalanced by a penny-pinching parliament, which would keep a close eye on the cost (and therefore the size) of the army. At the same time, by giving the Crown ultimate authority over military appointments, the army was believed secure against the undue influence of parliamentary factions. In reality, this distinction ensured that succeeding monarchs felt themselves to have the right of a royal veto over not just senior army appointments but all military affairs – and Victoria exercised this supposed authority to the fullest extent possible.

The bonds that knitted together monarchy and army were consolidated by the appointment of trusted friends and relations to the most senior military posts. In 1795, for instance, George III appointed his son, Prince Frederick, the Duke of York and Albany and a career soldier, as commander-in-chief of the army. The erosion of the military and civilian division of authority reached its acme in 1828, when the Duke of Wellington became prime minister while simultaneously occupying the post of commander-in-chief. Wellington was determined to ensure that 'the command of the army should remain in the hands of the Sovereign, and not fall into those of the House of Commons'[74] Henry Hardinge, who succeeded Wellington, was no less a defender of the royal prerogative. In Hardinge's view:

> The King, and not that House, was the disposer of grace, favour, and reward to the Army... It was of the utmost importance that the army should look up to no authority but that of the King. It was by his Majesty's direction that punishments were inflicted, and by him alone should rewards be conferred. This was the constitutional doctrine.[75]

In the opinion of Victoria, a soldier pledged an oath of fidelity not to Parliament but 'to defend Her Majesty, her heirs and successors, Crown and dignity, against all enemies' and 'to observe and obey all orders of Her Majesty, her heirs and successors, and of all Generals and Officers set over him'.[76] In January 1855, when, under pressure from both Parliament and the public, the Duke of Newcastle, Secretary of State for War in the Aberdeen administration, sent a despatch to Lord Raglan seeking explanations for the poor management of the war, Victoria chided him:

> The Queen has only one remark to make, viz. the entire omission of her name throughout the document. It speaks simply in the name of the People of England, and of their sympathy, whilst the Queen feels it to be one of her highest prerogatives and dearest duties to care for the welfare and success of her Army.

Victoria was conscious of the fact that her father, Prince Edward, Duke of Kent, had been a soldier, and that she had been taken by him as a baby to a military review on Hounslow Heath. Although he died when she was just eight months old, in 1876 she presented new colours to her father's old regiment, the Royal Scots, saying: 'He was proud of his profession, and I was always told to consider myself a soldier's child.'[77] In 1838, her coronation year, she supervised a large review of the army in Hyde Park and such reviews became a regular feature of her reign. She even formally approved army uniforms; during the Crimean War Panmure informed Victoria that he understood and respected her 'sole right to determine... all patterns for the arms, clothing, and accoutrements and equipment of the Army'.[78]

Victoria had no desire to dissolve the innate conservatism of the army, yet the introduction of an inherently democratic military honour flouted the established order. For her, the VC was no more than an extension of *noblesse oblige* into military affairs; for many senior officers, it threatened a dangerous erosion of their status, for which they had often paid large sums of money out of their own pocket. In retrospect they had much and nothing to fear: the creation of the VC certainly helped open the way for more profound army reform, including the abolition of the commission purchase system, but the preservation of the officer class as an elite, separate from and socially superior to the other ranks, was left intact.

The VC was therefore born out of a ghastly shambles. More positively (at least as far as the monarchy was concerned), it helped deflect public anger and dissipated the wrath of the press. It massaged that justified anger into an enhanced reverence for the Crown, thereby staving off the inevitable decline of royal authority over the armed forces. Queen Victoria saw the VC as a personal gift of the monarch, helped by Albert's astuteness in naming the decoration for his spouse. The VC publicly symbolized Victoria's gratitude to 'her' armed forces and cemented the affectionate loyalty the military extended to her.

The Times loftily dismissed the Victoria Cross when it first appeared as 'a dull, heavy, tasteless affair' and 'coarse-looking… mean in the extreme'. The newspaper held its nose and sneered at the VC's ugly appearance, apparently unaware that the decoration's unadorned crudity was deliberate:

> Much do we suspect that if it was on sale in any town in England at a penny a-piece, hardly a dozen would be sold in a twelve-month. There is a cross, and a lion, and a scroll or two worked up into the most shapeless mass that the size admits of… Valour must, and doubtless will, be still its own reward in this country, for the Victoria Cross is the shabbiest of all prizes.[79]

The Cross's down-at-heel look was widely deprecated, not merely by the metropolitan press. The 'Private Correspondent' of a regional newspaper remarked:

> The ungainly Victoria Cross has already disappeared from the breasts of those who can afford to get rid of it for something smaller, and therefore less conspicuous in its ugliness. A London jeweller occupies himself in making miniature decorations, and these are worn by many commissioned officers in place of those given them by their Queen and their country.[80]

But The Times's rhetorical flourish was disingenuous. Valour is not and has never been its own reward; successive generations of VC winners have tried to leverage their moment of battlefield prowess, whether by arguing for more rapid promotion, publishing a book, becoming a public speaker, or maybe just advertising themselves in a pub, like Hitch.

The New York Times naturally saw the Cross through a different prism; democracy was on the march in Britain, and the VC was 'a further indication that the British Government are resolved to make some concession to the democratic principles which, steadily and surely, are in course of progress in the realm of Victoria... It is, in effect, an "Order of Merit" for the humblest persons in the army and navy.'[81] The deliberate eschewal of ostentation in the VC's design certainly burnished its democratic image, by distancing it from the glittery pomp of Thistles, Garters and Baths; but appearances deceive. Despite its humble appearance, the VC out-glitters a whole chest full of honours. Most of the British press concurred with the *New York Times*; rare were critical comments such as this from the republican *Reynolds's Newspaper*:

[T]he preamble of QUEEN VICTORIA'S proclamation, instituting the 'VICTORIA CROSS,' is positively insulting to the lower ranks of the army, for she says the necessity for founding it has originated from the impossibility of conferring the Order of the Bath upon 'any but the higher ranks of the service.' This is tantamount to saying, that not even the bravest man in the ranks of the British army, whatever services he may have rendered his country, is qualified to be placed on a level with such miserable, blundering, timid old dolts, as the SIMPSONS, RAGLANS, and DUNDASES, which the present war has turned up![82]

Some contemporary newspaper coverage was remarkably level-headed. *Tinsley's Magazine*, which specialized in popular fiction, considered that:

Select though the sacred circle of Knights of the Victoria Cross be, it would be uncandid to pretend that there is universal satisfaction in the service with all to whom it has been adjudged. Nor are those wanting who rail against the institution, and hint that it has an evil effect, and creates irritating distinctions. But those are the men who have never earned it. Nobody despises pedigree so much as the knave without a grandfather. Still, it is true that there is reasonable complaint that many who ought to have got the Cross have not got it, and that many who have deserved it less than the unsignalized have got it. All the accident of war.[83]

For some correspondents, the VC perpetuated a very different and deeper social division. The *Cheshire Observer* published this from an irate civilian:

> Where is a class of men more deserving and unpitied than our merchant sailors, yet, what surprising and astounding feats do these poor fellows kindly and voluntarily perform to save the lives of the crews and passengers of the sinking vessel. Then there are our firemen, policemen, coalpitmen, and numbers of others... men who have to risk their lives by performing actions of gallantry which are appalling to reflect upon... Such is the class of civilians to whom the presentation of the 'Victoria Cross for Valour,' would be but a just and graceful act of encouragement, and a royal and official acknowledgement of their truly meritorious services, and would be the means of stimulating others to the performance of perilous and heroic deeds.[84]

Even the art world took notice. Louis Desanges, an English painter of French extraction, capitalized on the popularity of the VC by mounting a highly successful exhibition in London of fifty oil paintings, executed between 1859 and 1862, each taking a particular VC episode for its subject matter. Desanges's Victoria Cross Gallery was exhibited at the Crystal Palace throughout the 1860s and remained there until about 1880.[85]

The Victoria Cross has been depicted as marking 'the moment when... common soldiers ceased to be regarded as cannon fodder rounded up by the likes of Lord Cardigan, but were seen to be the equals of any peer of the realm in the face of the enemy'.[86] The reality is that common soldiers would still be cannon fodder, and the new award merely ushered in new uncertainties, not the least of them being disgruntlement among senior officers, some of whom felt the VC would undermine discipline and order, and others who were annoyed that this new and prestigious decoration was beyond them, simply because the opportunity for displaying such courage was usually unavailable to high-ranking officers. Jostling to be considered for the new award, and complaints of having been overlooked, swiftly followed.

Sergeant William McWheeny of the 44th Foot gained his VC in part for his rescue of Private John Keane who, according to the citation, was

dangerously wounded on the Woronzoff Road, at the time the sharp-shooters were repulsed from the Quarries by overwhelming numbers... [he] took the wounded man on his back, and brought him to a place of safety. This was under a very heavy fire. He was also the means of saving the life of Corpl. Courtney. This man was one of the sharp-shooters, and was severely wounded in the head, 5 Dec. 1854. Sergt. McWheeny brought him in from under the fire, and dug up a slight cover with his bayonet, where the two remained until dark, when they retired.[87]

This account was disputed by William Courtney in a letter to *The Times* in March 1857. Courtney claimed that he had carried Keane on his back to a place of safety and continued:

as to Sergeant M'Wheeny [sic] having saved my life, that is also entirely untrue. I was left on one side for many hours after I was wounded; and as to the assertion that I and M'Wheeny retired after dark, anyone with common sense must see how impossible it was. I received three balls in my head at once, and my right eye was shot out, besides other injuries. Of course, I was utterly incapable of moving, and it was equally impossible for anyone to have covered me, &c., as M'Wheeny is said to have done... I ask not praise; I did my duty to my Queen and country; all I request is justice.[88]

At this distance, no one can say with any certainty if Courtney was right or simply chancing his arm.

For junior officers and the other ranks, the VC was and is a grand lottery: a previously obscure nobody could achieve overnight fame. Editors quickly exploited the VC's potential as a source of colourful, dramatic copy, attractive to both readers and advertisers, and much better than the usual run-of-the-mill military reporting, such as another dull despatch from a commanding officer. The *Aberdeen Journal*, for example, ran a series from March 1857 of 'some of the more striking incidents' which had gained the VC in the Crimea, beginning with the Naval Brigade. Even in her dotage, Victoria cultivated opportunities to promote the indissoluble link between herself, the Cross and 'her' soldiers. In 1898 she visited the Royal Victoria Hospital at Netley in Hampshire to pin the VC on the tunics of two wounded soldiers, both of whom were found sitting down.[89] 'They were ordered to rise, but the Queen said, "Most certainly not," and raised herself without help (a very unusual thing) and stood over them while she decorated them with the cross.'[90]

By the end of the first investiture of the VC on 26 June 1857, much had changed, although in many respects everything remained the same. Holders of the VC found themselves entitled to take precedence over the highest peer of the realm on any ceremonial occasion; but few of those peers regarded VC holders as their equal once the ceremonies and ritual obeisance were over. Of greater long-term significance was that the establishment of the VC opened the way for a subsequent rash of new distinctions, which, by trying to distinguish more finely different grades of courage, helped restore the social divisions dissolved by the VC.[91] In novels, journalism and popular ballads, the VC winner was to be depicted as an icon of courage, on whose valiant shoulders rested the empire. Victoria could not foresee what a Pandora's Box she and Albert had opened: if merit was to be the principal means of selection in the recognition of supreme courage, why should merit not become more widespread in the armed forces, for promotion to its higher ranks? The course of the rest of the VC's history has been one in which a gradual rise in the level of courage demanded and expected, has imperceptibly taken hold. A new military aristocracy – the elite class of VC winners, no women and very few civilians allowed – was born on 26 June 1857.

3

Small Wars

'I have heard it said that no one could be so immodest as
to ask for the Victoria Cross. Poor deluded souls!'
LIEUTENANT GENERAL H. J. STANNUS[1]

'Christianity and thirty-two-pounders are better than
swords and spears and heathenism.'
CHIEF THAKAMBAU OF FIJI[2]

In the forty-five years between 1856, when the VC was first created, and
Victoria's death in 1901, no challenge to the empire went unpunished.
British soldiers fought 200 greater or lesser wars in Abyssinia, Africa,
China, Egypt, New Zealand, Sudan and India, as Britain gobbled up
land and peoples, quadrupling the size of the territory it controlled.
Colonel Charles Callwell summarized in a textbook for officers the
nature of these 'small wars': 'Small wars include... campaigns of
conquest when a Great Power adds the territory of barbarous races to
its possessions; and they include punitive expeditions against tribes
bordering upon distant colonies.'[3] This extension and consolidation of
empire turned the world map pink, while spattering red across jungle,
desert and bush, as British rule was imposed with varying degrees of

brutality. Indigenous peoples were subjugated, while domestic British opinion developed an appetite for heroes; men were needed to police new territories, and the struggles to defeat skilled, often poorly armed yet fierce opponents, placed a steadily rising premium on military professionalism. For readers of most of Britain's newspapers and periodicals, these decades were a record of gallant armies 'civilizing' natives, extending and deepening Britain's might against supposedly merciless barbarian hordes. To the Victorian mind, every soldier was potentially a Homeric hero, an evangelizing agent bent on imparting the values of Christianity. Over most of these campaigns were sprinkled the imparted 'glory' of Victoria Crosses, some deserved, some undeserved, and others obtained by the kind of machination that never occurred to Victoria and Albert when they put flesh on what was, in principle, a noble ideal. One who truly deserved the VC, Winston Churchill, who in the late nineteenth century fought in four wars in as many years, was, as we will see, excluded from the club, probably the victim of a capricious senior officer whom he had offended. Leaving aside larger ethical considerations of how the empire was gained and managed, it became clear that human frailty – ambition, greed, selfishness, posturing – was to become a consistent strand in the history of the Victoria Cross, entangled with the collective tale of exceptional individual courage. Senior officers had little compunction about using the VC to reward favourites and build their own careers; individuals who wanted the Cross and thought they deserved it exploited personal connections to achieve their aim. Noble idealism and ignoble politicking are but the obverse and reverse of the same medal – of all medals, perhaps; but the higher the reward, the greater the temptation to resort to corrupt means of obtaining it.

The Indian Mutiny of 1857–8 provided the perfect opportunity to test precisely how much independence officers in the field might have over the bestowal of this relatively new decoration. The seventh clause of the founding warrant of the VC in 1856 permitted the VC to be provisionally – and subject to confirmation by the sovereign – conferred on the spot if the deed had been performed 'under the eye and command of an Admiral or General Officer commanding the Forces'. Immediate subordinates of the admiral or general in overall command had the same authority. Clause eight further refined the witness/proof requirement: if no commanding officer witnessed the action, then individual soldiers, sailors or marines were able to lay claim to the VC, so long as they were able to prove 'to the satisfaction of the Captain or officer Commanding his Ship or to the Officer Commanding the Regiment to which the Claimant belongs' that the deed was sufficiently worthy. If one of these tests was passed, the claim was then to be passed up to the highest ranks for consideration, who 'shall call for such description and attestation of the act as he may think requisite and on approval shall recommend that grant of the Decoration'.

On 29 October 1857, while the fighting was continuing, the Indian Mutiny gave rise to the first amendment of the VC warrant, extending eligibility to the military forces of the East India Company. On 10 August 1858 another amendment was made, stating that cases of bravery not before the enemy were admissible. And on 13 December 1858, civilians who had served the Crown courageously during the Mutiny were also rendered eligible, by virtue of yet another amendment. Unhelpfully, this last revision did not seem to limit the scope purely to those civilians who had fought during the Mutiny; the key ambiguous phrase merely said 'against the mutineers at Lucknow and elsewhere'.[4] These *ex post facto* amendments were resisted by War Office civil servants who had the task of ensuring that all VC recommendations complied with the strictures of the warrant, but they were overruled by forceful senior officers on the ground in India, who had an entirely different view of the VC; for them, it was simply a useful tool to reward, recognize and encourage. This tension – between civilian administrators determined to defend a strict interpretation of the grounds for awarding the VC, and senior officers who took a much more cavalier approach – endured until well into the twentieth century.

When the Mutiny finally ended, Victoria reasserted in her speech to Parliament on 3 February 1859 her sense of ownership of all things military: 'The Blessing of the Almighty on the Valour of My Troops in India, and on the Skill of their Commanders, has enabled Me to inflict signal Chastisement upon those who are still in Arms against My Authority, whenever they have ventured to encounter My Forces...'[5] Yet Victoria's unquestioned authority over 'her' army was already waning. The Indian experience, coming so soon after the narrow victory in the Crimea, jolted British self-esteem and focused minds on the need for army reform, and led to the transfer of India's administration from the East India Company into direct British government control. En passant, it also undermined Victoria's personal control over military affairs, although, with a sense of something precious slipping from her grasp, she clung to what petty authority remained:

> Whether the subject was the design of the gold lace sword belt worn by field marshals or the state of the barracks at Windsor or the dismissal of a particular colonel who had lost so much money gambling on horse races that he set a bad example for his troops, or the appropriateness of khaki as a uniform in which to fight battles or even the relative merits of different rifles... the queen invariably held and voiced an opinion.[6]

The farther flung the fracas, the more difficult Victoria found it to exercise personal control over the armed forces – and the VC. As the supervision of the confusing and sometimes contradictory VC regulations slipped from the hands of the sovereign who created it, and seamlessly passed into the nervous fingers of War Office bureaucrats, some senior officers seized the chance to exploit their authority to confer dubiously earned VCs.

In the early days, none was more questionable than that given to Lieutenant Henry Marsham Havelock, awarded the VC in the field by his own father, Brigadier General Henry Havelock, who died of dysentery shortly after, while besieged at Lucknow. The elder Havelock commanded a column which set forth from Allahabad on 7 July 1857, destined to relieve the garrison (eventually brutally massacred) at Cawnpore, before marching to relieve Lucknow. As it marched to Cawnpore, Havelock's force encountered a cannon in the hands of mutinous sepoys; he sent his aide-de-camp, who happened to be his son, to take command of the apparently leaderless 64th Regiment and lead an assault to destroy it. Mounted on horseback, Lieutenant Havelock failed to notice that Major Stirling, now on foot, his horse having been killed, was still in command of the 64th. Under fire from the cannon and rifles, Havelock junior duly captured the gun, along with others, and, much to the chagrin of Stirling, was granted the VC by his father on the spot.

Havelock senior justified his decision by referring to a favourable report from Major General Sir James Outram: 'On this spontaneous statement of the Major General, the Brigadier General consents to award the Cross to this... officer [who]might from the near relationship Lieutenant Havelock bears to him assume the appearance of undue partiality.'[7] The War Office found this VC difficult to swallow; but the field bestowal of VCs was legitimate and, not wishing to undermine the authority of local commanders, it let this one pass; but it declined to concur with a second VC recommended by Havelock senior to his son in an action shortly thereafter. For that second recommendation, Sir Colin (later Lord) Campbell, commander-in-chief in India, was called on to convene a board of inquiry, which came up with an appropriately legalistic reason to deny the award: it ruled that a bar (the second award of the same medal) to a VC could not be recommended for a first VC that had yet to be officially confirmed by the sovereign. On such legalistic cavilling rests much of the VC's history. The younger Havelock may have been denied a bar to his VC, but 182 Crosses were nevertheless sanctioned for the Indian Mutiny, 71 more than during the Crimean War. Was this a high number? No one really knew – the whole business of granting medals to individuals was too new for any sensible comparisons to be possible. Were there really 39 per cent more acts of exceptional courage during the Indian Mutiny than the Crimean War? Was it that senior commanders in India made free with the VC, with little care as to standards? Or was it that – unusually – the elective principle, with officers electing from their own number candidates for the VC, came into play on several occasions, thus inflating the number of VCs that were handed out?

The truth is that it was early days for the VC and no settled, widely agreed standard had yet been reached. That perhaps was inevitable – but it created ill-feeling and public complaints. The Times's letters page carried for months its own mutinous correspondence, as contributors – probably officers, as they adopted pseudonyms – complained about the unfair distribution of Crosses during the Mutiny. In January 1859 'Justitia' wrote:

> I know full well that the officers and privates of the Delhi army consider that they have not had their due share of reward. All India depended on Delhi. The troops know it, and Delhi fell; yet in 25 engagements, in storming the walls, and six days' street fighting afterwards, only six men performed acts of bravery sufficient to make their claims to the Victoria Cross incontestable, whereas 64 of those engaged at Lucknow and in [the state of] Oude are found worthy recipients of it. All who have it deserve it doubtless; but more than the six fortunate recipients in the Delhi army deserve it also.[8]

Some critics felt that the medal was being unfairly restricted to the rank and file, and that democracy was being carried too far. Others complained that insufficient recognition had been given to the *defenders* of Lucknow (as opposed to those who had relieved the city), for whom there was not a single VC.[9] The imbalance – if such it was – between the Lucknow and Delhi VCs came down to the vigour in pursuing the VC by the respective commanding officers. At the lengthy siege of Delhi, two successive generals, Barnard and Reed, were quickly struck down with cholera; the third, Major General Archdale Wilson, was weak and inept, and had failed to block the rebel sepoys' occupation of Delhi in the first place. At Lucknow the much tougher – and more politically astute – Major General Sir James Outram and Lieutenant General Sir Colin Campbell were in charge.[10] The highest number of VCs won on a single day – twenty-four – was given out for the second (and lasting) relief of Lucknow, on 16 November 1857, with four going to civilians. These latter went to Ross Lowis Mangles, William Fraser McDonell, Thomas Henry Kavanagh, all of the Bengal Civil Service, and George Bell Chicken – an unfortunate surname for a man deemed to be of exceptional courage – who was a civilian volunteer with the Indian Naval Brigade. At the time of their award, none of these civilians was actually eligible. Shortly after the Mutiny ended, *The Times* forcibly argued for civilians to be drawn into the VC ambit:

> [T]he difference between an Englishman and a soldier is but the colour of a coat. Although not professionally trained to arms, [civilians] defended positions, concerted operations, and performed feats of individual valour which the bravest soldier in the British army might have been proud to number among his achievements. They were soldiers in all but name, and we rejoice to see that the Queen has been advised to give a soldier's reward to two men who have done a soldier's work.[11]

The two men The Times had in mind were Thomas Kavanagh, Assistant Commissioner in Oudh, who, disguised as an Indian, guided Outram in and out of the Lucknow siege, and Ross Mangles, Assistant Magistrate at Patna, who rescued a wounded soldier of the 37th Regiment.

Some who felt they had been unfairly jilted of a VC at the Crimea had better luck in the Mutiny. Evelyn Wood fought at the Crimea as a midshipman, part of the Naval Brigade. He had sufficient foresight to appreciate that a decoration created by the Queen, and for which the Queen had great personal affection, might be a useful stepping stone for a military career.[12] Wood had served as an aide-de-camp to Captain Peel and joined a fellow aide-de-camp, Edward St John Daniel, in rescuing Peel once he was wounded in action. For this, Daniel received the VC; Wood did not. Wood's father, Sir John Page Wood, decided to pull some strings. He wrote to Lord Panmure, Secretary of State for War, on 4 March 1857, pleading for his son to be awarded a VC, adding that Daniel was unscathed, while his son was wounded yet still carried on. His letter ended with a rhetorical flourish: 'I appeal to your Lordship from the decision of the Admiralty, to do justice to this young man, who has fairly deserved this order, by his blood.'[13] Evelyn Wood had better luck in the Indian Mutiny. The London Gazette of 4 September 1860 announced that the Queen was 'graciously pleased to signify her intention to confer the decoration of the Victoria Cross' on Lieutenant Henry Evelyn Wood of the 17th Lancers. He gained his Mutiny VC for attacking 'almost single-handed, a body of rebels who had made a stand, whom he routed'. That 'almost' is a nice touch. Wood's case is an example of the tendency at the time to award VCs not simply for one but for several gallant acts – and for rewarding individuals who may have, for one reason or another, been unsuccessful on previous occasions. Wood's Mutiny VC was an instance of persistence, as well as courage, being rewarded.

Others lacked a Baronet to write to the War Office on their behalf. Private Dennis Dempsey of the 10th Foot very probably was semi-literate. Nevertheless he put forward a VC claim for himself on 14 March 1858 for his services at Lucknow, when he carried a powder keg out of a burning village. Dempsey's case was ignored by the War Office, loftily indifferent to a solicitation from a humble private. It took a strong letter of recommendation on 23 January 1860 – almost two years later – from Lieutenant Colonel (and former Lieutenant and Adjutant) Percy Beale, now in command of the 10th Foot, to gain sufficient notice for Dempsey. Beale had witnessed Dempsey's act:

> Captain Alderley the Adjutant, the storming party and myself saw Pte Dempsey creep up this native street alone, with the powder bag, exposed to a very heavy fire from the Enemy behind loop holed walls, and an almost still greater danger from the sparks which flew in every direction from the village which was on fire. I and in fact the whole Company expected to see Pte Dempsey blown to pieces by the powder, the men were astonished at his cool bravery: and expressed their admiration of his conduct at the time.[14]

Dempsey was finally gazetted VC on 17 February 1860.

Relatives, civilians, militias – all who had served in the Mutiny clamoured to be heard, despite efforts by the War Office to hold back the tide. The issue of posthumous awards was resurrected, after five individuals on whom Sir Colin Campbell had conferred VCs on the spot died before the decoration was confirmed by Queen Victoria. Campbell suggested a solution: why not send a batch of VCs to him in India for his personal distribution? Edward Pennington, the senior War Office clerk responsible for handling VC recommendations, proposed instead that a notice be published in the London Gazette, stating that the soldier concerned would have received the VC if he had survived.[15] This was backed by the Duke of Cambridge, commander-in-chief of the armed forces, and Victoria. Technically, the dead were ineligible, but this – the case of one awarded the VC but dying before confirmation by the Queen – was a grey area. The Panmure diktat against posthumous awards was inadequate in such cases, and a handful of Crosses were sent to surviving relatives, with a message from the Queen expressing the satisfaction it would have afforded her to confirm the grant of the VC, had the soldier survived – although the government, ever parsimonious, ruled that the gratuity accompanying the medal would not be paid. In the London Gazette of 28 December 1858, a memorandum appeared to the effect that Cornet Bankes of the 7th Hussars, deceased, would have been submitted to the Queen for confirmation of the VC had he survived; his relatives were sent the medal. In cases where the Queen had not yet received the VC recommendation for the deceased, no Cross was granted. This anomaly was clearly unjust, the consequence of long delays in communications between India and London, but the ruling – you had to be alive when recommended in order for your family to receive the Cross – was fairly consistently applied throughout the nineteenth century.

It was, perhaps, a charitable compromise; but it cracked open the door for posthumous awards. Some dead soldiers – or at least their relatives – had to wait many years to receive the VC for which they had been recommended by a senior officer. One such was Private Edward Spence of the 42nd Royal Highlanders, the Black Watch. On 15 April 1858, during the Indian Mutiny, Spence and Private Alexander Thompson volunteered to assist Captain William Martin Café, in command of the 4th Punjab Rifles, in recovering the body of a Lieutenant Willoughby from the ditch surrounding Fort Ruhya, coming under heavy fire as they did so. Thompson survived and got his VC almost immediately; Spence was severely wounded and died two days later, so was ineligible; but a decision by Edward VII in 1907 to grant posthumous VCs in a handful of cases meant that distant relatives of Spence were tracked down and received his Cross – forty-nine years after the event.[16] Later, during the First World War, although nothing in the VC warrant permitted posthumous awards, many were given. According to Michael Crook: 'The only authority therefore upon which the many posthumous awards of the First World War were awarded was that there was nothing in the rules that precluded it.'[17]

Debate over the supposed injustices regarding the distribution of the Indian Mutiny VCs prompted widespread suspicion that for promotion and reward in the British army it was not what you did, but who you knew, as the *Saturday Review* asserted:

> Merit stands a man in little stead in the British Army. The few prizes that exist are for the most part bestowed by jobbery... A friend at the Horse-Guards, or a long bill with a fashionable tailor may do more for an officer than all the merit and ability in the world. The power of writing self-laudatory letters has been said to go far towards obtaining a Victoria Cross; and possibly the adoption of the same method might prove the shortest road to a staff appointment.[18]

Few VC winners in the nineteenth century either thought their story worth recording, or were literate enough to do so. An exception was the civilian Assistant Commissioner of Oudh, Thomas Kavanagh, who in 1860 published a rather self-serving book, *How I Won the Victoria Cross*, with a suitably romantic engraving of himself opposite the title page, bearing the title 'Lucknow Kavanagh in his disguise', in which he was shown garbed in Indian costume, casually holding a sword across his right shoulder. Kavanagh almost failed to get his VC, not because of his civilian status but because, as the *Glasgow Herald* revealed, the directors of the East India Company, his employers, refused to back the recommendation by Lord Canning, the Governor-General of India, 'alleging that he would have the Lucknow medal in common with the other brave men who had earned it!'[19]

Lampooned and immortalized by George Macdonald Fraser in his 1975 novel *Flashman in the Great Game*, Kavanagh (or Kavanaugh as Fraser has it) is seen by Flashman – not the most reliable of narrators – as a buffoon:

> It's a fact that Kavanaugh stole all the limelight when the story came out... he broke off the kneeling-and-praying which he was engaged in, looked up at me with his great freckled yokel face, and says anxiously:
>
> 'D'yez think they'll give us the Victoria Cross?'
>
> Well, in the end they did give him the V.C. for that night's work, while all I got was a shocking case of dysentery. He was a civilian, of course, so they were bound to make a fuss of him...[20]

But Kavanagh was prophetic in his judgement of British rule in India:

> No government was ever actuated by better intentions, or had more talented servants. But it made the mistake (and will go on doing so till another rebellion,) of endeavouring to govern an immense empire by very few and almost irresponsible subordinates... the interest of the State was considered to be of greater importance than the welfare of the people, who were, almost without exception, treated as rogues and liars.[21]

This critique sullied Kavanagh's reputation and he returned to India a profoundly bitter man. He regarded his £2,000 gratuity as insufficient,[22] and as he wrote to *The Times* on 10 August 1859, the VC was only an honourable bauble:

> I desired the Victoria Cross, and I wear it with pride where it was pinned by our good and gracious Sovereign. But it is only a badge of valour. The State has only recognized the great service rendered to it by the bestowal of a decoration no one is bound to respect... I am merely endeavouring to induce [my superiors] to reward me according

to my deserts. Caste prejudices are so strong in the India-office that I have hitherto failed, and I grieve to add that one of my superiors thought proper to threaten me...[23]

Another East India Company employee, Frederick Roberts, eclipsed all other Mutiny VC winners in later life. Born in Cawnpore in 1832, Roberts was a sickly but determined child; his sisters nicknamed him 'Sir Timothy Valliant'. After Eton, Sandhurst and the Addiscombe Military Seminary – the training academy for young officers of the East India Company – Roberts sailed for Calcutta; apart from a brief interlude in Natal he was to spend the next forty-one years in India. In letters published in 1924,[24] Roberts recounted his Indian Mutiny experiences, including the brutality on both sides. From Amritsar on 11 June 1857 he wrote:

> We have come along this far, doing a little business on the road such as disarming Regiments and executing mutineers. The death that seems to have the most effect is being blown from a gun. It is rather a horrible sight, but in these times we cannot be particular... A man (a native) who was at Delhi during the massacre told me he saw 8 ladies let out, and shot one after the other, they nearly all had children with them, who were killed before their eyes.

Present at the capture of Delhi, Roberts gained his Cross – a classic VC action, in which he galloped off alone to retake a captured standard – while attached to the staff of Sir Colin Campbell in the build-up to the relief of Lucknow. Was his gallantry inspired by being under the eyes of Sir Colin? Might he have thought better of it had no senior officer been present? We shall never know.

Certainly, Roberts could hardly contain his delight when he wrote to his mother on 11 February 1858, 'My own Mother, I have such a piece of news for you, I have been recommended for the *"Victoria Cross"*...

Is this not glorious? How pleased it will make the General [his father]. *Such a Medal* to wear with *"For Valour"* scrolled on it.' Under the watchful eye of generals such as Sir Colin Campbell, who groomed talented and dedicated officers such as Roberts, imperial VCs went to those who showed themselves unafraid, dashing and plucky. As a man who rose to be perhaps the most powerful, and certainly the most popular soldier of his day, feted by Kipling in several ballads, Roberts sealed his public fame in September 1880 when, as commander of a field force of 10,000 troops, he marched across 300 miles of harsh terrain to relieve Kandahar. Five years later, he was appointed commander-in-chief in India, his imperial prowess owing much to those two initials, VC.

As the Indian Mutiny dragged on, more minor incidents elsewhere prompted some remarkable revisions to the original VC warrant, revealing the extent to which luck played its part in gaining the Cross in its early days. On 11 November 1857, the coal-fired steamship *Sarah Sands* was carrying reinforcements to India in the form of the 54th Foot – and a lot of gunpowder – when she caught fire 800 miles off the Indian coast and the crew abandoned ship. Despite a severe squall, the soldiers who remained on board threw most of the gunpowder kegs into the water, preventing the fire reaching either the explosive or the coal stores, and the ship managed to limp into Port Louis, Mauritius, ten days later. Although there was an imminent threat to life, the soldiers did no more than their duty and were, no doubt, guided as much by self-preservation as any heroic instinct; there were not enough lifeboats on the *Sarah Sands* to ferry everyone out of danger, and those who managed to escape might not have been able to row fast enough to avoid death or injury if the *Sarah Sands* had blown up. Those who stayed to toss the powder kegs overboard made the only rational decision; it took nerve and discipline, certainly, and fulfilled one definition of courage – the overcoming of fear – but the alternatives were unattractive. As matters stood in November 1857, none of the 54th who fought the blaze or prevented an explosion was eligible for the VC; the fifth clause of the 1856 warrant stated that it 'shall only be awarded to those Officers or Men who have served Us *in the presence of the Enemy* and shall then have performed some signal act of valour or devotion to their Country...' [author's emphasis]. No enemy was present; the case should therefore have been cut and dried, and in this instance bravery should have been truly its own reward.

But public opinion – which so often has influenced the course of the VC's history – swayed events. When the *Sarah Sands* arrived in Port Louis, the soldiers of the 54th were treated to a sumptuous banquet, and the general stationed at Mauritius issued an order praising the soldiers as heroes. In London, the Duke of Cambridge issued an order to be read before every regiment in the army, recording 'the remarkable gallantry and resolution displayed by the Officers and soldiers of the 54th Regiment, on board the ship *Sarah Sands*, under circumstances of a most trying nature, namely, when the vessel took fire at sea, having at the time a large quantity of ammunition on board'. The British press lapped up the story, and the swell of public acclaim eventually washed across the desk of General Sir Colin Campbell in India.[25] On 29 January 1858 he wrote to the Duke of Cambridge, wondering if the VC might be suitable for the 54th on this occasion. The Duke agreed that a relaxation of the statutes seemed justified in this case, as did General Jonathan Peel, Secretary of State for War. Peel went so far as to say in the House of Commons on 30 July 1858 that the Queen supported bending the rules in this instance:

> At present it was requisite that some extraordinary proof of valour [for gaining the VC] should be given in the presence of the enemy. There were, however, instances of valour exhibited not in the presence of an enemy that ought to be rewarded, such for example, as the case

of the men on board the *Sarah Sands*. He was happy to say that he had received the sanction of Her Majesty to such an extension of that order as would include them and persons in similar situations.[26]

Thus an amended warrant, signed by General Peel and dated 10 August 1858, extended VC eligibility to officers and men of the naval and military services who displayed 'instances of conspicuous courage and bravery under circumstances of extreme danger, such as the occurrence of a fire on board Ship, or of the foundering of a vessel at Sea, or under any other circumstances in which through the courage and devotion displayed, life or public property may be saved'. The lone defender of rules being rules, Edward Pennington, the civil servant responsible for the VC at the War Office, counselled that this revised warrant should not be published in the *London Gazette*. It was therefore left in limbo, its existence widely known but not officially acknowledged.

Rumours of its existence reached Canada, from where, early in 1867, the commanding officer of the British forces expressed his curiosity about the revised warrant. In March 1867 Sir Edward Lugard, parliamentary under-secretary at the War Office, declined to forward to Canada a copy of the 1858 revision, stating that 'the Warrant in question has never been printed, or published in the London Gazette' and that it was not 'expedient' to distribute it.[27] In Pennington's view, the 1858 revision cheapened the VC and he, for one, regarded it as his duty to block awards made under it.[28] On his return to London in July 1860, former Major (and now Lieutenant Colonel) Brett, who had taken command of the 54th regiment on the *Sarah Sands* during the crisis,[29] wrote a letter to the new regimental CO, Colonel Michel, applying for a VC to be awarded to Private Andrew Walsh of the 54th Foot. Private Walsh was out of luck; despite being endorsed for the VC by the Duke of Cambridge, Lugard took the advice of Pennington that the unpublished revision of the warrant was not retrospective, even though it had been created specifically to cover the incident of the *Sarah Sands*. Walsh fell foul of a diligent if now forgotten civil servant.[30]

Only six VCs, all of which today appear aberrations, were granted under this revised and obscure warrant. Perhaps the oddest case was that of Private Timothy O'Hea of the 1st Battalion, Rifle Brigade. Stationed in Canada, on 9 June 1866 O'Hea was travelling on a train when a fire broke out in a truck loaded with ammunition. The truck was disconnected from the train while a sergeant dithered over what to do. O'Hea grabbed the key to the truck and opened it, called for a ladder and water to extinguish the fire, and apparently single-handedly put it out after more than an hour. The indefatigable Pennington raised objections to O'Hea's VC, the strongest being that what O'Hea did might be considered an act of duty and that doing one's duty had never been sufficient to merit a VC. Had this stipulation been implemented, then many subsequent VCs might never have been awarded. Pennington must have imagined that his killer blow was to reiterate that, as the 1858 revised warrant had never been invoked, then to do so after eight years might set an unfortunate precedent. But the board of officers which met to consider VC recommendations passed O'Hea's, no doubt confident in their judgement thanks to General Peel's return to the War Office as Secretary of State. So O'Hea got his unusual VC, gazetted on 1 January 1867, the only VC to be awarded on Canadian soil, and the only one to have been published in the *London Gazette* stipulating that it was awarded under the terms of the warrant signed and dated 10 August 1858.[31]

Equally bizarre were the VCs awarded for a single incident on Little Andaman Island, in the Bay of Bengal. On 21 March 1867 the British captain and seven crew members of the *Assam Valley* went ashore and disappeared. A few days later a small expedition went in search of them, but retreated after they were attacked by a group of Onge, the island's indigenous population. On 6 May 1867 a larger expedition landed on the shore, but again came under attack from the Onge and had to be rescued; four privates under the command of an assistant surgeon of the 24th Regiment landed and rescued the seventeen officers and men stranded on shore. Apart from the lavish distribution of VCs on this occasion – all five of the rescue party got one – this incident is notable for the debate as to whether the VCs were awarded under the original warrant or the revised 1858 version. The official notice in the *London Gazette* of these VCs made no mention of the 1858 warrant – unlike the O'Hea case – but nor did it refer to any enemy being present. Even today it is not entirely clear under what terms the five Andaman VCs were awarded. This case was particularly anomalous because the Albert Medal (named for Victoria's deceased husband, and with two classes) had been established by royal warrant on 7 March 1866 and was specifically designed to be awarded for the saving of human lives at sea. But in one sense it does not really matter. The Andaman VCs demonstrated a determination to recognize the bravery of the men concerned in the most public way possible; the Victoria Cross suited that larger political consideration much more than the rather less well-known Albert Medal. The Andaman VCs went to men who were, no matter how bathetically, defending the empire; their example was felt at the time to demand the highest recognition the empire could offer.

Such were the vagaries and rule-bending in the early years of the VC; it was not so much a matter of what you had done, but what allies could be pulled upon to back your case. Some VCs, such as 'Sir Timothy Valliant's', were virtually nodded through; others had to be fought for, both on and off the battlefield. The case of Charles Heaphy illustrates the extent to which lobbying for a VC could succeed, if pursued with sufficient tenacity and with the right political influence.[32]

British-born Heaphy was a talented draughtsman and water-colourist who gained a bronze and a silver medal from the Royal Academy before he was seventeen. In 1839 he took a job as draughtsman with the New Zealand Company (NZC), established in 1837 to colonize the country. Heaphy settled in Auckland and spent the next decade surveying and exploring the country, at a time when the indigenous people of New Zealand were fighting a lengthy guerrilla campaign against the NZC's land-grabbing rapacity. An eager imperialist, Heaphy volunteered his services to the local militia, whose task – backed by regular British forces – was to repress local resistance. He learned the Maori language and, according to his obituary in The Times, 'by his judicious mediations he prevented much native heartburning and bitterness of spirit towards the colonists'.[33] Judiciousness was in scant evidence in 1864.

On 11 February that year, the now Captain Heaphy was in command of a small force of local irregulars involved in a skirmish at the Mangapiko River. Heaphy went to the aid of a fatally wounded militiaman and was himself slightly wounded. Major Sir Henry Havelock VC of Indian Mutiny fame was in command of the regular forces during the Mangapiko episode, and saw fit to recommend Heaphy for a VC to Major General Galloway, a regular army officer and local commander of all forces. Havelock at least was unlikely to be ignorant of the formal VC regulations of the 1856 warrant, which did not embrace the type of local colonial forces to which Heaphy belonged. Up the chain went Heaphy's recommendation, first to Sir George Grey, Governor General of New Zealand, who in turn sent it to Edward Cardwell, then Colonial Secretary in London, until finally it reached the War Office – which, obedient to the terms of the warrant, refused the VC. Heaphy appealed, exploiting a loophole in the 1856 warrant, arguing that the phrase 'our military and naval forces' was open to interpretation in his favour. Heaphy's VC became a political issue: it was a matter of denying a great honour to a new colony. On 11 August 1865 the General Assembly of New Zealand heard a statement from the Governor-General, expressing regret that technicalities should prevent Her Majesty bestowing this distinction on officers and men of a colonial militia; the New Zealand government asked for an extension of the VC warrant. Heaphy wrote to Lord Palmerston to push his case, pointing out that Palmerston was acquainted with his father. Palmerston died before he could act on Heaphy's letter, but – such was the political necessity of placating a remote colonial government, in this case that of New Zealand – that the rewriting of the regulations of the VC was of lesser significance. The VC warrant was thus amended and promulgated on 1 January 1867 to include 'persons serving in the Local Forces of New Zealand' – and Heaphy got the VC he so craved, gazetted the same day, almost three years after his act.[34]

Did Heaphy merit his VC? At this distance the question is unanswerable, if we restrict the discussion purely to a consideration of the degree of courage displayed. The success of a VC recommendation has always depended, in part, on considerations of the broader political usefulness that might be gained. Heaphy's case might be seen as highlighting and overcoming an unhelpful ambiguity in the phrasing of the original warrant. On the other hand, it might equally be felt that rules are, after all, rules; what is the point of having them if they are to be altered simply by tugging at a few influential strings? By the time Heaphy's case cropped up, there had already been so many anomalies in the decoration's brief history that he, no doubt, felt entirely justified in pursuing his VC so assiduously.

Some – very few – dared to ask the question: was the VC such a marvellous creation? The senior ranks of the British army had a spectrum of views, ranging from those who thought it might be useful as a means of rewarding favourites or outstanding examples of gallantry, to the indifferent, through to those who regarded it with outright hostility. Few senior officers devoted much time and energy to a serious analysis of the Cross; those that did generally kept their doubts private. One who publicly attacked the VC was Lieutenant General Henry

James Stannus, an Irish career officer in the Indian army. Stannus loyally served queen and country for almost forty years before ultimately being squeezed out of the army and the only life he had known and loved, at the age of fifty-seven. A deeply conservative figure, Stannus was pushed into becoming something that he had previously given no sign of – an outspoken and highly critical maverick. If Stannus had not been shabbily treated by the tight nexus of power that operated between Simla, the Indian viceroy's summer residence, Horse Guards, the London army HQ, and Whitehall, he may never have committed to paper just how much contempt he felt for the army's highest ranks, or how much he and – so he claimed – others of his rank despised the Victoria Cross.

Stannus's condemnation of the VC is logical, detailed and principled, and was the view of one of Britain's most senior officers; yet his critique has been overlooked by the many books devoted to the VC that have appeared over the years. This neglect reveals the extent to which the received opinion of the VC quickly settled into place; most books on the Cross settle into the same format, the telling and retelling of tales of individual VC winners who all are deemed heroes, no matter what their individual circumstances might have been. Stannus was the first to apply a little bit of analysis, the first to look at the Cross more forensically. He disapproved not only of the VC but of all medals, decorations and military honours – although he received several himself – for the impeccably logical reason that to 'reward a man, as is frequently the case, for doing what he would be ashamed not to do, and for neglecting to do which he would deserve to be tried by court-martial, is acknowledged even by the recipient of the honours to be perfectly ridiculous'.[35] His acceptance of honours when they came his way may be thought hypocritical, but it was a necessary hypocrisy; to decline the CB he was awarded would have been to commit professional and social suicide. But once his career was finished and he was free of the yoke of silent obedience, Stannus returned to Horse Guards all his honours and medals.

Up untill shortly before he left the army, Stannus had enjoyed a glittering career. He joined the 5th Bengal Cavalry in India as a cornet. In the First Afghan War, from 1839 to 1842, he so distinguished himself at the age of nineteen that he was made adjutant of his regiment. In 1848, when the Second Anglo-Sikh War broke out, Lord (Hugh) Gough, commander-in-chief of the British forces in India, appointed Stannus head of his personal bodyguard. Stannus again shone, at the Battle of Gujrat on 21 February 1849, when thirty chainmail-clad Afghan cavalry tried to capture Gough. Leading a small band against the Afghans, Lieutenant Stannus and his men found their swords useless against chainmail and used their pistols instead. He was badly wounded in this skirmish, for which – had it existed at the time – he almost certainly would have been recommended for the VC. He was immediately appointed captain and brevet major – he held three different ranks in three days – and in 1852 took command of the 1st Punjab Cavalry. In 1862 Stannus was given command of the newly raised 20th Hussars, formed from the East India Company's European (i.e. non-Indian) cavalry regiments. Five years later, Sir William Mansfield, then commander-in-chief of the armed forces in India, appointed Stannus commander of a brigade based at Agra. By December 1871 Lieutenant Colonel Stannus was now a CB and in receipt of a good-service pension. A short while later the viceroy, Lord Napier, gave Major General Stannus command of the division based at the city of Umballa, today's Ambala.

In December 1872 the 20th Hussars were withdrawn from India and Stannus had no option but to leave too. By 1874 he was back in Ireland on the unattached army list, kicking his heels and wondering what his next appointment might be, when – to his bitter disappointment and anger – he learned that two more junior generals, Crawford Chamberlain and Donald Stewart, had been given commands of divisions in India. In an army where seniority was acquired by length of service, this could only be construed as a deliberate snub to Stannus, who complained to the commander-in-chief of the British army, the Duke of Cambridge, that he was a victim of injustice and possible nepotism. He drew attention to the fact that Sir John Lawrence, the viceroy of India from 1864 to 1869, loved to play croquet, and that a party comprising Lawrence, Chamberlain and Stewart (the latter two both then colonels) regularly met at Simla to indulge in a game. Digging deeper, Stannus discovered that his fate had probably been sealed in 1867, when he had been censured by Mansfield for an incident that was so trivial that Stannus had forgotten all about it.

During the heat of the Indian summer, Brigadier General Stannus and his staff at Agra usually donned white linen uniforms, following widespread practice. Major General Troup, a notorious bully who liked to boast of his rudeness to subordinates, commanded the Meerut Division of the Bengal army and was thus Stannus's immediate superior. When Troup turned up at Agra to inspect Stannus's command, he expressed surprise at being greeted by a cool but – for Troup – peculiarly dressed Stannus, who immediately offered to conform to Troup's more regular style of uniform. Troup dismissed the matter and led Stannus to understand he had no objection; Stannus mistook this for approval and he and his staff appeared at all inspection parades and official dinners in white linen uniforms. Throughout his stay at Agra, Troup gave no hint of displeasure; but once back at his own base Troup issued orders banning the white uniform throughout his command. Troup then left the division for a period and, as the next most senior officer, Stannus took over command. As he was entitled to, Stannus issued his *own* orders as to what to wear during the heat – white linen. Stannus may have lacked tact or political sense, but he had done nothing wrong. Nevertheless, Stannus was formally reprimanded by Mansfield for his infringement of official regulations regarding uniform.

In his plea to the Duke of Cambridge, Stannus dug his own grave deeper by, among other things, bluntly accusing Napier, the viceroy, of being surrounded by sycophants. He called Napier 'the greatest jobber the Indian Army ever had at its head... A long residence in India had given Lord Napier a host of personal acquaintances to provide for.' After a lengthy, private and – for Stannus – frustrating correspondence with the deeply unpopular Military Secretary at the time, General Sir Alfred Horsford, who was the Duke of Cambridge's gatekeeper, Stannus made public his grievances in the forlorn hope that the establishment would be embarrassed into giving him justice. He published in 1881 his lengthy letter to the Duke of Cambridge, and much else besides, in My Reasons for Leaving the British Army – a book that momentarily ruffled feathers and then disappeared, leaving his career in tatters. Clearly, Stannus was never going to win this struggle with the great beasts of the army and Raj politics, but he was driven to distraction by the financial difficulties resulting from his unsought retirement: he was left with an income of £456 a year (equivalent to about £37,000 in 2013 terms) to support five eligible daughters and a household in Dublin, while less distinguished juniors now commanding divisions in India were earning several times more. The Examiner of 21 August 1880 commented on his case, which Stannus quoted:

> It is a sorry tale that an officer who can show a Companionship of the Bath, a good-service pension, a wound pension for life, and nine medals and clasps, should find himself superseded, and obliged, in regard to his own honour, to retire from the service of a country which could furnish him neither employment nor adequate provision.[36]

Stannus was a victim of... what? Jealousy? Rivalry? His own bloody-mindedness? We will probably never know. His story, that of an angry and bitter senior British officer allegedly brought low by sycophancy and nepotism, is obviously partial, but nonetheless illustrative of how an exceptional career in the military could be humbled by trivia.[37] But we should be grateful, for his humiliation unlocked an absorbing critique of the VC, one that is all the more powerful because of its source. His brochure (as he called it) on the Victoria Cross aimed at demolishing the public mystique that had by the 1880s enveloped the VC: 'it is incontestable that by a great majority of the community outside the service the decoration of the Victoria Cross has an extraordinarily fictitious value, and one which it would no longer retain, but that the public generally cares so very little to dive below the surface.'[38] In 1881 Stannus plunged below the surface and pinpointed a major flaw endemic to the Cross – that the encouragement of ambition for individual recognition on the basis of exceptional courage also promotes distortion, hyperbole and heartache:

> The mischief the system entails throughout the Army can hardly be exaggerated; it induces to put the whole machinery of the service out of gear. Inflated despatch-writing is one of its most prominent evils, and the most niggardly economy of truth is its result... From the cradle to the grave of their military service a large proportion of the Officers of the Army are struggling for the possession of these baubles and shams, and in their acquisition all sense of modesty and decency is set aside and effaced.[39]

As we shall see, 'inflated despatch-writing' remains today a necessary *sine qua non* to stand a chance of winning a VC. For Stannus, it was axiomatic that professional soldiers clearly understood their duty, and that to offer inducements to go beyond that – to go off on a frolic of one's own – was folly:

> A man 'going on by himself,' or separating himself from his men should be severely censured, likewise an officer who exposes himself 'to the full fire of the enemy,' instead of keeping out of it, are not fit

recipients of the decoration. Such hair-brained [sic] folly if encouraged as a virtue would be fatal to success and ensure wholesale slaughter where an enemy was in any way enterprising. But... the authorities consider these deviations from the fundamental principles of all warfare deserving of special favourable recognition.[40]

Stannus also condemned the creation of 'new' acts of courage that resulted from the invention of the VC:

> Who can unravel the mysterious fact that these acts of heroism for which the Victoria Crosses are now given were never heard of *before* the institution of the order, and that ever since there have been periodical and spasmodic attacks of valour, and these epidemics are now coincident with the commencement of every petty campaign... All these marvels we now hear of have occurred since the institution of the Victoria Cross, a sufficient proof what a degenerate set we were in the good old days when Victoria was first Queen.[41]

The 'marvels' Stannus referred to could often easily be mistaken for simple acts of duty. Lieutenant Colonel F. C. Elton, for instance, of the 55th Regiment in the Crimea, gained his VC on 4 August 1855, for showing a splendid example to his men by continuing to lead the regiment while under fire at night; in other words, for doing what would generally be assumed to be nothing more than his duty. For Stannus, the VC set a dangerous precedent; the identification of individuals to be placed on a pedestal was, by definition, a subjective business, heavily dependent on luck, and this, he asserted, fostered wide disgruntlement. Worse, it bred mendacity:

> No-one, moreover, contests the received opinion of the service, that the element of merit is in no way mixed up with their distribution, and the shifts resorted to make the bestowal of the Victoria Cross appear plausible on paper, are extremely entertaining... I have known

men who could hardly write their own names... men whose brains were severely taxed to remember the proper side of the horse on which to mount... I have known such men get honours and rewards, and been thrust into exalted staff positions, solely because they brazed it out with those in power, and had back-stairs influence to assist them.[42]

No doubt Stannus had in mind the example of Charles Heaphy.

If Stannus was a lone voice, we might simply disregard his views as motivated by bitter prejudice. But there were others – less outspoken perhaps, because they had positions to protect – who worried that the VC caused more harm than good. As early as 1859, Sir William Fraser, MP for Barnstaple and a former captain in the Life Guards who idolized Wellington, spoke for many officers. Fraser feared the VC would encourage soldiers to seek individual glory, to the detriment of broader interests:

> Of all the despatches written by that great man [Wellington] there was not one in which the word 'glory' did occur, nor one in which the word 'duty' did not occur. Such was the mode of modern warfare that it was next to impossible for an officer of any rank to attain the honour of the Victoria Cross, and he doubted whether its being attainable by subalterns, corporals, and men of the line would not lead them to neglect duty in the pursuit of glory.[43]

Henry Hardinge, commander-in-chief of the army, spoke in the same Commons debate. Remarkably, given his close proximity to the Crown, Hardinge asserted that the British army owed its historic success to its discipline, conformity and uniformity, and that the VC undermined these virtues:

> the great object in the English army should be to preserve the correct formation of regiments and brigades in line, and not to encourage

officers to step out of the line and mar its completeness for the purpose of signalizing themselves by some special action of gallantry; and an order of this sort which was given for such actions might have its disadvantages.

Unlike Hardinge and Fraser, Stannus had nothing to lose by the time he published his *Curiosities of the Victoria Cross*. In this he considered seven VC citations from the recently concluded Afghan War, unravelling some of the nonsense of early VC citations. His second case was that of Gunner James Colliss of the Royal Horse Artillery.[44] Recommended for the VC by General Roberts for his bravery on 28 July 1880, the citation for Collis read in part: 'For conspicuous bravery during the retreat from Maiwand to Kandahar... when the officer commanding the battery was endeavouring to bring in a limber, with wounded men, under a cross-fire, in running forward and drawing the enemy's fire on himself, thus taking off their attention from the limber.' Stannus found this 'childish twaddle... the idea of any one isolated man drawing off the fire from a limber of wounded men whom it is reasonable to suppose had some escort or protection!'[45] Discounting Stannus's satirical stabs, his point is valid: why would the enemy fire on Collis rather than the bigger and better target – the loaded limber?[46]

Stannus's fourth case concerned Reverend James William Adams of the Bengal Ecclesiastical Service. The Adams VC is a perfect illustration of how powerful and influential figures could obtain the Cross for favourites. Stannus was incredulous at the following 1881 citation of the VC for Adams:

> During the action at Killa Kazi, on the 11th December, 1879, some men of the 9th Lancers having fallen, with their horses, into a wide and deep 'nullah' or ditch, and the enemy being close upon them, the Reverend J. W. Adams rushed into the water (which filled the ditch), dragged the horses from off the men upon whom they were lying, and

extricated them, he being at the time under a heavy fire, and up to his waist in water. At this time the Afghans were pressing on very rapidly, the leading men getting within a few yards of Mr. Adams, who having let go his horse in order to render more effectual assistance, had eventually to escape on foot.[47]

A hasty reading of this citation might conclude that Reverend Adams was clearly tough and courageous on that December day in 1879; why not give him a VC? Does it matter? If we buy into the mythology of an unbroken line of heroes who represent Britain at its finest, then it matters, as the Adams VC is dubious in the extreme; once one citation is doubted, all risk being tainted with suspicion. Stannus inserted his scalpel into the pugnacious parson:

Having had the misfortune during my career to have more than once had a horse lying on the top of me, I am some authority in this matter. Why forty parson-power could not have accomplished what is attributed to this enterprising ecclesiastic! Has the reader ever seen a London cab horse in difficulties? Try even to assist in moving him when on the ground. The physical labour required to alter his position even by a dozen men is surprising. I have never seen the Reverend gentleman who accomplished the marvel above described, and neither know nor have heard anything of his physical proportions, but I should not care to meet him in a lone alley on a dark night.[48]

The idea of a forty-year-old man pulling several struggling horses off other men, who are trying to get out of a water-filled ditch, is rather difficult to swallow. Under the terms of the 1856 VC warrant, Adams's eligibility for the VC was in any case a grey area. Formally, he was a civilian attached to the Bengal Establishment and, although three VCs had been bestowed on civilians of the Bengal Civil Service during the Indian Mutiny, forcing an extension of the VC warrant on 13 December

1858 to embrace 'non-military persons' who had performed 'deeds of gallantry', that extension was regarded by the War Office in London as being specifically limited to the Mutiny. So what may have lain behind Adams's VC?

The word 'Reverend' conjures up images of a meek-and-mild dog-collared individual. Nothing could be further from the truth in the case of Adams, a tough, stern, Irish-born 'muscular' Christian who, at the age of sixty, managed to supervise five services and preach three sermons every Sunday. Adams was an excellent horseman and athlete, and according to contemporaries, he was considered to be the strongest man in Ireland while at Trinity College, Dublin. Ordained in the Church of England in 1863, three years later Adams went to Calcutta, where he joined the East India Company's Bengal Establishment. In December 1876 Adams was placed in charge of the cavalry and artillery camp for the 1877 Delhi Durbar, attended by the Prince of Wales. He was clearly a successful organizer, for in November 1878 General Roberts selected Adams to accompany him as part of the Kabul Field Force. Adams, along with the Presbyterian chaplain, the Reverend J. Manson and Father G. Brown, the Roman Catholic priest, were Mentioned in Despatches by the deeply religious Roberts for being 'unremitting in their attention to the spiritual wants of the troops'. By the time of his action at Killa Kazi in December 1879, Adams had a firm ally in General Roberts.

Whitehall resisted giving the VC to Adams, not because of the possible absurdity of the citation but because he was strictly speaking a civilian. In the view of the Military Secretary of the time, Lieutenant General Sir Edmund Augustus Whitmore, the 1858 extension of the warrant was to be strictly interpreted. But by 1879 General Roberts was Britain's most successful soldier; he brooked no opposition from War Office desk wallahs. His imperial military success – avenging the murder of Sir Louis Cavagnari, British envoy in Kabul, and his victory at the Battle of Kandahar on 1 September 1880 – made him a darling at court; the Queen created him Knight Grand Cross of the Order of the Bath (GCB) on 21 September 1880. He was lionized as a national hero, and his own VC status suggested he knew what courage was. Roberts could, more or less, do what he wanted. Against this the pen-pushing Whitmore was powerless.

Roberts wrote to Whitmore and suggested that, as had happened after the Indian Mutiny, an amended warrant should be drawn up, specifically to accommodate Adams. The Duke of Cambridge – as impatient with bureaucracy as Roberts – saw no real need for a new warrant but inevitably backed Roberts. Whitmore was correct in his strict interpretation of the VC rules; but the rules had stacked against them the two most important military officers in the land. The result was inevitable – just rewrite the rules to accommodate all concerned. Thus on 24 August 1881 the *London Gazette* notified that the Queen had altered the VC warrant to include 'members of the Indian Ecclesiastical Establishments'; just two days later, and almost two years after the event took place for which he was being decorated, Adams's VC was gazetted.

The strong bond between Roberts and Adams continued; when trouble broke out in Burma in 1885, Roberts asked Adams to accompany the field force sent there to quash the rebellion. At Killa Kazi Adams may have been brave, but the courage involved in trying to help struggling officers escape a tense situation was merely a suitable peg on which to hang the reward. The Reverend Adams was never politically powerful; he merely inhabited the outer reaches of influence. But his VC consolidated his toe-hold at court. Before he died in 1903, having retired from India and taken up a living near Oakham, Adams was made Honorary Chaplain to Queen Victoria and then, after her death, was appointed one of a dozen Chaplains in Ordinary to Edward VII. For Stannus, Adams's VC was to be judged purely on the basis of its citation, and that appeared ludicrous; for the rest of the world, and perhaps for history, it is more obvious that the Reverend's VC was clearly a reward for good, loyal service to Roberts not just for a single day, but for years.

In his principled and very public condemnation of the VC, Stannus was a lonely voice. Popular opinion, at least as represented by the jingoistic and imperially minded press, adored the Cross. Newspapers and periodicals gained tremendously useful copy in stories of individual heroism, as exemplified by the VC – a boon for the press that continues to this day. As the conquest of indigenous peoples came to be justified as extending 'civilization', the general public needed some of the 'civilizers' to be towering heroes. The VC became indelibly associated with a romantically inclined adulation of individual heroes, embodied in texts such as T. E. Toomey's Victoria Cross and How Won, published in 1889.[49] Toomey, a former colour-sergeant of the 1st Battalion, The Royal Irish, compiled from the London Gazette the names, rank and regiment of the VC winners, together with a brief description of their deeds. Toomey's unquestioned assumption that winning the VC marked an individual out as indisputably heroic – he dedicated his book to 'The Heroes of the Victoria Cross' and, in a sign of a more deferential age, to 'The Officers under Whose Command it was Won' – remains the dominant mode for understanding the Victoria Cross. The VC, although a perfect example of the paternalism on which the hierarchies of Victorian industrialized society depended, was widely depicted as exercising a beneficial, socially unifying influence. According to one contemporary newspaper, the Cross was 'the most democratic of distinctions, since on its roll of fame there are the names of Corporals and Sergeants, as well as those of Peers of the Realm and Generals. Here birth goes for nothing; and the trooper who has brought away his comrade under fire figures in the same list with the Commander-in-Chief of the Indian Army.'[50]

97

Certainly the distribution of the VC was, in the nineteenth century, fairly evenly balanced between officers and other ranks: of the 404 VCs awarded by 1889, the year of Toomey's compendium, 223 had gone to other ranks, 181 to officers. This amounted to little more than a democratic façade, however; existing social and military divisions were left intact. Stannus, Fraser, Hardinge and other officers or ex-officers who disliked the VC were no radicals; their critique of the Cross derived from an ultra-conservative position, a wish to defend the professionalism of the army from being, as they saw it, debauched by disruptive personal accolades. Their view, always a minority opinion, lost the debate, and by 1880 Stannus's fundamental criticism of the VC, that it showered praise on men who were merely doing what had previously been expected of them, was already anachronistic. On 15 September 1882, Israel Harding, a gunner on board the *Alexandra*, was gazetted VC. The year before, on 11 July, the *Alexandra* was engaged in a very minor action against the forts of Arabi Pasha, at Alexandria, when the ship was hit by a shell that lodged on the main deck. On hearing shouts of alarm, Harding dashed up from below deck, saw the fizzing fuse, doused it in water, and then put the shell in a nearby tub. A hero? Or someone who simply did his duty? For Stannus these were key questions – and they remain so today – but they had been lost sight of by 1882. By then the received opinion was that the leaden dullard of a private soldier could be transmuted into a golden hero by performing an action that could, with suitable embellishment, be made to look astonishing; on occasion, might even *be* astonishing. As a contemporary commentary on the VC put it: 'The private, graced with such a distinction, is no longer a plebeian. He is not one of the multitude. Even if his social and military rank should remain unchanged, he is raised morally much above his former self.'[51]

As Stannus was struggling with his personal fate, British redcoats were about to suffer their most humiliating defeat at the hands of 'uncivilized' soldiers in the heart of Natal, South Africa, as Lord Chelmsford led a punitive expedition against the Zulu nation. The deeply republican *Reynolds's Newspaper* struck a cautious note, little knowing that the disaster it feared had already happened. On Sunday, 2 February 1879, *Reynolds's* warned:

> An attack on such a nation with a small army, in a difficult country, and with so large an unfriendly population behind, even though every possible precaution has been taken, involves some serious risks. The result of a struggle in the long run cannot of course be doubtful. We are, however, very likely to be once more reminded of the difficulty, if not impossibility, of engaging in a little war. A single mistake in the first hostile operations which should give a well-prepared enemy a momentary success might lead to lamentable disasters.

The first lamentable disaster had already happened. On 22 January, Lord Chelmsford foolishly failed to entrench his troops, declined to build a defensive laager, and divided his force, taking half with him supposedly to pursue the Zulu force. He left behind at Isandlwana almost 2,000 British and natives troops; the majority of these were slaughtered by Zulu impis, some of whom then went on to threaten a tiny British-held frontier post at Rorke's Drift.

The British expedition to subdue Zululand was in some respects a repetition of the Crimean disaster; it is difficult to say whether Lord Chelmsford suffered more from arrogance or ignorance. London's newspapers had assumed the fighting would be so brief and one-sided that it was not considered worth the expense to send special correspondents – which did not prevent some from publishing remarkably colourful accounts. *The Graphic* of 15 March 1879 depicted the final moments of Lieutenants Nevill Josiah Aylmer Coghill and Teignmouth Melvill of the 24th Regiment as they failed to cross the turbulent Buffalo River and were killed by pursuing Zulus: 'We may presume that the wound of Coghill necessitated dismounting. The other, tending him with all the care of a comrade, must have witnessed his death. He himself, too, spent with loss of blood, could not remount, and with the colours wrapped around him, sank down to die, happy in the soldierly conviction that honour was saved.' This was fiction parading as fact: Melvill and Coghill, whose final moments cannot possibly be known – there were no British eye-witnesses, and no Zulu account has been recorded – were thrust forward for public adoration and hero worship. They were not the only British officers who, rather than be slaughtered, chose to gallop away from Isandlwana – an option unavailable to the horseless rank-and-file redcoat. Some officers at Isandlwana were fortunate to be wearing their dark blue-and-black patrol uniforms; the Zulus had been ordered to ignore those dressed in black, who were presumed to be civilians. Captain Allen Gardner of 14th Hussars, who fled the scene and survived, was one such; he later justified what could have been seen as desertion by asserting that he thought it vital to warn Chelmsford, who warmly commended Gardner. Gardner was prematurely talked of in the British press as having gained the VC; but as the scale of the disaster slowly emerged, the honour of British officers began to be questioned, and Gardner's mooted VC was quietly forgotten.[52]

The bigger the military catastrophe, the greater the need to boost national morale; and Isandlwana was the greatest military defeat for British forces up till then. It was time for a few ennobling and attention-diverting VCs. Thus Lieutenants Coghill and Melvill were swiftly depicted in the British press as having sacrificed themselves to save the quasi-mystical soul of the regiment, the colours. The Zulus, however, were so indifferent to this scrap of woven cotton that it was later found 500 yards downstream from Coghill's and Melvill's corpses. Next day at Rorke's Drift honour was partially restored, thanks to the stalwart defence by 150 British and colonial troops of the tiny garrison against 4,000 Zulus. Rorke's Drift, no doubt because of the eleven VCs given to its defenders, has come to symbolize for the British national psyche all that is 'best' in the tradition of military heroism. The two senior officers at Rorke's Drift, Lieutenants John Rouse Merriot Chard and Gonville Bromhead, became nationally feted as heroes, although Colonel (as he then was) Evelyn Wood, part of Chelmsford's expeditionary force, thought Chard a 'most useless officer fit for nothing... a dull, heavy man, scarcely able to do his regular work',[53] while Major Francis Clery, who was garrisoned at Rorke's Drift with Bromhead after the battle, commented: 'Reputations are being made and lost here in an almost comical fashion... [Bromhead is a] capital fellow at everything except soldiering.' Lieutenant Henry Curling, also at Rorke's Drift with Bromhead after the battle, wrote: 'It is very amusing to read the accounts of Chard and Bromhead... Bromhead is a stupid old fellow, as deaf as a post. Is it not curious how some men are forced into notoriety?'[54]

Whatever the truth about Bromhead and Chard personally, they at least stayed at their posts – although flight was not really an option – and fought with determination, unlike Coghill and Melvill. The drama played out in Zululand that January – a desperate, and successful, 'last stand' by brave white men against hordes of 'savages', a bloody defeat redeemed by the valiant defence of a handful of individuals from the same regiment that had been so badly let down by an inept commander – was perfectly suited to the contemporary mores of the VC. Britain's newspapers did their utmost to secure Coghill and Melvill posthumous VCs, despite that being technically impossible; posthumous VCs had only gone to the families of those who had been granted the decoration but died before it could be bestowed. This was of little consequence to the *Morning Post*, which in March declared: 'Such heroes as Coghill and Melville [sic] would certainly have been accorded the Victoria Cross had they lived. Is it too much to suggest that this grand deed should be recorded in the Official Gazette, and that the Cross should be awarded as an heirloom to their families?'[55] An innovation of this sort would not come for almost three decades; in 1907 Edward VII, against his better judgement, succumbed to pressure to grant posthumous VCs to Coghill and Melvill and a handful of others.[56]

General Sir Garnet Wolseley, who took over from the disgraced Lord Chelmsford in Natal, confided to his South African diary his scepticism regarding the 'heroism' of Coghill and Melvill: 'I am sorry that both of those officers were not killed with their men at Isandlwana... I don't like the idea of officers escaping on horseback when their men on foot were killed.'[57] In all likelihood the tale of Coghill and Melvill riding to save the colours was entirely fictitious, the spurious creation of a British press that was developing an appetite for heroes. There were no eyewitness accounts – a direct infringement of the seventh clause of the 1856 warrant, which required the deed to have been performed under the watchful eye of a commanding officer, or, failing that, that the claimant of the VC 'shall prove the act to that satisfaction of' a senior officer. In his memoirs, Horace Smith-Dorrien, then a young subaltern transport officer (and later a fine First War general), one of five surviving officers at Isandlwana, suggested that although the two bodies were found together, the men had retreated separately, and that the river swept them downstream to the spot where they met before being killed.[58] Coghill's ride may have been 'no more than an entirely human, and in the context of a rout a permissible if unheroic, attempt to save his life, something that, as a well mounted staff officer, he was better placed to do than the ordinary soldiers'.[59] The deaths of Coghill and Melvill did produce one sensible change: the carrying of regimental colours into battle was thereafter banned, to prevent rash soldiers from risking their lives to defend or rescue a piece of cloth.

At least 150 VCs prior to 1890 were awarded for the rescue or attempted rescue of a fallen comrade. Many of these acts more appropriately merited the Albert Medal, which in 1877 was extended to cover the saving of life on land, but that medal lacked the prestige – and certainly never attracted the same publicity as the VC. And one key element of the original 1856 VC warrant – the principle by which officers and men could elect one or more of their number to be put forward for a VC – was implemented inconsistently. Cases such as that of Private J. Divane, who gained his VC by election of his peers, were rare.[60] Divane, of the 60th Regiment, led a successful charge against rebel trenches during the Indian Mutiny; a clear case of a VC that was merited – if Divane's peers thought he deserved it, who could with justice deny it? Other examples, such as that of Private W. Griffiths, who rescued seventeen comrades from drowning close to the Andaman Islands in the Bay of Bengal on 7 May 1867, were clearly wrong, even at the time. Yet the VC, once bestowed, joins all winners in a hallowed club of the heroic.

Winston Churchill never won the VC, although arguably he deserved it for his personal courage in battle on several occasions. Yet paradoxically he also represents a good illustration of what Stannus particularly disliked about the Cross: the encouragement it gave to a young and dashing officer, who so eagerly sought a decoration that he was prepared to risk his life whenever the opportunity arose, indifferent to larger questions of battlefield strategy. Churchill's courage was of the type that, had his friends at court been sufficiently powerful (or his enemies less formidable), he would have got the VC. Churchill joined the 4th Hussars in 1895 after passing out from Sandhurst eighth of the 150 cadets in the previous year. As a subaltern he fought in campaigns on the Northwest Frontier, the Nile, in the South African and First World Wars, and served in turn with the 31st Punjaub Infantry, the 21st Lancers, the South African Light Horse, the Oxfordshire Yeomanry, the Grenadier Guards, the Royal Scots Fusiliers, and the Oxfordshire Artillery, the unit changes driven by his self-acknowledged lust for action. About the only thing he was afraid of was being shot in the mouth, as that might have stopped him from being able to talk.[61] Hungry for medals, Churchill found the colonial campaigns in which he fought full of 'fascinating thrills. It was not like the Great War. Nobody expected to be killed. Here and there in every regiment or battalion, half a dozen, a score, at the worst thirty or forty, would pay the forfeit; but to the great mass of those who took part in the little wars of Britain in those vanished light-hearted days, this was only a sporting element in a splendid game.'[62] He participated in the last great cavalry charge, that of the 21st Lancers at the Battle of Omdurman on 2 September 1898, where Captain Raymond de Montmorency received a VC for having recovered the corpse of Lieutenant Grenfell.[63]

In October 1899 Churchill arrived in South Africa, where he was to experience his fourth war in as many years. Churchill was at the time the correspondent of the *Morning Post*, having resigned from the army on 3 May 1899 to fight a by-election in Oldham. It was in South Africa where he displayed, before a very public audience, the kind of bravery that unquestionably merited the Cross. At dawn on 15 November 1899, Churchill left Estcourt aboard a train carrying some Dublin Fusiliers and a company of the Durham Light Infantry, destined for Colenso, close to Ladysmith, where a beleaguered British garrison was under siege. He had been invited to accompany the trip by a friend, Captain James Haldane, DSO, of the Gordon Highlanders. As Churchill recalled: 'Out of comradeship, and because I thought it was my duty to gather as much information as I could for the *Morning Post*, also because I was eager for trouble, I accepted the invitation without demur.'[64] The train was ambushed and partially derailed, and three Creusot cannon, a thousand rifles and one Maxim gun poured fire onto the stranded train, stuck in the open. Winston rallied the driver and promised that, if he 'bucked up', he (Churchill) would ensure he got a medal. As they tried to pull the derailed trucks from blocking the engine's path, Churchill's party came under intense rifle, Maxim gun and artillery fire, killing four soldiers and wounding thirty more, at a range of around 900 yards. According to Haldane's later account, Churchill supervised the work to clear the line:

> I knew him well enough to realise that he was not the man to stand quietly by and look on in a critical situation... his self-selected task, into which he threw all his energy, was carried out with pluck and perseverance, and his example inspired the platelayers, the driver of the locomotive, and others to work under the fire which the Boers were directing on the train.[65]

Churchill's working party managed to clear the rocks from the rail, allowing the tender and engine, laden with the wounded, to chug laboriously back towards Estcourt. After a few hundred yards, when he knew the train would escape, Churchill dismounted to go back to the stranded Haldane. The remnants of the small force, including Churchill and Haldane, became prisoners. Private Walls, a soldier who had been aboard the train, wrote to his sister, who sent the letter to Churchill's mother: 'Churchill is a splendid fellow. He walked about in it all as coolly as if nothing was going on, & called for volunteers to give him a hand to get the truck out of the road. His presence and way of going on were as much good as fifty men would have been.'[66]

The story of Churchill's subsequent escape from captivity is well known; of greater significance here is the tangled tale of how he failed to win any decoration for his remarkable courage on that day. There was plentiful testimony of his exceptional bravery under fire; in London, the weekly *Black & White* reported on 23 December 1899 that it was 'rumoured that both Mr Churchill and the engine driver [Charles Wagner] will be recommended for the Victoria Cross which they appear to richly deserve'. Not for the first time, the press rumour proved false. In his report of the action Haldane said that he had 'formally placed' Churchill under his command and he 'could not speak too highly of his gallant conduct'.[67] Despite the testimonies of Churchill's conspicuous courage and the precedents already set for civilians to gain the award, he received neither decoration nor any official recognition for that day's skirmish. Why not? He had made too many enemies in the preceding years; one in particular regarded him as an appalling whipper-snapper.

Churchill's skill with the pen, as well as the sword, was enviable – but not envied by all. When Churchill sought to join the Sudan forces in 1898, he 'became conscious of the unconcealed disapproval and hostility of the Sirdar [commander] of the Egyptian Army, Sir [Horatio] Herbert Kitchener'.[68] Kitchener refused his solicitations, but through connections Churchill persuaded Sir Evelyn Wood, himself a former Sirdar, and by then Adjutant General to the forces, Kitchener's superior, to intercede on his behalf. Kitchener's dislike of reporters and journalism was almost as profound as that for superiors who gave him instructions. A young and openly ambitious interloper such as Churchill was innately suspicious; that he also worked as a reporter was beneath contempt.[69] In his account of the Sudan expedition, The River War, Churchill honestly – but unwisely – publicly condemned the Sirdar for desecrating the tomb of the Mahdi, the Dervish leader, and for carrying off the Mahdi's head in a kerosene can:

> [I]t was an act of vandalism and folly to destroy the only fine building which might attract the traveller and interest the historian. It is a gloomy augury for the future of the Sudan that the first action of its civilised conquerors and present ruler [Kitchener] should have been

to level the one pinnacle which rose above the mud houses... I shall not hesitate to declare that to destroy what was sacred and holy [to the Dervishes] was a wicked act, of which the true Christian, no less than the philosopher, must express his abhorrence.

Churchill also referred to Kitchener's brutality towards wounded Dervish troops: 'The stern and unpitying spirit of the commander was communicated to his troops, and the victories which marked the progress of the River War were accompanied by acts of barbarity not always justified even by the harsh customs of savage conflicts of the fierce and treacherous nature of the Dervish.' General Sir Ian Hamilton, who had himself been deprived of the VC in South Africa and was a gifted writer, considered that Kitchener had 'magnificently primitive' ideas, and 'was never himself amidst the complexities of Western civilisation'.[70] Much later, in his memoirs, Churchill returned to the incident: 'the Mahdi's head was just one of those trifles about which an immense body of rather gaseous feeling can be generated. All the Liberals were outraged by an act which seemed to them worthy of the Huns and Vandals. All the Tories thought it rather a lark.'[71]

Thus humiliated by a mere writer, the perpetually dyspeptic Kitchener, who moved up from chief of staff to take overall command of the South African forces from Lord Roberts in November 1900, never forgave Churchill. The evidence is circumstantial, but Kitchener would have been required to pass on to London any VC recommendation for Churchill's epic work on the railway line to Colenso; no such recommendation was ever made. Even Churchill's mother, a formidable networker on behalf of her son, would have been unable to persuade Kitchener to consider decorating such a scoundrel as Winston.[72]

If one valiant young officer who miraculously survived cannons and bullets in South Africa was automatically ruled out of the VC for having failed to ingratiate himself with influential officers, another, who futilely died, was granted his, because one senior officer felt guilty. The first commander of the forces in South Africa, General Sir Redvers Henry Buller VC, suffered a series of humiliating defeats during the 'Black Week' of 10–17 December 1899, during which Lord Roberts's son, Frederick, a lieutenant in the King's Royal Rifle Corps, was killed, for which Roberts senior never forgave Buller.

Young 'Freddy' Roberts was on Buller's staff during the Battle of Colenso on 15 December 1899. Buller incorrectly believed Colenso was only lightly defended by the Boers; when his mistake became clear, Buller lost control of the battle and became obsessed with saving the guns of the 14th and 66th Batteries, which had been abandoned by their commander, Colonel Chris Long, who had in any case positioned them where they were completely exposed. The Boer commandos, firing smokeless cartridges (which concealed their positions) from a mile distant, stalled the advance of the British infantry, and forced the artillery's horses and limbers back to shelter about 800 yards behind the guns. The guns fired more than 1,000 shells but after an hour ran out of ammunition; Colonel Long, along with a quarter of the gunners, was injured and put out of action, whereupon Major A. C. Bauward took over command and ordered the crews back to shelter while they waited for resupply. Buller, by now on the scene with his staff, ordered Captain Harry Norton Schofield to take out some teams and drivers to recover the guns, but they were forced to turn back under a hail of bullets. Captain Walter Norris Congreve and others – including Freddy Roberts – then attempted the same, but were wounded or forced to turn back, Roberts managing to get only thirty yards before a shell exploded nearby, killing his horse and mortally wounding him. Another attempt succeeded in hauling back two of the guns, but the remaining ten were captured by the Boers after Buller ordered a withdrawal. Buller recommended Freddy for the VC, but VCs at that date were not for the dead.

The awarding of VCs to men who had died before they could officially be gazetted had prompted a question in the House of Commons on 21 May 1897, when the MP for Pembroke and Haverfordwest, Lieutenant General John Wimburn Laurie, asked William Brodrick, Under-Secretary of State for War,

> whether the Secretary of State for War would reconsider his decision... with respect to Trooper Frank William Baxter, of the Buluwayo Field Force, in which it is stated that on account of the gallant conduct of this man in having, on 22nd April 1896, dismounted and given up his horse to a wounded comrade, Corporal Wiseman, who was being closely pursued by an overwhelming force of the enemy, would have been recommended to Her Majesty for the Victoria Cross had he survived; and, in consideration of the self-sacrificing act of devotion to his wounded comrade which cost Trooper Baxter his life, would he recommend to Her Majesty that the Victoria Cross should be conferred on the late trooper on the date of his gallant action, and that the decoration so heroically earned should be forwarded to his nearest relative?

Brodrick stated the situation according to the prevailing VC statutes:

> I can assure my hon. and gallant Friend of the full sympathy of the Secretary of State in his wish to commemorate the noble deed of Trooper Baxter; but the statutes of the Victoria Cross do not contain any provision under which a man who is already dead can be recommended for the distinction. Many cases have occurred in which the Cross would have been awarded had the soldier or sailor survived, but no exception to the rule I have stated has ever been made.

Other VCs Buller recommended that day – Captain Congreve and Captain Hamilton Lyster Reed (7th Battery, Royal Field Artillery), who had brought three teams from his own battery to attempt to rescue the guns – received theirs. The guns themselves were deserted; a cardinal military sin. Buller was acutely aware that he had not only disgraced himself at Colenso, but had also managed to oversee the pointless death of the son of the man who was shortly to replace him as commander-in-chief.[73] The wording of Buller's recommendation, published in the *London Gazette* on 26 January 1900, carefully avoided revealing that Roberts had been fatally wounded:

> Captain Congreve, Rifle Brigade, who was in the donga, assisted to hook a team into a limber, went out and assisted to limber up a gun; being wounded he took shelter, but seeing Lieutenant Roberts fall badly wounded he went out again and brought him in. Some idea of the nature of the fire may be gathered from the fact that Captain Congreve was shot through the leg, through the toe of his boot, grazed on the elbow and the shoulder, and his horse shot in three places. Lieutenant the Honourable F. Roberts, King's Royal Rifles, assisted Captain Congreve. He was wounded in three places. Corporal Nurse, Royal Field Artillery, 66th Battery, also assisted. I recommend the above three for the Victoria Cross.[74]

Frederick Roberts was not gazetted with the VC until the *London Gazette* of 2 February 1900 – where it was acknowledged that he was 'since deceased'. Timing was everything: a dead Roberts was ineligible for the VC, but a 'since deceased' Roberts was a different matter. The most that gallant but dead officers and men, who might otherwise have been granted the VC, might expect to receive was an official note in the *London Gazette* that they *would* have been recommended for the VC, had they survived. Buller may have felt the VC for Freddy Roberts was the least gesture he could make to a heartbroken Lord Roberts, but it was yet another example of a senior officer using sleight of hand to bestow an illegitimate VC. Nor should Roberts's corpse have been so honoured; all he did was die, perhaps fearlessly but certainly pointlessly.

On 14 November 1900, with more than two years of the Boer War to run, Lieutenant General Sir Charles Warren, the hapless commander of British soldiers slaughtered by Boer commandos at Spion Kop, gave a rousingly patriotic speech in the town hall of Chatham, in Kent.[75] According to *The Times*, Warren praised the unknown and unrecognized heroes who had fought the Boers and helped preserve the empire. He thanked those 'men who had performed heroic deeds – men whose names had never been mentioned, and never would be mentioned. He had seen men do heroic deeds in bringing in the wounded, and he could not get the names of them... It was that modest and retiring spirit among so many Englishmen that made this nation what it was. (Cheers.)'[76] Warren's speech prompted a thoughtful response published in *The Times* on 26 November 1900, in which 'Old Soldier' referred to what he called 'the unpopularity of the Victoria Cross':

> There are dozens, I might almost say hundreds, of officers and men now in the service quite as worthy of reward as those which under luckier circumstances have earned the V.C, and these very naturally look with disfavour on a decoration in the earning of which luck has to be combined with merit... the standard of valour required varies enormously, for whilst one general will recommend anybody and everybody, another will recommend no one.[77]

The Boer War established beyond all doubt the truth of 'Old Soldier's' assertion. Without luck, all the courage in the world could not win the VC. The VC is at heart a roulette wheel. If you had the bad luck to be in a regiment or ship whose commanding officer – either from laziness or on principle – did not put names forward, or put them forward to the wrong person, then you could be a Hercules and still go unnoticed.

Before Lady Roberts sailed to Cape Town to join her husband in South Africa, Queen Victoria handed her a small parcel, saying: 'Here is something that I have tied up with my own hands, and that I beg you will not open until you get home.' The parcel contained the VC awarded to her dead son.[78] Lord Roberts had glided into legend in Afghanistan and India, been lionized as 'Bobs' by Kipling in an 1893 ballad, and, by the time he took command in South Africa at the advanced age of sixty-eight, was a national military hero; but his involvement with the VC was less than glorious.

On the evening of 30 March 1900, a British column of about 1,800 soldiers, commanded by Brigadier General Robert George Broadwood, bivouacked close to Sanna's Post, near Bloemfontein in South Africa, unaware that a Boer commando was close by. Next morning the British were shelled and, amid the chaos, formed up and tried to move off. The Boers, under the command of Christian de Wet, captured the British supply wagons. Broadwood ordered U and Q Batteries of the Royal Horse Artillery to follow the supply train and cover the retirement of the force. U Battery was ambushed and captured, but one of its officers managed to signal the impending disaster to Q Battery. There was pandemonium, with panicking artillerymen and soldiers trying to flee while others tried to regroup to fight. The survivors of Q Battery lost one gun and two ammunition wagons before establishing themselves in buildings at Sanna's Post, where they unlimbered the guns and tried to fire on the Boers at a range of some 1,000 yards. The gunners immediately came under intense accurate fire from the Boers who occupied well-concealed positions. Under the order of Major Edmund Phipps-Hornby, Q Battery withdrew to behind the buildings to avoid being picked off and left behind a further gun, taking four back by hand. The British that day lost seven guns and suffered 570 casualties. Astonishingly, Lord Roberts exercised his right as a commander in the field to confer a provisional VC on Major Phipps-Hornby, and instructed the battery to elect three members to receive the same.[79] He also forwarded to the War Office three more recommendations for VCs.[80] Brave the troops may have been, but this was yet another humiliation and to give away four VCs, albeit provisionally, in such circumstances was unheard of. The words of the Duke of Newcastle, the Secretary of War at the time of the Crimean conflict – that 'great care would be required to prevent abuse' – were but a faint echo. But for London to deny them so soon after Roberts had taken over command in South Africa would have undermined his authority; the most that could be done was to refuse the three further recommendations. The provisional 'conferment in the field' clause was quietly dropped in the 1920 redrafting of the VC warrant.[81]

Victoria ended her reign as she had begun it, a staunch and sentimental supporter of 'her' soldiers. Sir Frederick Ponsonby, Acting Private Secretary to Victoria at the time of the Second Boer War, recalled: 'In 1899 the Queen had started an album for photographs of all the officers killed in the war... After a year, the Queen came to the conclusion that the book was too sad to look at.'[82] In the photograph album was her favourite grandson, Prince Christian Victor – a gifted amateur cricketer who played a match at first-class level, and the first member of the royal family to attend school (Wellington College) rather than be tutored at home – who died in Pretoria of enteric fever. A few days before her death on 22 January 1901 Victoria received the final visitor from outside her immediate family circle. It was, appropriately enough, Field Marshal, now Earl, Frederick Roberts VC.

4

Big War

'There's no good having decorations unless they are given the right way!'
BRIGADIER FRANK CROZIER[1]

'Few countries muddle along without an honours system of some sort, for it
is quite simply the cheapest method of rewarding and encouraging those the
state holds in esteem or to whom it may even consider it owes its survival.'
MICHAEL DE-LA-NOY[2]

At the start of the twentieth century old soldiers were still fighting the
battles of the nineteenth century – at least, when it came to deciding
who, and what, deserved the Victoria Cross. Pseudonymous correspondents – obviously serving or former officers – skirmished back
and forth across the letters' page of *The Times* in 1902, clashing over
whether or not the recent South African war had seen a subtle altera-
tion of the standards required for gaining a VC. 'Pretoria' was annoyed
that senior officers, colonels and above, had apparently been excluded
from the Cross:

> In *The Times* History of the South African War it is stated that General
> French recommended Colonel Ian Hamilton for the Victoria Cross,

but... it was not considered wise to grant this decoration to so senior an officer for a purely personal act of bravery... If it has been decided that senior officers are not eligible for the decoration, the Victoria Cross warrant should certainly be at once amended.[3]

Field Marshal Sir Charles Brownlow sternly reminded readers that the gallantry of senior officers was usually regarded as no more than their duty:

Nearly forty years ago... Lord Straithnairn, then Commander-in-Chief in India, decided that personal gallantry on several occasions during a hard-fought campaign, on the part of certain majors in command of regiments was no more than their duty, and should be recognized by other rewards than the V.C., for which they had been recommended in his published despatches by the general under whom they had served [Sir Neville Chamberlain];[4] they received instead a step of rank and the C.B., as more conducive to their future promotion and usefulness... In a profession, the members of which are all supposed to be brave, a badge of superior courage, in addition to the usual rewards of a successful Commander, is more or less an invidious distinction.[5]

More jaded correspondents, such as 'An Unamazed Veteran', voiced a widespread sense that chance had displaced gallantry:

The young officer, or, for the matter of that, the old officer, who has never seen service has an exceedingly exalted view of the V.C. and what should win it; but as he serves on campaign after campaign and sees who get the cross, how easily it is often obtained, and how unequal the standard, his estimate of it falls lower and lower till he joins with the general ante-room verdict that 'luck,' not necessarily bravery, is the predominating factor... only conspicuous bravery or devotion to the country should be rewarded, irrespective of rank or wounds or any other consideration. It is the deviation from this strict interpretation of the warrant that has, I assume, raised the present outcry.[6]

Twelve years after this was written, the yearned-for 'strict interpretation of the warrant' was in tatters, and luck – and politics – were exercising as much sway as ever over who gained a VC.

Few were luckier than the Canadian pilot Billy Bishop, who rose from complete obscurity to acclaimed hero during the First World War, thanks to social connections and his own aggressively tear-away self-promotion. When William 'Billy' Avery Bishop was gazetted with the VC on 11 August 1917, the citation spoke of his 'most conspicuous bravery, determination and skill'.[7] The skill thus acknowledged was for Bishop's so effectively handling his Nieuport 17 biplane, a plane that sometimes lost its wings in a steep dive and was slower and had less firepower than the Albatros D-III, the main German single-seater fighter in 1917; but many believe it could equally have been for Bishop's expertise at embellishment. For very few of Bishop's claimed forty-seven enemy aircraft kills with 60 Squadron in France were witnessed. This was unusual and definitely suspicious: 'for a claim to be confirmed it was customary for the name of a witness, or witnesses, to be included in the combat report. Only three of [Bishop's] claims were indisputably corroborated in that fashion... as for the thirty claims made while flying alone, obviously there could be no corroboration.'[8]

The specific action for which Bishop received his VC took place on 2 June 1917. At 3.57 a.m. that day Bishop took to the clouds alone, although he had asked others, including Willy Fry, his deputy flight commander, to join him in a planned raid on a German aerodrome.[9] Bishop flying solo was not unusual; his squadron commander gave him a very free hand. On his return, Bishop claimed to have destroyed seven enemy planes on the ground, and to have shot down three others that had managed to take off and pursue him. Controversy over the veracity of Bishop's claims for that day will persist; the scanty available evidence is contradictory.

Born to an upper-middle-class Canadian family, Bishop arrived in France as a junior officer with a cavalry regiment. Always a maverick loner, he soon tired of the grimness of trench life and sought out the greater independence – and glamour – offered by the Royal Flying Corps (RFC). During his first combat tour of duty as an observer in two-seater biplanes, his aircraft crashed and Bishop was hospitalized in England, thus avoiding the grisly summer of 1916, the meat-grinding Somme offensive. While in hospital, Bishop was taken up by an influential London socialite, Lady Mary St Helier, who, like many upper-class women of the day, had discovered a new outlet for their noblesse oblige through visiting injured troops in hospital. Lady Mary's son would have been the same age as Bishop, had he not died of typhoid in India many years previously; she took the young Canadian airman under her wing. Her London salon, a honeypot to the eminent, was regularly attended by some of the most influential political and cultural figures of the day. Among their number was Winston Churchill, the Canadian-born newspaper magnate Max Aitken, and F. E. Smith, attorney-general in Lloyd George's administration. Not only did they regularly sip Lady Mary's champagne; they were all personal friends of the commanding officer of 60 Squadron, Major A. J. L. (Jack) Scott, who was persuaded to take Bishop as a pilot officer in March 1917. Bishop had a baptism of fire; the following month was a harrowing period for the RFC, and thirteen of 60 Squadron's original eighteen pilots, and seven replacements, were shot down during the Battle of Arras. Bishop, however, proved relentlessly aggressive, and scored twelve of the squadron's thirty-five confirmed April victories. In late April he was promoted to captain. Bishop became Scott's protégé, his determination to take on the enemy and unquestioned bravery cementing a lasting friendship. Scott understood that medals had an extra-curricular function – that they were not simply for the brave but also had propaganda value. This view of gallantry decorations was shared by Major General Hugh Trenchard, the RFC commander, with whom Scott had a warm relationship. In turn, Trenchard was highly regarded by Field Marshal Sir Douglas Haig, who took command of the British Expeditionary Force in December 1915. These 'friends at Court', together with the coalition government's need to publicly identify and reward Canadian RFC fliers, set the stage for Bishop to be granted the highest military decoration.[10]

After the death of the RFC's leading fighter pilot Albert Ball on 7 May 1917, Bishop became lauded as the RFC's unquestioned rival to the German air ace Baron Manfred von Richthofen. Revelling in his status, Bishop was given command of the newly formed 85 Squadron; more than 200 pilots immediately put themselves forward to join it. As CO of his own squadron, Bishop could confirm his own claims. He registered a remarkable twenty-five victories in twenty-three days between the beginning of April and 19 June 1918, when he was ordered to return to Britain – a living hero had greater propaganda and recruiting value than a dead ace. Bishop's final and, in later years, much disputed tally was seventy-two, including two balloons. In June 1918 Bishop published a racy account of his flying days. Exceptionally thin on facts but surfeited with derring-do, the book was ghost-written by the Office of Public Information under supervision of the War Office, with the intention of boosting public morale. The final chapter details Bishop's VC investiture by King George V:

> Following some Generals and Colonels, who were being admitted to the Order of St. Michael and St. George [so much for the VC's precedence over all other decorations], it came my turn to march in... Imagine my consternation, when, at the first of those ten paces, one of

my boots began to squeak... approaching the King, he hooked three medals on my breast. These had been handed to him on a cushion. He congratulated me on winning them, and said it was the first time he had been able to give all three to any one person.[11]

A war-weary Britain – and Canada – got the charismatically glamorous, if perhaps morally ambiguous, hero it so desperately wanted, and probably deserved.

Bishop was a complex character who in later life seemingly spurned his First War braggadocio.[12] He owed his elevation to pilot officer status to a chance hospital encounter with a woman in perpetual mourning for her own son, but he made the best of that lucky break and pursued both glory and the enemy with complete dedication. He has been accused of being 'an inveterate liar; and no one but Bishop ever told one to get himself a Victoria Cross!'[13] But the case against Bishop is circumstantial and unproven; First War pilots often fought in single combat, far from the eyes of reliable (or any other) witnesses, and cast-iron confirmation of victory was often impossible. There is a broader question about Bishop's VC: did his courage stem from the lack of, or the overcoming of, fear? In a 1982 National Film Board of Canada drama documentary, *The Kid Who Couldn't Miss*,[14] Harold (later Lord) Balfour, who served in 60 Squadron, commented: 'Billy Bishop is one of those who I felt did not know fear. The definition of a brave man is someone who is frightened, and overcomes it. The definition of someone who does not fright is somewhat different.' Either way, the VC makes no distinction between those who were fear-less, and those who were fear-full, yet carried on.

It would be unwise and unfair, given the nerve it must have taken simply to get into a flimsy aircraft and seek out a skilful enemy equally intent on killing, to suggest that Bishop did not deserve his Cross. It is equally clear that Bishop was groomed for greatness, and that his

VC was not awarded for courage alone but served a wider political purpose, as did that bestowed on John ('Jack') Travers Cornwell.

Cornwell enlisted in the Royal Navy in October 1915 and was fatally wounded at the Battle of Jutland (31 May–1 June 1916), when aged sixteen. Cornwell was part of a deck gun-crew of HMS Chester, all of whom were killed or mortally wounded by shell splinters when the ship was bombarded by a squadron of German cruisers. When the battle was over, Chester's medical staff found Cornwell still at the gun-sight, apparently awaiting orders; he died of his wounds shortly after. Poor Cornwell was one of more than 6,700 Royal Navy deaths and one of four VCs awarded at Jutland, an indecisive engagement where both sides claimed victory. The other three names are largely forgotten,[15] but Cornwell's youth – which might have been politically embarrassing, even though boys aged fifteen could join the navy (the minimum age for army enlistment was eighteen) – helped ensure him a lasting place in the national mythology of heroism. Letters to The Times called for his photograph – or, better still, a brass plaque with his story engraved on it – to be 'placed in every school in the Empire'.[16] Cornwell was buried 'with every honour, military and civil' at Manor Park Cemetery in London, 'an extraordinarily impressive funeral both for its details and all that it implied', with a volley fired over the grave and the Last Post sounded.[17] King George V presented his mother, Alice Cornwell,[18] with the posthumous VC on 16 November 1916 at Buckingham Palace; the society painter Francis Owen Salisbury was commissioned by the Admiralty to paint 'Boy Cornwell in the Battle of Jutland', using Jack's brother Ernest as a model, and subsequently built his career as a specialist in royal sitters on the back of the painting; the 'Boy Cornwell Memorial Fund' was established; Robert Baden-Powell first awarded the Bronze Cross (the highest award for boy scouts, modelled on the VC) to Cornwell, and then created the 'Cornwell Scout Badge'; streets and schools were named in Cornwell's honour.

Yet Cornwell's VC was a flagrant infringement of the terms of the VC warrant, which the somewhat embarrassing citation – he 'remained standing alone at a most exposed post, quietly awaiting orders, until the end of the action, with the gun's crew dead and wounded all round him' – could do little to disguise.[19] If a wounded and no doubt traumatized child, either unable to leave his post or terrified of the consequences of doing so, deserved the VC, then who did not? Not all First War VCs were so obviously outside the prevailing rules; some, such as that of Alfred Oliver Pollard, one of Britain's most highly decorated First War soldiers, might be said to have over-fulfilled the VC warrant's stipulations.

Few First War VC winners committed to paper what it was that drove them to act as they did. Pollard was exceptional in this regard, writing a memoir of his wartime experiences in which his determination to kill as many Germans as possible is the central focus. Pollard had been an insurance clerk prior to joining up as a private in August 1914, and quickly became a specialist in trench raiding and bombing; after the war he became a prolific author of thrillers and crime novels. Pollard wrote that he felt more alive when bombing an enemy trench than at any other time. His account of the trenches of the Western Front – Fire-Eater: The Memoirs of a V.C. – is a refreshing counterbalance to the view that First War soldiers were sunk in despair, universally despising the mud, misery and murderousness. Some soldiers, such as George Coppard, a machine-gunner, found, if not joy, then a sense of shared community:

Of my memories of life in the trenches, the one thing I cherish more than anything else is the comradeship that grew up between us as a result of the way of life we were compelled to lead – living together under the open sky, night and day, fair weather or foul, witnessing death or injury, helping in matters of urgency, and above all, facing the enemy. Such situations were the solid foundation on which our comradeship was built.[20]

Received wisdom is that the First War was loathed by all participants, but this is incorrect; Pollard was intensely proud of being part of the Honourable Artillery Company, the oldest regiment in the British army, where, he said, 'every man was a potential officer'. He recalled with gusto his first night patrol into No Man's Land: 'I was thrilled to the core. This was man's work indeed... To me these excursions were everything. The danger acted like a drug quickening my pulses. At last I was doing something worthwhile. I was as happy as a sand boy.'[21] Pollard's memoir is no literary feast, but his reflections, although often clichéd, have a direct, earthy quality. His weapon of choice was the trench grenade which, with its highly destructive shrapnel, was much more efficient than a cumbersome rifle in shrouded trench mazes, where confusion often required instant reaction. Pollard, an irrepressible and perpetually optimistic survivor, who was wounded on more than one occasion, lacked the capacity for deep intellectual introspection, but was probably all the better a soldier for that. Siegfried Sassoon believed that the 'better the soldier, the more limited is his outlook... One cannot be a useful officer and a reader of imaginative literature at the same time... The mechanical stupidity of infantry soldiering is the antithesis of intelligent thinking.'[22] After recuperating from a wound, Pollard returned to the trenches as soon as possible: 'It was good to be back in the line again. One felt one was pulling one's weight for the Country, doing the right thing. I thoroughly enjoyed it. After a nine months' gap the knowledge that the Huns were just opposite waiting for an opportunity to kill me if I gave them a chance added a spice to life which I had missed.'[23] A typical letter home to Pollard's mother signed off: 'Best of spirits and having a good time. By the way, I have killed another Hun. Hurrah! Well, cheerioh!'[24]

Pollard gained his VC for action on 29 April 1917 at Gavrelle, France, when, under fierce attack and sustaining heavy casualties, troops of various units became disorganized and began to flee in panic. Pollard – by then a second lieutenant – took four comrades and started a bombing counterattack, pressing it home until his small band had broken the enemy attack, regained all lost ground, and gained much more. At Pollard's VC investiture at Buckingham Palace, twenty-four VCs were given, including six posthumously:

> I stood with my arms straight down by my sides and my chest swelling my tunic. 'God save our gracious King.' Wasn't that what we were fighting for? To save the King and all he stood for – our great Nation?... Every one of us had done his damnedest and we were there to receive our rewards. Not that we needed them. People do not go into action with the idea of winning the Victoria Cross. They go with the bare intention of doing their duty. The decoration merely happens.[25]

Clearly Pollard's VC was thoroughly deserved, both personally and politically, yet a total absence of fear, either in the moment or over a much longer term – not uncommon among VC holders – is difficult to see as courage. The American general George Patton believed of soldiers that 'the more intelligent they are, the more they are frightened'.[26] On that basis, Pollard was exceptionally dim; he did not know fear. This same point has been made by William I. Miller: intelligence finds 'good reasons for worry, whereas those without that ability sleep well and march blithely on'.[27] Is a trained killer – or even possibly a natural born one, such as Pollard seems to have been – unbalanced? In war, society needs determined killers; yet if unbalanced, even if they are as effective as Pollard, do they merit a VC? Pollard gained the VC, as did Albert Ball, the RFC pilot; but they had completely different attitudes to their task. Two days before Ball died, he wrote to his father: 'I do get tired of living to kill and I'm really beginning to feel like a murderer. Shall be so pleased when I have finished.'[28] Over the course of the First World War – as the certainty of victory receded, and, for monarchy, politicians and generals, the political and personal cost of possible defeat became more unbearable – Pollard's certainty rather than Ball's doubts was increasingly valued.

Bishop's and Cornwell's VCs were two of 634 distributed during the First World War, including one for the American Unknown Soldier interred at Arlington Cemetery.[29] Bestowed in November 1921, the British government had been backed into this overtly political gesture; the previous month Washington had given the Medal of Honor to Britain's Unknown Soldier, entombed in Westminster Abbey. London resisted pressure to give VCs to the other allies. In a curt memo from the War Office in 1924, the Parliamentary Under-Secretary brushed aside agitation to bestow the VC on France's Unknown Warrior, ignoring the 1921 US precedent. The view of the War Office was that 'we should be well advised not to re-open the question of the exchange of decorations for Unknown Warriors. We have already put the Italians off and we could hardly deal with one of the Allies without admitting the others.'[30] For approximately every 14,000 men mobilized in the British and Dominions' forces during the First World War, one VC was awarded – a parsimonious rate of distribution compared to the relative largesse of the nineteenth century. Between June 1857, backdated to the start of the Crimean War, and 1 August 1914, 522 VCs were given – more than one-third of the total awarded as of 2014.

That there was an informal tightening around the neck of the VC sack during the progress of the First, and even more evidently the Second World War, is clear. How is this to be explained? Not by reference to courage *per se*, however that might be defined, but by reference to how courageous acts were sliced and diced by the creation of new medals and awards, and by the increased propaganda and morale-boosting value of the VC. The VC came to be seen by the establishment not just as the pre-eminent military decoration, but as a useful tool that could be used to give heart to a nation. Too many heroes would dilute the overall impact and potentially have a diminishing return for national morale.

Some other military decoration sacks – usually those pertaining to officers – were not so tightly held. As Sir Martin Lindsay, a former officer, wrote, if you had the right connections you would in all likelihood get some very prestigious medals:

[I]n spite of the provision of the Royal Warrant which instituted the DSO, that it was for 'special service in action,' staff officers below the rank of general were awarded the DSO or the MC... Such was the indignation of the Brigade of Guards when the 6th Earl of Rosebery [Harry Primrose, who served as Camp Commandant and ADC to General Allenby] emerged at the end of the war with the DSO and MC earned at Army HQ without a day spent at the front with his regiment, that for a few years he was virtually ostracised.[31]

The creation of new gallantry decorations, particularly the Military Cross and Military Medal, served a dual function: the supposed distinctiveness of the VC could be preserved, by limiting the numbers handed out, while the authorities were able to reward clearly courageous acts according to different grades. The invention of the MC and the MM obviously had nothing to do with any objective change in the definition of courage, were such even possible; rather it was because from 1914 onwards there was too much courage. It was not merely the case that technology, with its manifold means of long-range destruction, depersonalized warfare; it was also that anonymous barbarity became ubiquitous. Officers who had gained their professionalism in the Victorian era struggled to cope with the loss of an important sustaining ideal – that killing another human being might be done chivalrously. General Sir Ian Hamilton, who led the failed expedition at Gallipoli, summed up the changed nature of warfare:

> From Ypres onwards trenches and barbed wire fastened their paralys-
> ing grip upon the field… war sank into the lowest depths of beastliness
> and degeneration. The wonder of war, the glory of war, the adventure
> of war, the art of war all hung on its shifting scenery. For years the
> Armies had to eat, drink, sleep amidst their own putrefactions. Bit by
> bit the old campaigner's memories and young soldier's dreams were
> engulfed in machinery and mud.[32]

The first commander-in-chief of the British Expeditionary Force (BEF) sent to Flanders in 1914 was General Sir John French, who, at sixty-two, was still physically vigorous; but French and many of his contemporaries had learned their profession on horseback and were baffled by the technicalities of the new warfare. War obviously meant killing, but that need not, should not, entail bestiality; French was unable to grasp that honour and glory died with the birth of the machine-gun, and that beastliness was endemic to the new battlefield. In 1919 French saw no absurdity in writing that soldiers, 'emulating the knights of old, should honour a brave enemy only second to a comrade, and like them, rejoice to split a friendly lance today and ride boot to boot in the charge tomorrow'.[33]

The VC was born in an era when Sir John French's understanding of warfare was a plausible model; by 1915 only Victorian soldiers could still cleave to that limited horizon. Prior to 1914 the individual could matter; a spirited gallop, a determined rally, the rescue of a wounded officer – all could be noble and practical acts that might not only be physically seen, but were regarded as intrinsically important for morale: a courageous battlefield act might inspire others to greater determination or bravery, or even turn the tide. By 1916 there was a need for heroes, not just to maintain morale at home, but to inspire the conscripted millions who were not professional soldiers. In a post-war committee investigating the incidence of shell shock, Lord Southborough referred to a witness statement by Lieutenant Colonel H. Clay, Chief Recruiting Staff Officer of the London District, who said 'that the men were trained to the last pitch when they went out in 1914. It was different with the unfortunate man taken suddenly out of an office. He was brought up and rushed in twelve weeks straight into the trenches.'[34]

As the First World War's Western Front settled into apparently endless trench warfare, the scope for the individual to make a difference shrank almost to the point of invisibility; the mass mattered infinitely more. A single word – attrition – came to define the nature of the battlefield. The war gained a lastingly gloom-laden reputation, assisted by Winston Churchill's ersatz Augustan rhetoric:

> No war is so sanguinary as the war of exhaustion. No plan could be more unpromising than the plan of frontal attack. It will appear not only horrible but incredible to future generations that such doctrines should have been imposed by the military profession upon the ardent and heroic populations who yielded themselves to their orders.[35]

Individual soldiers on the Western Front rarely saw the enemy; 59 per cent of casualties were due to artillery.[36] If Sir John French embodied the warrior spirit of the nineteenth century, Pollard spoke for that of the twentieth. Pollard's VC – single-minded aggression, the killing of the enemy, bestiality if necessary – would become the archetype for VCs awarded during the later stages of the First War and certainly throughout the Second.

When the war started in 1914, the War Office was swamped by demands from field officers who, in their own small quarter of the Flanders battlefields, almost daily encountered the kind of self-sacrificial bravery that they imagined – often correctly – might merit a VC.

The end result was that those senior officers based in London who had the task of sifting VC recommendations pushed the requirement for VC eligibility – bowing to pressure when necessary to award VCs such as Cornwell's – beyond anything previously seen, without any reference to the VC warrant. Their in-trays were lightened by two developments: the invention of new medals and the informal acceptance of posthumous VCs. Following the crumbling of Edward VII's resistance to posthumous awards in 1907, a dead soldier could get the VC, even though the extant VC warrant made no posthumous provision and would not do so before 1920.[37] And, steadily, the authorities realized that one way to measure supreme courage might, if the circumstances were right, be a gallant, or at least a useful, death.

Yet the informal acceptance of posthumous VCs merely allowed another anomaly to surface. During the First War posthumous awards of lesser decorations – the DSO, the MC, the DCM, the DSC (Distinguished Service Cross) and the DSM (Distinguished Service Medal) – were not permissible. This discrepancy provoked considerable resentment from soldiers, heartache for families of dead servicemen, and pointed exchanges in Parliament. The impossibility of posthumous decorations – other than the VC or a Mention in Despatches – led to some extraordinary anomalies. Corporal James McCarthy of the 1st Royal Irish Regiment, stationed at Ain Kanish in Palestine, was cleaning grenades in barracks on 24 January 1918, when the fuse of one grenade started fizzing. He carried it outside, intending to throw it to safety, but fellow soldiers were standing about and it must be supposed he realized it could not be thrown anywhere without risking the lives of others. He was last seen holding the grenade tightly in both hands and close to his body. The explosion killed him but no one else was injured. McCarthy received a posthumous gold Albert Medal, originally created for civilians who saved life at sea and in 1877 extended to acts 'performed on land... in preventing accidents in mines, on railways, and at fires, and from other perils on the shore'.[38] McCarthy was obviously no civilian, but the Albert Medal could at least be given posthumously; the only alternative military decorations that were posthumously available were the VC or a Mention in Despatches. There were ten incidents when more than one Albert Medal was awarded between 1914 and 1918, and sixty-nine occasions when a single medal was granted.[39]

The ruling against posthumous gallantry awards (other than the VC or MiD) was debated on 8 March 1916 in the House of Lords. Lord Sydenham,[40] a Liberal and a former lieutenant general with the Royal Engineers who had served in the Sudan expedition under Kitchener, highlighted the anomaly:

> [I]t cannot be said, when one order is posthumous, that the concession may not be conceded of other orders... in the allocation of orders for gallant action it is very difficult to say exactly where the line of the Victoria Cross comes and that of the next lower decoration. It is a question that cannot be decided with absolute certainty.

More precisely, the 'system' was a cracked veneer overlaying confusion and muddle, not simply with the VC but with the whole gamut of military decorations. Lord Sandhurst, Under-Secretary of State at the War Office, responded to Sydenham for the government with unhelpful sympathy, pointing out that families of dead VC winners would be sent the Cross, while in the case of the CB, CMG, DSO and MC, the insignia might be sent to the next of kin, so long as the man who gained the distinction survived long enough for it to have been gazetted. A posthumous VC might not be in strict accordance with the extant VC warrant but could nevertheless be given; a posthumous MC could not. Sandhurst said this was regrettable, but all he could offer was a promise that the 'whole matter will be dealt with at the termination of the war'. The government blocked posthumous decorations other than the VC because of the old anxiety – to permit them might mean a flood of retrospective demands. As Sandhurst put it: 'the selection of names is always a very difficult matter in the case of posthumous honours. Whatever system was adopted... it would be very difficult to satisfy every claim.'[41] There the matter rested until the end of the war.

As slaughtered heaps were interred in Flanders, London continued to be inundated with VC recommendations. Sifting the questionable from the deserving was taxing. Some early ones, such as this approved by Sir John French, received short shrift: 'On 24th August [1914], when retiring he [Lieutenant W. G. R. Elliott of the 1st Cheshire Regiment] ran back, picked up a wounded man, and carried him 100 yards to safety under a hot fire, being himself shot through both ankles.'[42] Courageous acts that formerly might have gained the VC were, if not ten a penny, certainly in far greater numbers than ever before, and many went unnoticed; indeed, the brave sometimes had to make do with compensations other than medals.

Frank Richards served as a private in the 2nd Battalion, Royal Welch Fusiliers, throughout the war. In his memoir *Old Soldiers Never Die*,[43] Richards tells of 'Broncho', an incorrigible troublemaker when out of the front line but 'a grand front-line soldier, and most of his crimes were caused by overbearing non-commissioned officers'. In trouble once more, Broncho redeemed himself by volunteering to carry a message to Battalion HQ, through an intense artillery barrage. 'I'll take the bloody message,' shouted Broncho, even though it 'was a hundred to one he would be blown to bits before he had gone sixty yards'. Broncho not only carried the message – he returned with an answer. The previous week he had carried to safety a man who was wounded during a night patrol: 'For these two acts [Broncho] had a term of imprisonment washed out and about six months accumulated Number Ones; but he got no decoration.'[44]

Max Plowman had started out the war as a member of a Territorial

Army Field Ambulance unit and later became a commissioned officer before finally turning conscientious objector early in 1918. In his memoir, Plowman recalled a 'remarkable soldier' called Side, a rag-picker in civilian life and a stretcher-bearer at the Somme:

> on the 1st of July he carried stretchers under fire continuously for twenty-four hours. Anyone who knows the weight of a loaded stretcher and remembers the heat, the condition of the ground, and what the firing was like upon that day, will agree with me that the Victoria Cross would have expressed rather less than Side's deserts. However, he for his bravery was promoted to full corporal in the fighting-ranks.[45]

But before new medals could be invented there was ready to hand another way of cutting the number of VC claims: change what was demanded. That had already happened to some extent, by making a posthumous Cross possible; death in the performance of conspicuous gallantry surreptitiously served to exclude conspicuous gallantry that did not quite result in death. In December 1914 General Sir Douglas Haig, commander of the 1st Division in Flanders, met King George V, in the course of which they discussed the VC. The king admired Haig's professionalism and had sanctioned his appointment as commander of the Aldershot garrison. Although both were taciturn, emotionally buttoned-up and highly conscious of status, Haig and the king were friends and had developed a mutual respect since they first met in 1898. According to Haig, the king thought a VC for rescuing a fallen comrade 'was justified and beneficial. I replied that each case must be judged on its merits but, as a rule in civilised war such efforts did the wounded man harm and also tended to increase loss of valuable lives.'[46] Superficially this appears callous, but Haig was merely espousing the conventional notion of what a 'civilised' war constituted. His mentor during the Sudan campaign (and later), Horatio Kitchener, had the same view of a VC for rescuing the wounded: 'I think that some steps should be taken to discourage recommendations for the Victoria Cross in civilised warfare in cases of mere bringing in of wounded and dismounted men.'[47]

For Haig and his contemporaries, civilized war was played according to clear, mutually understood rules; both sides showed mercy to a wounded and militarily uniformed enemy. An 'uncivilized' war had no such rule; a British soldier who fell into the hands of Sudanese Dervishes, mutinous Indian sepoys, Afghan tribesmen or Zulu warriors could usually expect torture and humiliation before a terrible death. British soldiers sometimes took no prisoners in colonial wars, but did not as a matter of course indulge in torture before the killing. In reality, there was a degree of hypocrisy in Haig's position. In the South African war he had seen nothing wrong in spearing fleeing and unarmed Boers with his cavalryman's lance, although he may have justified that butchery because the Boers were, in his eyes, renegades and not professional soldiers;[48] but Haig assumed that in a white man's war both sides would desist from torturing and then killing wounded prisoners.[49] It would be wrong to say that in such a casual way Haig changed the course of the VC's history; after all, he wanted each case 'to be judged on its merits' and in conversation with the king suggested that rescuing fellow soldiers from a burning building would certainly merit consideration for a VC. In any case, no formal changes were made to the VC's warrant during the 1914–18 war.

When Haig succeeded French as the BEF's commander-in-chief on 15 December 1915, he stuck to his word regarding the VC recommendations he sanctioned – each case was judged on its merits. This meant that quite a few 'rescue' VCs got through, particularly if they suited wider considerations, such as deflecting uncomfortable attention from British military disaster. On 1 July 1916, the first day of the Battle of the Somme, when almost 20,000 British soldiers were killed, temporary Lieutenant Geoffrey St George Shillington Cather, adjutant of the 9th Royal Irish Fusiliers, gained his VC 'for the most conspicuous bravery' (the conventional opening phrase used in First War VC citations) during the attack at Beaumont Hamel.[50] The 9th Battalion went over the top at 7.10 a.m., immediately coming under intense machine-gun fire; the bodies soon piled up. Twelve hours later Cather was the only surviving officer of the battalion. Between 7 p.m. and midnight Cather was out in No Man's Land with other volunteers, searching for wounded survivors and recovering three. Next morning Cather continued the search, rescuing another man, giving water to others and arranging for them to be collected later, all the while under direct machine-gun and intermittent artillery fire. Cather was killed mid-morning.[51] He showed considerable courage and selfless dedication, but his VC was of the type that Haig had apparently ruled out in December 1914. But in the days that followed the start of the Battle of the Somme, Haig needed all the 'good' publicity that could be mustered; in the absence of obvious battlefield victory, dead heroes were the best available means of garnering the sympathy of a critical press and a bewildered and appalled general public.

As the VC had grown in status and acquired greater mystique – despite the many anomalies of the nineteenth century – the establishment took care to limit, as much as possible, the number awarded. This happened in two ways. The adjudication process implemented by the hierarchy of committees raised the minimum bar for consideration for a VC, without public acknowledgement. Simultaneously, a multiplicity of alternative gallantry awards, which attempted to grade more finely the distinctions between supposed 'levels' of courage displayed, were introduced. In December 1914 the Military Cross was instituted, specifically for warrant officers (sergeant majors) and junior officers (captain and below), who were, because of their rank, ineligible for the Distinguished Service Order, of which almost 9,000 were distributed during the First World War. By the end of the war, many MC citations, published in the London Gazette, spoke of the kind of gallantry that in a previous era might have gained a VC. An example is the 1918 citation for Acting Major Norman Fielden Dare, of the Royal Field Artillery, for a second MC bar:

> For conspicuous gallantry and devotion to duty. This officer was in command of a battery when it was rushed by an overpowering number of the enemy. His judgment and coolness enabled him to extricate four of his guns, which he brought later into action in a forward position, from which, though much exposed, he directed their fire himself, inflicting severe casualties on the enemy and breaking up their attack.[52]

The partial rescue of previously deserted guns at Colenso in 1899 – an inglorious moment in British military history – had seen six Crosses awarded. Standards had clearly changed: more than 37,000 MCs were awarded during the First War, with almost 3,000 bars.[53]

Sir Frederick Ponsonby, successively private secretary to Queen Victoria, King Edward VII, and now King George V, witnessed the haphazard birth of the MC, as his role included the supervision of what he called the whole 'tiresome question' of decorations. A Conservative to his marrow, Ponsonby had long fought a rearguard action to prevent British honours from being cast away like birdseed on the deserving and the undeserving alike, as had happened with decorations in Germany, France, Italy and Russia. He regarded it as his duty to defend what already existed, not to create something new and possibly superfluous, such as the MC, but the pressure to reward courage on a vastly enlarged scale weakened even his resolve. If there was resistance to giving out VCs with the relative abandon of the nineteenth century, then clearly the bravery of some officers, particularly the junior ones who would bear the brunt of the fighting, was going to go unrecognized. Ponsonby summed up the position:

It had been for some time abundantly clear that our existing decorations were inadequate for a war of this magnitude, and that some
decoration other than the V.C. and D.S.O. would be necessary for
officers. There appeared to be some dissatisfaction at the front, and
while, of course, the whole standard [for the VC] had been raised,
there seemed no rewards for junior officers whose bravery did not
entitle them to the V.C. The D.S.O. was originally designed for this
purpose, but eventually it was restricted to senior officers; during the
South African War, too, it had been prostituted, as several officers who
had never left the base received it.[54]

The logical course would have been to broaden the scope of the DSO
to include junior officers, but that would have faced stiff resistance
from senior officers – many of whom had the DSO – who wished to
preserve the distinctive status of the decoration; it was an order, after
all, no mere medal. This snobbery helped produce a confusing pano-
ply of military decorations, only partially tidied up in the 1993 review
of gallantry awards.

In the discussions between George V and the military establishment
on how best to solve the medal 'gap' at the end of 1914, the king suggested extending the Distinguished Service Cross, an award limited
to the Royal Navy, to the army.[55] Kitchener jumped at the idea, but
the First Sea Lord, Winston Churchill – his bitter encounters with
Kitchener in South Africa an enduring memory – strenuously defended
the exclusivity of the DSC for the Royal Navy. The king was 'very much
opposed to the idea of the two Services having different decorations',
but Kitchener, thus rebuffed, furiously refused to have anything more
to do with the DSC idea. Instead he opted for a new, army-only cross
and formed a committee to work out the details, which was done in
such haste that Ponsonby was surprised 'that more mistakes were
not made'. Ponsonby wanted the new army decoration to be for

fighting officers only; staff officers, far from the front lines, would be excluded. Kitchener disagreed, reasoning that 'a staff officer in charge of intricate operations during an offensive deserved greater recognition than a man who performed an individual act of gallantry. One man was merely responsible for his life, whereas the other might be responsible for thousands of lives...'[56] Thus tension that had existed since the first days of the VC – between a desire to recognize individual acts of tactical gallantry and the need to reward strategically significant military planning – resurfaced once more. Kitchener chaired the small committee formed to produce the MC, on which Ponsonby, now Keeper of the Privy Purse after having served briefly with the 7th Division in France, also sat. The disorderly process by which the MC was created greatly contrasts with the deliberate planning that went into the VC. The MC was entirely Kitchener's handiwork:

> The word 'autocrat' can only give a feeble idea of what Kitchener was at that time. The War Office blindly carried out his orders, and no one ever thought of questioning his proposals or of attempting to argue with him. The committee was therefore a farce... When we came to the design I suggested we should have something really good, but Kitchener said it would take too long and there was no necessity to have anything damned artistic... Kitchener seemed to fancy himself as an artist, and was constantly engaged in drawing pathetic designs on the blotting-paper.[57]

Kitchener decreed that the MC should be silver, but only, Ponsonby believed, because he was presented with a rough sketch that had been coloured with silver paint. The choice of the MC ribbon was made in no less slapdash a fashion. Kitchener proposed various colour schemes, only for Ponsonby – with his encyclopedic knowledge of European decorations – to point out that Kitchener's suggestions were either identical to or closely matched the ribbons of other countries:

Kitchener became quite exasperated and said: 'This damned fellow contradicts me whenever I say anything. We'll have no nonsense; I've got it, plain black and white, simple and dignified', to which I remarked that that happened to be the Iron Cross. That broke up the meeting, and Kitchener said he would choose the ribbon with the King.[58]

Kitchener then consulted a book of Ponsonby's containing examples of all British and foreign ribbons. Ponsonby also left lying around a basket with a selection of ribbons, collected by his wife:

> Eventually I was sent for and shown with triumph a ribbon they had selected which was not in any book; I found they had chosen the one my wife had made out, mauve on a white ground... It was decided to call the new medal the Military Cross, but there was no guarantee that it would not be given for services at the base or on the line of communication, which was a great pity. The King then proposed to start a Military Medal.[59]

Having hastily created the MC for junior officers – thereby allowing the informal raising of the VC bar for those ranks – there inevitably arose pressure to do something for the enlisted men, although a perfectly respectable, indeed coveted award already existed in the form of the Distinguished Conduct Medal, awarded 'for distinguished conduct in the field'. On 4 April 1916, sixteen months after the MC was established, the London Gazette revealed that the king had got his way: the Military Medal (MM) was invented specifically for other ranks and initially only for men. The MM was a medal that really did not need inventing; for NCOs and other ranks the DCM had hitherto ranked just behind the VC. But the sheer numbers of men in the army evoked from the military establishment a desire to try to grade courage ever more finely, artificially inventing distinctions between acts, where such discrimination was hardly credible. In the first great round of savagery in the twentieth century, the military establishment almost forgot the DCM, awarding just 25,000 of them (including bars); and in the 1939–45 replay that number dropped to some 1,900.

Fifty-one VCs were won during the Battle of the Somme, twenty going to junior officers, twelve to NCOs and nineteen to privates; a third were posthumous. Some of the Somme VCs ought to have raised a few eyebrows, as they clearly fitted poorly within the extant VC statutes. Although one writer has suggested that 'surely the most heroic figure was Billy McFadzean',[60] a twenty-one-year-old private in the 14th Royal Irish Rifles, his act of 'most conspicuous bravery' involved only his own, particularly pointless death, at Thiepval Wood, where on 1 July he was in a densely packed trench. McFadzean, a specialist bomber, was ordered to unpack grenades ready for troops about to go over the top. He picked up a box and cut the cord surrounding it; but the box slipped from his hands, dropping two grenades on the ground and knocking out their pins. With only seconds to react before the grenades exploded, McFadzean threw himself on them; he died and a soldier nearby lost a leg. His citation read, in part: 'He well knew his danger... but without a moment's hesitation he gave his life for his comrades.'[61] It was an impossible, horrible moment, in which McFadzean can only have reacted instinctively. Yet however we look at it, McFadzean was responsible for mishandling the box, admittedly under dreadfully stressful circumstances – the Germans were shelling heavily the Royal Irish Rifles' position – and he brought about his own end. Given the circumstances, why did he not receive the Albert Medal? The answer is likely to have been nothing to do with the act itself, but the wider signals sent by the VC – signals that would have been entirely absent from the barely known Albert Medal.

McFadzean's VC-winning act, along with other VCs in 1916, served a much broader purpose: the public acclamation of a hero who died in battle. Six months before the Somme started, the government had, to mixed response, imposed universal conscription (except in Ireland), as the army's appetite for men seemed insatiable; yet victory was a more distant prospect than ever. The uncomfortable fact is that the dead McFadzean may have contributed far more to the war effort than if he had lived. It was newsworthy that his father was given a ticket (third class) to travel from Belfast to receive his son's Cross personally from the king.

Such royal gestures were, as in the nineteenth century, eagerly written up by the press; in November 1916 the *Illustrated London News*, under the heading 'The King Presenting the Victoria Cross to the Mother of a Fallen Hero', carried a full-page graphic of George V handing to his mother the posthumous VC awarded to Private Edward Warner of the Bedfordshire Regiment, sixteen months after Warner had entered a gassed trench alone at Hill 60, near Ypres. Warner went to find reinforcements and the deserted trench was held, but he died from ingested gas the next day. That same investiture also saw the VC handed to Alice Cornwell.[62] Such gestures not only celebrated heroes; they demonstrated that the king was 'with' the people and honoured the dead, who – the public was reminded – had not been forgotten. By late 1917, in the final days of the futile Battle of Passchendaele, Haig's paper-thin distinction between uncivilized and civilized war had become a bitter joke for those in the trenches: what was civilized about gas, flame-throwers, aerial bombing, or a sharpened spade in the back?

On the battlefields of the First War the VC performed its historic function, that of honouring the dead and knitting together humbled national morale. On the home front, where the ripples of war soon touched civilian life, there was, at the start of the war, no means of honouring those out of uniform. Civilian casualties during the war were minimal – 1,414 killed and 3,416 wounded, from fifty-one Zeppelin and fifty-two aircraft raids[63] – but the outrage was nevertheless considerable. The government came under pressure to create a new honour to award to those thought to have provided invaluable contributions to the war effort. Zeppelins first dropped bombs on British soil in December 1914, and airship raids continued throughout 1915 and 1916, but the real damage was caused by Gotha aircraft; the deadliest daylight air raid on London happened on 5 June 1917, which left 162 dead and 432 wounded. The timing was fortuitous; the previous day the government had unveiled a new decoration specifically for civilians. Unlike the VC and other military gallantry awards, the British Empire Order immediately reintroduced class-based stratification, with different grades – KBE, CBE, OBE, MBE – used to reward civilians according to their status.[64]

By August 1918, when the tide had turned in favour of an eventual allied victory, it was clear that the current VC warrant no longer covered all eventualities. Various technical and uncontroversial changes to the warrant – such as including the newly created Royal Air Force – were obviously necessary. In July 1918 Sir Reginald Brade, Permanent Under-Secretary of State for War between 1914 and 1920, raised with senior figures of the armed services the question of a new wording for the VC warrant. Rear Admiral Norman Craig Palmer seized the opportunity provided by Brade to suggest that the merchant navy should be included in any new warrant:[65] 'It would appear to me to be highly desirable that Officers and men of the Mercantile Marine should be eligible for this very highly valued Decoration, in view of the unprecedented conditions which prevail.' As well as the merchant navy, there was the anomaly of (commonplace but prohibited) posthumous VC decorations; there was the clear possibility that a civilian might deserve a VC; and there was the thorny issue of women in uniform, if not in action.

On 7 August 1918 the War Office published a press release, notifying the establishment of an interdepartmental committee 'to consider and advise His Majesty' on amending the VC warrant, to make the VC more 'in keeping with the requirements of modern warfare', to draw up a 'new clause to support posthumous award of the VC as the existing Warrant does not legislate for such awards', and, most sensitive of all, to consider 'the advisability or otherwise of extending, in certain circumstances the award to women and to civilians'. The Military Secretary at the War Office, Lieutenant General Sir Francis Davies, solicited opinions from various ministries and the armed services.[66] The air force, the Colonial Office and the army raised no objection to including women, so long as the prevailing high (albeit ill-defined) standards were maintained. However, the Naval Secretary, Admiral Sir Allen Frederic Everett, was opposed. He privately wrote to Lieutenant General Davies on 7 August 1918:

My Dear General,

At first blush, it seems logically indefensible to debar the fair sex from being awarded the V.C. provided of course they 'have performed some signal act of valour or devotion to their country'... It must be fully realized that the standard of 'valour and devotion to duty' for the Victoria Cross is now very much higher than it was in the earlier years of its introduction. In fact, it may be said that the standard now required for the award of a V.C. is far, far higher than the actual words express... if women are to be eligible, will not the ordinary gallantry of man render his judgment lenient; will he not be soft-hearted towards the woman (marriage proves this) and give her the benefit of the loosest interpretation of a female act of valour or devotion to duty; will he not be inclined to say 'By Jove (Mars or Venus), for a woman that was a splendid deed', and assess her award by virtue of being influenced by her sex?... let us hypothecate a retreat where some bloody-minded virago W.A.A.C is overtaken by a Hun, might she not be the more induced to take up a bundook [old British army slang for a rifle] and battle with a Hun, might she not be all the more tempted to take some very unladylike action or conduct herself in such an unseemly manner from the universal standard expected of the fair sex that the enemy would proclaim all women combatants and shoot them at sight?... There are enough bickerings in the masculine line as to whether this man or that should or should not have been awarded a VC, but if the hysterical female world is to be allowed in, God help the poor devils who have to make decisions...[67]

Everett next day delivered to Lieutenant General Davies a memo, 'Eligibility of women for the Victoria Cross', which used less emotive language but maintained the same opposition.

When the eight members, all men, of the 'Committee on Co-ordination etc. of Warrants Relating to the V.C' first met on 30 August 1918,[68] Ponsonby, acting as chairman and representing the king,[69] opened by saying that there was 'a lot of very simple work in front of us, and a certain amount of rather intricate work. I do not think, however, there is anything that requires any acrimonious discussion.' It was a forlorn hope. Everett was adamant about not allowing women in:

we think that the words 'some signal act of valour or devotion to their country' as a matter of fact should be very severely interpreted. It is only artificially that the V.C. has reached the very high standard it has reached at present and if you are going to bring women in that particular definition would cover all sorts of petty things.

Ponsonby asked: 'Your suggestion is that we should stiffen up that definition.' To which Everett simply replied: 'Yes.' Colonel Graham said: 'You cannot compare the V.C. in this war with any previous war because people are getting the Military Medal now for what would have won the V.C. in the South African War.' This recognition by Everett and the army's Deputy Military Secretary that the VC standard had been surreptitiously elevated could have been a pivotal moment; but there was no interest from those assembled in even considering a lowering of standards to bring the VC back into line with its earliest history. By August 1918 Billy McFadzean's self-sacrifice would probably not have gained him a VC: at the meeting, Colonel Graham commented on 'cases where a man gets an arm or a leg blown off in picking up a bomb, or loses his life by throwing himself upon a bomb. That is pure self-sacrifice, and not really valour, I mean.' The debate was confused and confusing; might self-sacrifice not also be valorous?

Quite remarkably, it emerges at this point of the proceedings that there existed 'local rules' regarding the distribution of the VC, demarcating the Royal Navy from the army; while the army required 'first-hand evidence of two witnesses', the navy had no such requirement. Colonel Graham pointed out that the 'two witnesses [requirement] is *merely a domestic arrangement* on the part of the Field Marshal [Douglas Haig] in France' [emphasis added]. The meeting agreed that the phrase 'conclusive proof' should be included, and Everett wanted to see 'conclusive' italicized for emphasis, adding that 'one might almost, after "conclusive" put in "backed by two witnesses" or words to that effect'. Colonel More raised an obvious point: 'Might not there possibly be a case in which it would be difficult or impossible to get two witnesses, and is it not better to leave it rather open.' He was ignored; Ponsonby merely said: 'I think the word "conclusive" covers all that is necessary.'

Everett and Graham's acknowledgement that the VC standard implemented in the war had been 'artificially' raised was only partly right; it was rather that the VC Committee began to reward aggression much more than selflessness. In 1915, 117 VCs were awarded, 35 per cent of them for rescuing or tending to comrades; in 1917 such acts gained 13 per cent of the 174 VCs for that year; in 1918, 203 Crosses were gained, 6.5 per cent for rescuing the wounded.[70] But Everett was isolated regarding his *bête noir*: none of the rest of the committee objected to including women or civilians, so long as high standards were maintained. Ponsonby read out submissions which supported the inclusion of women and civilians, including this from Major General Sir Godfrey Paine, of the Air Ministry: 'it is only logical that they [women] should be included subject to precise definitions as to eligibility.' General Ruggles-Brise, meanwhile, who as Haig's Military Secretary at GHQ in France can be assumed to have spoken for Haig, said:

> [while] it is difficult to conceive that a woman could perform services sufficient to merit an award of the V.C. at the present standard [army commanders] are generally of the opinion that there is no objection to civilians, and therefore women, being eligible for the Victoria Cross, so long as the present high standard is maintained and any tendency to forward recommendations for sentimental reasons is sternly repressed.

Ponsonby teased out the implications of including women: 'A woman might save a life, might possibly bring a man back or anything of that sort but the idea the V.C. is now given for, exceptional service in the presence of the enemy, means that women will have in future to be considered as combatants... [for the VC] you have to do a bit of fighting.' Colonel More pointed out that that was not true; chaplains and medics had got the VC. Everett bluntly said it was the job of chaplains and medics to 'go into the firing line and be in the fighting'. Chaplains and medics became temporary combatants, suggested Everett, but it was absurd to imagine women being temporary combatants. Colonel Gordon suggested they might be in the front line helping, to which Everett retorted: 'they ought to clear out'.

What is interesting about the meeting, however, is that Ponsonby did not reveal what he must have been aware of – that King George V was deeply opposed to the inclusion of women and civilians. In a letter dated 7 March 1919, Lord Stamfordham, the king's private secretary, wrote to Winston Churchill (by then Secretary of State for War):

> As I mentioned to you in conversation, The King was averse to the inclusion of women and civilians among those eligible for the Victoria Cross. I explained to His Majesty the points which you raised in favour of allowing the terms of the Warrant to remain as recommended by the Army Council. The King has, therefore, signed the [new] Warrant, but His Majesty hopes that its publication may be deferred until we are no longer in a state of war. This would insure no question of making the Warrant retrospective.

Having granted women over the age of thirty the right to vote in November 1918, and thus enfranchising more than eight million women, it might have been politically difficult to so publically exclude women from the highest military decoration.

The committee – all save Everett – and even the king grasped the obvious fact that the events of 1914–18 had shown that the battlefield was without geographical limits; civilians and women might find themselves in positions where they could conceivably demonstrate exceptional gallantry. The most the committee could do to limit VC distribution and thus preserve its exclusivity was to hope that the military would block any attempt to award the VC to a civilian or a woman. And this hope has so far been realized. In a parting shot, Everett requested that the preamble to the committee's report should note the Admiralty's disapproval of women being eligible for the Cross; that too was overruled. The committee met again on 12 November 1918, by which date Everett had been replaced by the new Naval Secretary, Admiral Sir Rudolph Bentinck, who raised no objections to women or civilians being drawn under the VC umbrella. It dispensed with some minor points and nodded through women, civilians and the merchant navy into a revised warrant, together with posthumous awards. Some of those present wanted to tighten the regulations by excluding non-combatant actions; but as the only two men to have won bars to their VCs were medics, and they had gained them in a non-combatant role, that was clearly indefensible.

On 22 May 1920 a new warrant, superseding all previous, was signed into being by Winston Churchill. Clause three of the 1856 warrant – 'It is ordained that the Cross shall only be awarded to those Officers or Men who have served Us in the presence of the enemy, and shall have then performed some signal act of valour or devotion to their country' – was rewritten thus: 'It is ordained that the Cross shall only be awarded for conspicuous bravery or some daring or pre-eminent act of valour or self-sacrifice or extreme devotion to duty in the presence of the enemy.' 'Conspicuous bravery', the phrase that had come to be used in the First War for all gazetted VCs, was a clear step up from 'signal act of valour'.

That the war had indeed made exceptional courage a much tougher proposition was the view of many who fought, as expressed by Squadron Leader W. Tyrell DSO, MC, of the Royal Air Force Medical Service, when he gave evidence to the 1922 inquiry into shell shock, chaired by Lord Southborough: 'The old Regular Army had a much fiercer way of looking upon anything approaching cowardice, because their standards were based upon wars previous to this war in which the calls made upon a man's courage were as nothing compared to this war.'[71] The minimum requirements for a VC had been surreptitiously raised during 1914–18 with scant regard to what the VC warrant actually stipulated, forcing the warrant to be revised to take account of changed circumstances.

On Saturday, 26 June 1920, King George V and Queen Mary held a garden party at Buckingham Palace for 305 surviving holders of the VC and their relatives, those who 'stood for courage in every form,

from the sudden deed all unpremeditated that changed a whole position in action, to the patient, calculated venture that culminated at
Zeebrugge'.[72] As the band of the Welsh Guards played, the guests
drifted through rose-filled marquees while sampling strawberries and
cream, cakes and sandwiches, and glimpsing Field Marshal Earl Haig,
Air Marshal Sir Hugh Trenchard and Winston Churchill. Newspaper
reports of the assembly were suitably deferential:

> There were about half-a-dozen babies in arms, and their fathers –
> proud of them as of their Crosses – gently manoeuvred that the wife
> should come into the line that was being followed. In no case did the
> Queen fail to give these little mites a distinction to be recalled to the
> end of their days by a pat on the cheeks, and some gracious words of
> enquiry to the delighted young wife.[73]

The physically able VC winners had marched from Wellington Barracks
amid thousands of cheering onlookers, photographers and autograph-
hunters. Doyen of the throng was General Sir Dighton MacNaughton
Probyn, aged eighty-seven and now severely hunched. Probyn was an
Indian Mutiny survivor who, as a twenty-four-year-old captain in the
2nd Punjab Cavalry, had gained his VC over several actions, including killing an enemy standard-bearer and capturing the standard.[74]
Just sixty years had passed between Probyn's VC and that of Patrick
Joseph Budgen of the 31st Battalion, Australian Imperial Force (AIF),
who fought at Polygon Wood from 26 to 28 September 1917.[75] Budgen
twice successfully attacked enemy pillboxes against 'devastating fire
from machine guns' and captured the defenders; had rescued a corporal who had been taken prisoner, shooting dead one German and
bayoneting two others; and 'on five occasions' rescued wounded men
under 'intense shell and machine-gun fire, showing an utter contempt
and disregard for danger'. He was killed on the last such rescue mission.[76] What linked Probyn's and Budgen's VCs was their individual

bravery, the one frenziedly slashing with his sabre at sepoys, the other equally desperately charging machine-gun posts; what separated their VCs was the requirement of death, an imposition that became more exigent in the bigger war to follow.

5

Go Home and Sit Still

'Armies are self-evidently political institutions.'

HEW STRACHAN[1]

'Every combatant soldier knows how chancy is
the whole business of decorations.'

ANTHONY EDEN[2]

The foundation stone of the VC was gender-specific; the fifth clause of the 1856 warrant stipulated that the VC would only 'be awarded to those Officers or Men who have served Us in the presence of the Enemy'. By 1918 this stipulation was, formally at least, antiquated; uniformed women had for two years been serving king and country in many different capacities, though not in the front line, nor in any combat role. But relatively few women wore uniform during the First War – by November 1918 around 90,000 had served in the auxiliary services, mainly in the Women's Army Auxiliary Corps (WAAC) – and even fewer were near the front line, 'able to be injured and killed in warfare but not able to fight for their country'.[3] The very suggestion that a woman might gain a VC was anathema to the nineteenth-century military and, indeed, civilian establishment; most Victorians or Edwardians, male or female, would have found the term 'woman soldier' a repellent oxymoron. The prevailing assumption in the nineteenth and well into the twentieth century was that women were fragile, hysterical creatures, dependent on a protective male. Yet the idea that women were incapable of exceptional courage or self-sacrifice was as nonsensical as the assumption that all soldiers were brave.

In 1869 Elizabeth Desborough Harris, wife of Lieutenant Colonel Webber Desborough Harris of the Peshawar-based 104th Bengal Fusiliers, found herself in the midst of a devastating and, for many of the soldiers, fatal outbreak of cholera. She nursed the sick and dying with complete indifference to her own safety, and the grateful band of officers clubbed together to have a gold replica of the VC manufactured for her. On the reverse of the medal the officers had inscribed that it was in recognition of her 'indomitable pluck'. No one thought Mrs Desborough Harris a serious candidate for the real VC, but twenty-two years later London's newspapers were briefly full of the stirring tale of intrepid courage shown by Ethel Grimwood, who *was* seriously spoken of as meriting a VC.

Ethel was married to Frank St Clair Grimwood, the British political agent in Manipur, a highly sensitive posting in a remote, mountainous region on India's north-east frontier. Such agents were intended to be the eyes and ears of the Indian government, keeping Calcutta apprised of all relevant developments in those princedoms and regions where local *rajas* nominally ruled with a degree of independence, pledging submission to Calcutta in return for financial support. Apart from a nine-month interval in another district, the Grimwoods were based in Imphal, Manipur's capital, from 1888 to 1891. They were turbulent years, during which the ruling *raja* and his seven brothers jostled for power, their continual internecine intrigues playing out against a background of deceptive tranquillity. Handling this viper's nest called for all of Grimwood's tactful sensitivity; he learned Meitei, the local language, and befriended all of the squabbling brothers while favouring none. This scrupulous diplomacy was wrecked when a simmering dispute between Tikendrajit – the *Senaputti* or commander-in-chief of the Manipuri troops – and another brother, over who would have the right to take as a bride a beautiful sixteen-year-old girl, turned violent. Tikendrajit orchestrated the removal from his throne of Surachandra, the *raja*, in September 1890 and installed another brother, Kulachandra; Tikendrajit was named the *jubraj*, or heir. Surachandra temporarily took refuge with Grimwood in the residency before subsequently fleeing to Calcutta, from where he lobbied the viceroy, Lord Lytton, son of the novelist Edward Bulwer-Lytton, to restore him to a tawdry throne. The British authorities opted to accept Kulachandra as *raja*, but – unbeknown to the Grimwoods, who accepted the *fait accompli* and maintained good terms with Tikendrajit – they decided to punish Tikendrajit by arresting and banishing him.

In late March 1891, Grimwood's superior, James Wallace Quinton, Chief Commissioner in Assam, along with 400 Gurkhas under the command of Lieutenant Colonel Charles Skene, arrived unannounced in Manipur. Quinton was an old Indian government hand – he had been with the Indian civil service for thirty-three years – but all his time had been spent on the north-west frontier; he knew nothing of the local language and little of the complexities of Manipuran politics. Quinton's plan was based on treachery. He proposed to invite Tikendrajit and his general Thangal to a *durbar* in an Imphal building, lock all the exits, and arrest them at bayonet point. Quinton informed Grimwood of this underhand trap the day before it was to be sprung; the man on the spot, in other words, was not consulted until too late. According to Ethel: 'To be obliged to arrest a man himself with whom he [Grimwood] had been on friendly terms for nearly three years, and see him treated like a common felon, without being able to defend himself, was naturally a hard task, and my husband felt it bitterly.' In one of his final letters Grimwood lamented that 'a native Administration is a dreadful thing to have to do with. It seems impossible to improve it.' The same might have been said of the white authorities in Calcutta whose ineptitude, as much as Tikendrajit's cannon, did for Grimwood.

Tikendrajit was no fool; the arrival of a senior figure such as Quinton and a contingent of Gurkhas inevitably aroused his suspicions. On 24 March 1891 Tikendrajit and Thangal feigned illness and stayed away from the *durbar*, and when Quinton tried to force their arrest, a mêlée broke out. Quinton, who had foolishly brought no artillery with him, found himself facing cannon and rifle fire from several thousand Manipuri troops, safe within an impregnable citadel. The bombardment quickly reduced Grimwood's residency – converted to a makeshift hospital where Ethel helped tend the wounded – to a dismembered shack. Grimwood, Quinton, Skene, a Mr Cossins and a Lieutenant Simpson went unarmed to the palace to see if they could negotiate a ceasefire, under which they might withdraw from Imphal. In the confusing ruckus outside the palace, Grimwood was speared and died immediately; the other four were seized and clapped in irons. That same evening, after a brief deliberation, they were taken outside the palace and beheaded, their blood 'sprinkled over the mouths of two idols, which stand in the shape of dragons in front of the Royal Palace'.[4] To recover the shackles from the corpses their feet were hacked off.

Seven Gurkha officers and 150 troops thereupon fled, taking Ethel Grimwood with them. Where other trussed-up pampered Victorian women might have succumbed to despair on their flight to safety, Ethel was fearful but steadfast. Her footwear was quickly torn to shreds, as for a week she and the raggle-taggle band trekked, with little food or water and covered in leeches, until they reached safety at Lakhipur on 1 April. The local correspondent of *The Times* reported that 'Mrs Grimwood displayed the greatest heroism, attending the wounded under heavy fire. After the Residency was evacuated she acted as guide, her knowledge of the country proving invaluable.'[5]

In the House of Commons on 5 June, Sir John Eldon Gorst, Under-Secretary of State for India, was asked if there was an appropriate Indian order for Mrs Grimwood; to loud cheers, Sir John replied that, when he had reviewed the full official reports, he would 'gladly consider whether it is open to him to make any recommendation on Mrs Grimwood's behalf'. Three days after Gorst addressed the Commons, Queen Victoria – or more likely, as Victoria, now seventy-two, was ailing, her advisers – pre-empted Gorst by awarding Ethel the Royal Red Cross, 'in recognition of her devotion to the wounded under most trying circumstances'.[6] This medal was then so little known that *The Times* thought it necessary to publish an explanatory note from *Burke's Peerage*, pointing out that it was worn by the Queen herself, Florence Nightingale and more than fifty 'other ladies'.[7] The award of the Royal Red Cross to Ethel did not placate *The Times*, which intoned on 12 June:

> The fact that the Order of the Royal Red Cross has been conferred upon Mrs Grimwood must not be taken as an indication that her case is finally disposed of. If it is found that the official despatches confirm the reports cabled to the English newspapers as to the lady's bravery during the attack on the residency and the subsequent retreat, it is probable that Lord Cross [Secretary of State for India] will recommend her Majesty to confer upon her the Victoria Cross.[8]

The Times evidently based this assertion on a well-placed leak – but the source was inaccurate. Sir John would not have dared to create such a precedent, even though the official reports supported the account of Ethel's courage.

The subsequent tale of the indomitable twenty-four-year-old Ethel Grimwood is an example of how the press in Victorian England could conjure a celebrity out of the ashes of a disaster, only to drop them at the first whiff of scandal. Any remote chance that Ethel might be the first female winner of the VC was ruined by the ill-judged decision of her sister to send to The Times a letter of Ethel's, published on 29 April, which criticized Quinton and by implication Calcutta. Ethel's bald statement that Quinton 'kept us in the dark as to the real reasons for coming until they arrived on 22 of March' deeply embarrassed the establishment by diverting attention from Tikendrajit's wickedness.[9] By no coincidence at all, rumours soon circulated of the Grimwoods' extra-marital activities, about which nothing had been heard prior to the Manipur debacle.[10] The only Manipur VC to be awarded was the entirely conventional – and, by conventional standards, thoroughly deserved – one given to Lieutenant Charles Grant, a twenty-nine-year-old Scot with the Madras Staff Corps. On learning of the Manipur shambles, Grant had volunteered to lead a tiny force of eighty Punjabi and Gurkha troops from his base at Tamu, and this small force held at bay a much superior advance army of Tikendrajit's until reinforcements arrived.[11]

This long-forgotten incident on the outskirts of the empire trundled inexorably to its destined conclusion; the rebellion was put down and in London there were demands to find a scapegoat. Dissembling, squirming and fudge helpfully obscured matters. The only persons punished – apart from Tikendrajit, Thangal and others of the Manipur elite, who were captured, tried and hanged – were the officers who fled the scene. These were disgraced and cashiered, although without ammunition and facing overwhelming odds their only alternative was to have stood their ground until they too were slaughtered.[12] In November 1891 Ethel published an account of her Manipur days, in which she wrote:

I think that the honour of England is as dear to us women as it is to the men; and though it is not our vocation in life to be soldiers, and to fight for our country, yet, when occasion offers, I have little doubt that the women of England have that in them which would enable them to come out of any dilemma as nobly and honourably as the men, and with just as much disregard for their own lives as the bravest soldier concerned.[13]

A finer statement of why women might sometimes deserve a VC would be difficult to imagine.

Valiant women were not, therefore, to be subject to the erratically applied slide-rule used to gauge VC worthiness in the nineteenth century. This exclusion was perhaps understandable in an era when usually brief military campaigns were waged far from Britain, with armies numbered in thousands, the dead in tens or hundreds, and women kept far distant from the battlefield, restricted to tending for the sick or wounded. But Zeppelin raids on London and elsewhere in Britain dragged women and civilians into a front line that now existed everywhere in reach of long-range attack by air. Men were conscripted in 1916, and there were numerous calls for the same for women: 'Official attitudes appeared to have come full circle: from rejecting women's offers of voluntary labour in 1914, the War Office was actively considering their conscription by 1916.'[14] But no one seriously contemplated giving a rifle and bayonet to a woman; any conscription for women would be for auxiliary duties, and the creation of the Women's Army Auxiliary Corps (WAAC) in March 1917 was represented as an organization that was essentially feminine rather than military.

The hope in August 1914 that the fighting in Flanders would be brief had faded by Christmas that same year. Very few politicians or soldiers – with the notable exceptions of Lord Kitchener, Secretary of State for

War, and General Sir Douglas Haig – had believed that it would last more than a few months. While men rushed to join up, eager to see some action before the war was over, women who early volunteered their services usually encountered the kind of patronizing attitude Elsie Inglis, a medical doctor, experienced when she put herself forward in August 1914. A War Office official told her: 'My good lady, go home and sit still.'[15] Little had changed in more than 2,500 years, when Homer had Hector, about to go off to fight with Achilles, instruct his wife Andromache to 'Go home, attend to your own handiwork/ At loom and spindle/ As for the war, that is for men.'

Women were not seen as fighters: their role in war 'was to symbolise the society for which the men were fighting'.[16] By 1916 the war gripped almost every British home and, over the next two years, the British army reached its maximum strength of four million, pulling large numbers of women into jobs previously done by men, including roles close to the fighting. With a sprawling front line extending from the Channel coast to Switzerland, and territory gained or lost measured in yards rather than miles, individual supererogatory acts of courage became much more difficult to easily identify and almost too numerous to mention. Eyewitness accounts of supremely gallant acts by senior officers were infinitely more problematic on battlefields of such vast scale, while the scope for creative hyperbole in the writing-up of VC recommendations created even more uncertainty about their reliability than in the past. The ascending hierarchy of committees engaged in adjudicating VC recommendations faced many more such recommendations than in the past, giving them a difficult choice: either give the VC in quantities proportionate to the numbers engaged and the duration of the conflict, even though it was much larger and longer than anything seen before; or dismiss all but truly exceptional acts, in which case to gain a VC meant the risk of almost certain death. In choosing the second course, not just for the First World War but also for the Second, one category of potential VC candidates would become inescapably excluded: women. Partly this was because, even when the war ended in November 1918, women who donned uniforms were still widely regarded, by men *and* women, as merely *playing* soldiers.[17] It was only with the deepest reluctance that the military hierarchy accepted women; women medics – nurses and doctors – working alongside the Royal Army Medical Corps were graded and paid according to army rank, but could not be commissioned and were denied badges of rank. In 1919 Winston Churchill, Secretary of State for War, refused to grant commissions to women doctors, primarily to avoid setting precedents.[18]

The arrival of the Military Medal (MM) was a step forward in one sense: women who might show bravery near the combat area would clearly never have been considered for the DCM (let alone the VC), but they were eventually drawn under the umbrella of the MM. A supplement to the *London Gazette*, published on 27 June 1916, announced that the MM, 'under exceptional circumstances, on the special recommendation of a Commander-in-Chief in the Field, [might] be awarded to women, whether subjects or foreign persons, who have shown bravery and devotion under fire'.[19] This was a radical departure: for the first time, women were formally eligible for a military decoration. It was such an unusual step that next day *The Times* commented:

> It is curious to note how few are the rewards for public service or decorations or any sort hitherto conferred upon women. In England [for which read 'Britain'] there were none until the reign of Queen Victoria, when there were instituted for ladies the Royal Order of Victoria and Albert (of which no fresh conferments have been made for a considerable time), the Imperial Order of the Crown of India, the Royal Red Cross, and the Order of St. John of Jerusalem. Women may also receive the Order of Merit. . . Foreign countries are more generous in their bestowal of rewards on women.[20]

The death of Kitchener, drowned on 5 June 1916 when HMS *Hampshire*, the cruiser on which he was travelling on a diplomatic mission to Russia, was sunk by a mine, perhaps helped clear the way for women to be granted the MM; one stalwart misogynist had disappeared.[21] Of some 115,600 MMs awarded during the First World War, just 138, or 0.12 per cent, went to women, both military and civilian, of all nationalities. On 2 September 1916, *The Times* reported the first women MMs, awarded to five members of the Army Nursing Service, alongside a lengthy list of other MM winners, 890 names in all.[22] Sixteen members of the FANY – the First Aid Nursing Yeomanry, a civilian organization – were awarded Military Medals in the First World War. The citation for seven of these stated the award was for 'conspicuous devotion to duty during an hostile air raid. All these lady drivers were out with their cars during the raid, picking up and in every way assisting the wounded and injured. They showed great bravery and coolness and were an example to all ranks.'[23]

The invention of new medals during wartime was politically acceptable; but tinkering with existing decorations always ran the risk of retroactive claims, something to which the War Office was congenitally opposed. Thus a consideration of the VC warrant and how it might be altered was postponed until August 1918, when the war turned decisively in favour of the Allies. There followed dilatory deliberations over almost two years, resulting in a complete revision of the VC warrant that superseded all previous warrants and amendments. Signed on behalf of King George V by Winston Churchill, then Secretary of State for War, in 1920, the third clause reiterated what had to be done to be considered for the VC: 'the Cross shall only be awarded for most conspicuous bravery or some daring or pre-eminent act of valour or self-sacrifice or extreme devotion to duty in the presence of the enemy.' But the most radical departure from the past came in the sixth paragraph of clause six: 'Matrons, sisters, nurses and the staff of the Nursing Services and other Services pertaining to Hospitals and Nursing, and civilians of either sex serving regularly or temporarily under the Orders, direction or supervision of any of the above mentioned Forces shall be eligible for the decoration of the Cross.' Against fierce opposition, as we have seen in the previous chapter, from some senior officers, women and civilians have been formally eligible for the Cross since 1920.

While most of the (all-male) 1918 Committee on Co-ordination etc. of Warrants Relating to the VC accepted that women and civilians should be included in the 1920 VC warrant, none could imagine that within two decades the twentieth century would witness an even greater conflagration than that just ended – and that women and civilians would have an even bigger role than during the years between 1914 and 1918. Ignoring Admiral Everett's prejudices against women was only logical; in a total war none were safe from danger, all might display exceptional courage. And if civilians were to be included, it was obviously impossible to prohibit women. But Everett's entrenched hostility was the tip of a very deep iceberg; to contemplate awarding the VC to women offended not only his sensibilities but those of many lower-ranking officers, and men generally. And the development of other military awards gave the military hierarchy a wider selection of medals to choose from. It became easier to deny someone a VC, or to downgrade a VC recommendation; after all, they could be given something else, instead – and who was to judge whether a particular act really was worthy of a VC or not? The inclusion of women and civilians in the 1920 VC warrant proved a hollow gesture.

And it became all the easier to avoid considering women for the VC once yet another medal pair was created, shortly after the start of the Second World War. At one of the lowest points of the war, on 24 September 1940, nine days after the Luftwaffe launched its biggest raid on London, King George VI signed into being the George Cross and the George Medal;[24] the first awards were gazetted a few weeks later.[25] The previous evening wirelesses across Britain played the king's address. For eleven minutes the king spoke from a bunker beneath Buckingham Palace, while outside could be heard the eerie wails of air raid sirens. In a speech carefully constructed to uplift the nation's spirits, George VI said

> civilian workers... worthy partners of our armed forces and our police... [who] earn their place among the heroes of this war... In order that they should be worthily and promptly recognized I have decided to create at once a new mark of honour for men and women in all walks of civilian life. I propose to give my name to this new distinction, which will consist of the George Cross, which will rank next to the Victoria Cross, and the George Medal for wider distribution.[26]

The king's words were unhelpfully ambiguous about the status of the newly created GC. It is widely but incorrectly assumed that 'rank next to' means of equal stature, but the VC 'outranks' the GC in order of precedence.[27] Simultaneously, Downing Street issued a statement specifying that 'there will be a small Military Division of the [George] Cross to permit of its award to members of the Fighting Services who have performed acts coming within the terms of the Warrant'. The announcement of the new decorations was made in haste; as the king spoke, no designer of the GC had been contracted. The sixty-seven-year-old Admiral of the Fleet, Lord Chatfield, was given the job of supervising recommendations for the George Cross and Medal. He seemed in little doubt that they were primarily for civilians: 'This task that has been entrusted to me by the Prime Minister is to watch over the recommendations for gallantry in civil defence and for the award of the two new honours created by his Majesty the King. We have to ensure that... no acts of gallantry meriting these new awards fail to receive recognition.'[28]

According to his biographer, George VI inherited 'a great interest' in medals and honours; as their real power dwindled, the ceremonial, ritualistic distribution of decorations gave British monarchs a revitalized sense of purpose and majesty, particularly in wartime. George VI had, at his own initiative, established in 1939 the Committee on Honours, Decorations and Medals in Time of War,[29] with the intention of clearing up 'a thoroughly confused situation... [The king] was also incensed by the bland Whitehall view that civilians were not fighting "in the face of the enemy".' But the king was dissuaded from any root-and-branch rationalization of military decorations: 'Lloyd George, fully aware of the jealousies and competition between the services on these matters, persuaded him not to.'[30] The 'bland Whitehall view' permeated all levels of the country's wartime administration and helped perpetuate the exclusion of men and women from the VC. By definition, civilians rarely faced the enemy in the nineteenth-century sense of literally seeing the whites of an opponent's eyes, but many of those sheltering in tube stations trying to hear the king's speech through the Blitz would have been surprised to learn they were not 'facing' the enemy. By introducing the GC and GM, George VI may have boosted flagging national morale, but inadvertently he also did a disservice to future generations of courageous men, women and civilians, who instead of gaining the GC might have been considered for the VCs to which they were, theoretically at least, entitled.

The 1939–45 war saw more women in uniform than ever before, not merely lending medical support but engaging in tasks of utmost peril. In December 1941 the National Service Act made it compulsory for women aged between twenty and thirty (excluding, initially, married women) to register for military service. During the Second World War some 600,000 women served as commissioned officers or other ranks in the three main auxiliary services. We do not have to delve too deeply to find instances of exceptional but neglected female courage during the war; there are many unsung heroines. A fine example is that of Margot Turner, who died in September 1993 at the age of eighty-three; that she lived as long as she did was in some ways miraculous, for at the age of thirty-two Turner endured a protracted period of cruelty that today is difficult to fathom, during which she consistently displayed remarkable fortitude.

In 1937 Turner joined Queen Alexandra's Imperial Military Nursing Service (QAIMNS), part of the army's medical services.[31] By 1942 she was a theatre sister – a rank then equivalent to lieutenant in the army – in Malaya. As the invading Japanese forces swiftly moved down through the east coast of Malaya, Turner helped evacuate patients from a hospital on the Johore Strait. When the last patient had been removed, a fresh outbreak of shelling forced her and a fellow nurse to retreat beneath a billiards table, taking with them a bottle of brandy from the medical stores. 'After a number of swigs,' she later recalled, 'the barrage became nothing like as terrifying.' Along with other nurses, civilian women and their children, Turner then boarded a ship destined for Singapore, but this vessel was shortly after sunk by Japanese aircraft. She then spent three days on a deserted islet before being picked up by another boat, only to be sunk yet again, this time by a Japanese warship. Turner then assembled sixteen survivors, including two babies, on a raft. After three days, everyone save Turner had died; she survived by eating seaweed and collecting drops of fresh water in her face-powder compact. On the fourth day she was picked up by a Japanese cruiser, her skin so blackened that her captors did not initially believe she was British. At some point in her early captivity a Japanese soldier knocked out two of her front teeth, when Turner failed to bow with sufficient alacrity. She was handed over to the *Kempei Tai*, Japan's version of the Gestapo, who meted out harsh treatment and accused her of being a spy. Turner then endured six months of interrogation in a prison in Palembang, on Sumatra, from where she was transported to a camp. When liberated, Turner resumed her military nursing career, was appointed Chief Military Nurse in 1964, and created a Dame of the British Empire in recognition of her services to nursing. Turner's story, along with those of other women imprisoned by the Japanese, inspired the 1981 British TV series *Tenko*.[32] Turner helped to save lives; faced extreme cruelty with exceptional courage; inspired others bravely to face their own horrors; wore a uniform; was under the direct command of officers of the British army; and displayed 'extreme devotion to duty in the presence of the enemy'. That it never crossed anyone's mind to recommend Turner for the highest British military decoration sits uncomfortably with the 1920 VC warrant.

But the most egregious examples of valour by women who were not considered for the highest honour are to be found in Special Operations Executive (SOE). Their commissions may have been temporary or honorary but, following the 1920 warrant, that should not have barred them from being considered for the VC. According to M. R. D. Foot, doyen of SOE historians, SOE employed some 13,000 people, a quarter of them women; more than half of the women in the FANY were seconded to SOE. The inspiration behind SOE was Winston Churchill, who in 1919 had resolutely blocked military commissions for women doctors, but in the desperate days of 1940, when Churchill instructed Hugh Dalton, then Secretary at War, to 'set ablaze' Europe, quibbling over gender seemed less important.[33] Women were not simply accepted into SOE, which, as Foot said employed anyone 'from pimps to princesses', but actively sought as field operatives; their femininity provided additional cover for underground work, and might help protect them from the worst of abuses if captured. Moreover, the women SOE recruited usually had the required steeliness. In Foot's words:

> Not many women who seemed promising enough from SOE's point
> of view to be worth interview would be likely to quail at the thought

of a singularly nasty death, perhaps preceded by outrageous torture,
if caught; and fighting enthusiasm can be quite as strong in one sex
as the other.[34]

Selwyn Jepson, the recruiting officer for F [French] Section of SOE,
faced stiff opposition to the recruitment of women, on the basis that
under the Geneva Conventions women were not to be regarded as
combatants, a variation of the argument put forward twenty years
previously by Admiral Everett.[35] Jepson evaded that obstacle by arguing that although women were not strictly permitted to fire guns, in
reality some did: 'I discovered that the anti-aircraft units always had
ATS [Auxiliary Territorial Service] Officers on their strength and that
when it came to firing an anti-aircraft gun the person who pulled the
lanyard that released the trigger was a woman.'[36]

General Sir Frederick Pile, Commander of Air Defence in Britain,
was an enthusiast for uniformed women of the ATS being permitted
to fire guns, particularly as, in his estimate, Britain's air defences were
short of more than 1,000 officers and almost 18,000 other ranks during
the Blitz in late 1940. By the middle of 1941, combing-out of men serving in home defence capacities saw 30,000 searchlight operators being
removed from Air Defence, posts that were filled by women, who could
thus be killed or injured fighting for their country. Officially, women
remained non-combatants – an artificial distinction that fooled no
one, least of all the women themselves. Pile commented that 'there was
a good deal of muddled thinking which was prepared to allow women
to do anything to kill the enemy except actually pull the trigger'.[37] This
artificial distinction between combatant and non-combatant status
meant that women working on anti-aircraft batteries were ineligible
for the service medals their male colleagues could receive; they were
also paid a third less. By June 1945 there were more than 190,000 ATS
members, more than 6 per cent of the total British army; the statistic

was even higher for the Women's Auxiliary Air Force (WAAF), whose members formed almost 14 per cent of the Royal Air Force.[38]

SOE agents were well aware that the Geneva Conventions offered no protection against the Gestapo. Wearing military uniform was obviously impossible behind enemy lines, thereby ensuring SOE agents were at much greater risk than any uniformed combatant, particularly after Hitler issued his 'Commando Order' following the Dieppe Raid of August 1942, which instructed that 'all sabotage troops will be exterminated, without exception'. Women SOE operatives were largely drawn either from the WAAF – the Royal Air Force, more willing to accept women than the army or Royal Navy, regarded the WAAF as an integral part of itself – or from the FANY. They were generally employed as wireless operators or couriers, but SOE training made no distinction between men and women; it emphasized aggression and daring,[39] and included 'weapons handling, unarmed combat, elementary demolitions... map reading, fieldcraft and basic signalling... the sort of training that any army recruit might expect to receive'.[40] If captured and interrogated, SOE agents were often tortured. One female trainer recalled after the war that

> someone who had been tortured more than once said it was the smaller things that were hardest to bear, such as pulling out teeth or nails or sticking pins into a woman's breast, not the beatings, hangings by the wrists, electric shocks or near-drownings. These made them semiconscious after a time. Most agreed that if you could withstand the first quarter of an hour without 'talking' you probably wouldn't talk at all.[41]

If we focus purely on F Section of SOE, it is clear that anomalies exist in the recognition of gallantry. F Section employed 480 agents, 130 of whom were captured. Between 17 July 1942 and 7 July 1944 it sent thirty-nine female agents into France – thirteen did not return

– the first being a forty-five-year-old grandmother, Yvonne Rudellat, who was born in France, had married a British waiter, and settled in London.[42] She entered France in July 1942 and lived a clandestine existence for almost a year before being arrested by the Gestapo. Rudellat was then incarcerated in Bergen-Belsen concentration camp, where she died from typhus shortly after the camp was liberated in April 1945. To the end, she maintained her alias of 'Jacqueline Gautier' and, before her true identity was known, died and was buried in a mass grave. Lost amid the secrecy surrounding SOE at the end of the war, Rudellat received no posthumous award.

One SOE F Section agent who did receive appropriate recognition – although not by Britain – was Virginia Hall. An American citizen working for the *New York Post* before America joined the war, Hall had the disadvantage of a wooden leg, the result of accidentally shooting herself in 1932 while in Turkey. Her disability meant SOE had little hope that Hall would be of much service, but her work as a journalist in Vichy France provided good cover, and she was asked by SOE to keep her eyes open. She did that – and also organized rescues of stranded SOE agents, managed the finances for Resistance groups, blew up bridges and much else. Hall was recommended for a CBE by SOE, but that was downgraded to a civilian MBE. In 1944 she joined the newly opened Office of Strategic Services (OSS), precursor of the CIA. For her OSS work she became the first woman to be awarded the Distinguished Service Cross, the US Army's second-highest military decoration after the Medal of Honor.

After the war some SOE female agents were, understandably, angry at being fobbed off with what they regarded as inappropriate decorations: 'Pearl Witherington… was strongly recommended for an MC, for which women were held ineligible; and received instead a civil MBE, which she returned, observing she had done nothing civil.'[43] At the end of her SOE training Witherington's instructor had commented: 'This student, although a woman, has leader's qualities. Cool, resourceful, and extremely determined. Very capable, completely brave... the best shot, male or female, we have had yet.' Witherington parachuted into central France in September 1943, where she worked as a courier between Resistance groups. She took over as head of one branch of the Limousin region's Stationer circuit, which had been split into two when Maurice Southgate, its original SOE organizer, was captured by the Gestapo. Witherington was awarded by France the Croix de Guerre, the Légion d'Honneur and the Resistance Medal and, later, the British CBE. Much later she gained the honour she most coveted. During her SOE training she had completed four instead of the required five practice jumps, and had therefore been refused the paratrooper's insignia. In 2006, aged ninety-three, Pearl was finally granted her 'wings' as a parachutist. Southgate was tortured and narrowly escaped execution at Buchenwald concentration camp; when liberated he received the DSO.

Nancy Wake was an Australian who, after she ran away from home aged sixteen, landed in France, where she married a French industrialist in 1939 and settled in Marseilles. Dubbed by the Germans the 'White Mouse' because she was so elusive, Wake established an escape route across the Pyrenees for Allied servicemen and, fleeing the Gestapo, left for England in 1943. There she joined SOE and returned by parachute to the Auvergne, where she welded together several Maquis groups into a 7,500-strong force, allocated their weapons and controlled the financial support from London. The rest of the war she spent ambushing German convoys and blowing things up, with a five million franc reward for her capture posted by the Germans. Contemporary witnesses spoke of Wake's ferocity: she was said to have killed an SS guard with her bare hands, and in later life she said her biggest regret was not having killed more Nazis. She died in 2011, aged ninety-eight. On 13 July 1945 a small entry in the *London Gazette* read: 'Awarded the

George Medal: – Miss Nancy Grace Augusta Wake, First Aid Nursing Yeomanry. For brave conduct in hazardous circumstances.'[44]

Throughout the Second World War the all-embracing terms of the 1920 VC warrant were studiously ignored; there was little obvious interest from any senior politician (and certainly no officer) in pushing for either women or civilians to be granted the VC. Nevertheless, some contemporary Members of Parliament prodded for a wider distribution of the Cross. On 18 January 1944 the Tory MP Alexander Critchley asked Winston Churchill

> [if,] having regard to the courage displayed by women in this war and their devotion to duty in the tasks allotted them, any woman serving in the branches of His Majesty's Forces has been recommended for the Victoria Cross; if such honour has been open to women since the commencement of hostilities; and if he will give an assurance that no discrimination will be used against women being awarded such an honour.

The prime minister's reply, while strictly accurate, was evasive:

> No recommendation in favour of a woman has been made during the war so far for the Victoria Cross, which is given only for services in active operations against the enemy. The Naval, Military and Air Force Nursing Services and the Women's Auxiliary Services have been eligible for the award since the outbreak of war...Women are also eligible for the George Cross for services not in active operations against the enemy... I can, therefore, readily give my hon. Friend the assurance he desires and I should like to take this opportunity of paying tribute to the courage and devotion to duty displayed by women in all walks of life and forms of service during the present war.[45]

As a young man, Churchill had craved the VC and indeed probably deserved one. For him, the VC was the ultimate military accolade, the defining symbol of what it meant to be a hero – and a man. The newly created George Cross had in 1944 none of the cachet of the VC. Churchill's comment that women were also eligible for the George Cross for services 'not in active operations against the enemy' was wily in the extreme; he was fully aware, for example, that courageous women were, as he spoke, engaged in 'active operations against the enemy' in occupied France and elsewhere on the Continent. He may not have said it, but in his heart Churchill was wedded to the nineteenth-century notion that the VC should be reserved for acts of supreme courage by *men*; by all means let women and civilians have the George Cross instead.

The first official public word on women engaged behind enemy lines in France came on 6 March 1945, when Sir Archibald Sinclair, then Secretary of State for Air, said in the House of Commons that the WAAF had 'been to the fore' of organized resistance within occupied Europe: 'several young WAAF officers were dropped by parachute at night [one of whom] took charge of a large Maquis group... reorganised it and, displaying remarkable qualities of tact, leadership and courage, contributed to the success of many supply-dropping operations and to the destruction of enemy forces.' He then undermined this homage by venturing a joke: 'In another case, a WAAF W/T [wireless transmitter] operator landed and trained three French operators. This brave young woman's parachute stuck and opened only just in time. So she fell heavily and declares that she owes her life to bundles of paper francs which she was carrying wrapped around her like a cushion.'[46] Of the contribution of the FANYs, Sir Archibald was silent.

The minister who had official responsibility for SOE, Roundell Cecil Palmer, 3rd Earl of Selbourne, strived to stifle all reference to SOE's existence. Dame Irene Ward, an MP at the time, later wrote that the earl, 'popularly known as "Dumbo"', had told her that 'it was vital that the existence of the "Org" operating under our direction should not be disclosed. It is not for me to comment on the different viewpoints and, indeed, actions of Ministers of the Crown.'[47] Ward, the redoubtable Conservative Member of Parliament for Tynemouth, was a maverick with a deep loathing for injustice where she thought it existed.[48] A dogged campaigner for equal pay for women, Ward in 1956 fought – and failed – to obtain a posthumous VC for Violette Szabo, an SOE agent who was captured in France, tortured and possibly raped, then transported to Ravensbrück concentration camp, where she died in September 1944, probably shot in the back of the neck. Szabo was given a posthumous GC, a 'decoration her outstanding gallantry had amply earned already, while she was still free', according to Foot,[49] but arguably she merited the VC. Ward's lobbying on Szabo's behalf was ignored by the government. On 6 March 1956, Ward wrote to Anthony Eden, then prime minister, reminding him that

> this highest of all Orders can be awarded to women as well as men – though in the nature of things there are likely to be very few women who can quality [sic]: but I think, as there does appear to be one, that it would be significant if a posthumous VC could in this centenary year [of the VC] be awarded to Violette Szabo.

The *Atticus* columnist, writing in the Conservative *Daily Sketch*, then edited by Herbert Gunn,[50] supported Ward's effort in his newspaper:

> this would be an excellent idea if it were possible to be done... women have their full share of the final courage that nothing can break. It would be good if the long roster of VC's could contain at least one woman – not only in recognition of the gallantry of one, but the gallantry of countless others whose deeds of suffering have ennobled the human race.

Irene Ward's abrasiveness in her agitation on behalf of a VC for Szabo did not help Szabo's cause, but there are deeper reasons why Ward was unsuccessful in her campaign. For one thing, the George Cross had become the highest possible award to which the most courageous SOE agents, men or women, might aspire: after the GC citation for Wing Commander Forest Yeo-Thomas, who survived the war, was published in the *London Gazette* on 15 February 1946,[51] it was clear that the VC was not for SOE personnel, even though Yeo-Thomas had performed not just one but several supremely courageous actions in the field and shown tremendous bravery while suffering medieval cruelties at the hands of the Nazis. If the likes of Yeo-Thomas were not to win a VC, then it was obvious that the authorities would not award the Cross to a woman, no matter what she had done.

More deeply, Yeo-Thomas and other SOE operatives were ruled out of the VC because beyond its own portals SOE was an unloved orphan. The Foreign Office and the Secret Intelligence Service (SIS, now MI6) sneered at what it felt was SOE's amateurism, a charge dismissed by Foot, even though some SOE agents, such as Noor Inayat Khan, proved themselves hopeless blunderers when in the field. Khan, a wireless operator who was tortured and executed at Dachau in September 1944, was awarded a posthumous GC unusually late, in April 1949,[52] her case neglected for so long largely because of the uncertainty that surrounded the circumstances of her death. Noor was a particularly lax agent, leaving her codes lying around, contacting French friends she had known before the war and disclosing to them that she was a British operative; a poor agent, if a courageous woman, Noor's highly strung nervousness and inability to lie should have seen her weeded out at the training stage.[53] Other SOE critics, such as Sir Arthur 'Bomber' Harris, RAF Marshal, regarded clandestine operations as a waste of scarce resources that needlessly risked the lives of aircrew.

A further factor explaining the lack of SOE VC recommendations is that the head of Section F was Colonel Maurice Buckmaster, who proved himself almost equal to Noor when it came to making elementary blunders that cost the lives of captured agents. Before the war Buckmaster had been a journalist with *Le Matin*, and subsequently joined the Ford Motor Company in France. He left France when the war started and joined the British army just in time to experience the Dunkirk retreat. Buckmaster was no professional soldier and was plagued by uncertainty in an organization that officially did not exist. He ran F Section with insufficient guardedness, ignoring warnings that some circuits in France had been penetrated and were being used by the Germans to transmit disinformation to London and trap agents when they arrived in the field. His superior and overall head of SOE was Brigadier Colin Gubbins, an archetypal professional soldier who gained an MC for rescuing men under fire during the First World War. Gubbins did not need to make his view of the VC known; the unquestioned assumption of all long-service senior officers was that only men serving in the armed forces were really eligible, no matter what the 1920 warrant said. SOE's agents – men and women – were the overlooked and unofficially distrusted soldiers of a secret army.[54]

But perhaps the most compelling explanation why Ward's fight to get a retroactive VC for Szabo failed is that SOE and its mostly courageous, sometimes fallible agents were tainted with an aroma of personal and professional scandal. Traitors, double agents, poor management, outright incompetence – SOE suffered from them all. What little information about SOE did filter out after the war's end merely fed the appetite for sensationalism, the ill-informed and deliberately misled press doing what it always does with espionage – focus on glamour.

The story of Odette Sansom was seized upon by the post-war press, who in the grim days of 1946 could hardly believe its luck. Here was an attractive female agent whose adventures titillated the sadomasochistically inclined; but it was also a story with a happy ending – she survived and was about to marry a male war hero. A wave of publicity followed the official notification of Odette's GC on 20 August 1946 in the *Gazette*; several newspapers the following day published her citation in full. Her tale of tussles with Nazis, physical and mental abuse, the concentration camp, ultimate freedom and romance was captured (and perhaps embellished) in a bestselling biography and subsequently a 1956 film, *Carve Her Name With Pride*.[55] Irene Ward later suggested to Anthony Eden that giving Odette the first George Cross awarded to a woman was a blunder:

> I have nothing to say about her bravery in captivity, but I think it must be well known to you – as it is to many people – that she and Peter Churchill would not have been arrested at the time they were had they not disobeyed orders for their own personal reasons, and that those in full possession of the facts asserted that as a result some valuable lives were lost. I, of course, have always thought it unfortunate that the George Cross should have been awarded in this instance without waiting for news of some of the other girls; and we are all only too painfully aware of how the light of publicity is shed on a few individuals while others equally or more eligible for it are passed by. I don't think anyone reading Violette Szabo's citation for her G.C. would be left under any illusions as to her contribution both in the field and in captivity; and I can see only one way to ensure that posterity recognises that her contribution was, in fact, far greater than Odette's.[56]

Irene Ward's main objection to Odette's GC was that she had disobeyed orders and that this had led to the deaths of other agents in her network; the fact that Odette was also technically married to Mr Sansom while she was conducting an affair with Peter Churchill,[57] another SOE agent, offended Ward's strait-laced morality, but the greatest sin was unprofessionalism.[58] Against strict orders, Odette, who was already in France, went to meet Peter Churchill when he landed by aircraft on

15 April 1943. Odette was already known to the occupying authorities; she had been negotiating with Hugo Bleicher, an Abwehr agent, again defying London's orders. Peter Churchill was ordered to avoid Odette until she had broken contact with Bleicher. Nevertheless, the couple returned from the landing ground to the Hôtel de la Poste in Saint-Jorioz. Next day Bleicher arrested them both and rounded up members of their network.

Ward was not alone in questioning Odette's GC; doubts were raised by several contemporaries in SOE and later by Foot in the first edition of his history of F Section of SOE, the damning comment there being that Odette's experiences in Ravensbrück had 'induced in her a state of nervous tension so severe that she had considerable difficulty for many months in distinguishing fantasy and reality'. Foot amended a subsequent edition following legal action by Odette that was settled out of court. Selwyn Jepson, Odette's original interviewer at SOE, wrote privately to the Treasury that she 'was so keen to be a martyr that she ought to be tied to a bedpost and whipped'.[59] Yet although Odette is likely to have made some appalling mistakes, blinded by her sexual desires, it would be unfair to castigate her from the comfort of an armchair; no one who has not suffered at the hands of the Gestapo can imagine what mental and physical terror had to be endured. On 1 January 1946 Major-General Sir Colin Gubbins signed Odette's GC recommendation:

> The Gestapo tortured her brutally to try to make her give away this information [the whereabouts of other operatives inside France]. They seared her back with a red hot iron and, when that failed, they pulled out all her toe-nails; but Ensign Sansom continually refused to speak and by her courage, determination and self-sacrifice, she not only saved the lives of these two officers but also enabled them to carry on their most valuable work.[60]

1. Hyde Park, London, 26 June, 1856: Victoria unveils her Cross for the first time.

2. The VC's other creator: Francis Albert Augustus Charles Emmanuel, Prince of Saxe-Coburg and Gotha, and husband to Victoria.

3. Winter in the Crimea, 1855: men of the 77th Regiment.

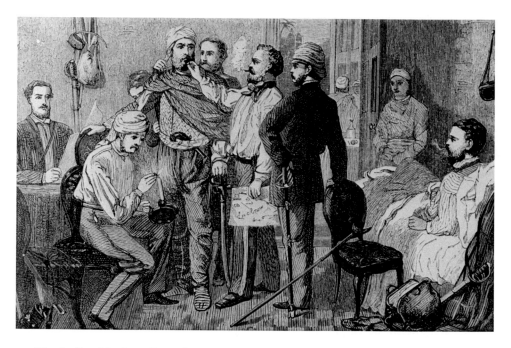

4. The Indian Mutiny, 1857: Thomas Henry Kavanagh (*third from left*), a civilian in the Bengal civil service, volunteered to lead a relief party during the siege of Lucknow to the beleaguered Garrison in the Residency. Here he is depicted preparing his disguise.

5. No VC for women: Ethel Grimwood, heroine of the Manipur massacre in 1891, wearing the Royal Red Cross.

6. A miserable Winston Churchill (right) among a group of Boer prisoners in 1899.

He did his duty.
Will YOU do YOURS?

7. Lord Kitchener, depicted on a poster in 1915. Kitchener took the lead in creating the Military Cross, whose appearance was the result of haphazard selection and whose purpose was questionable – unlike the carefully designed VC, whose intent was consciously framed by Victoria and Albert.

8. 1916: a depiction of a national hero, Earl Roberts VC, who died in 1914. Trotting out earlier national heroes at times of grave crisis is one of the uses to which the VC is put – even if, like Roberts, the hero helped push through some very dubious VCs.

9. John 'Jack' Travers Cornwell (1900–1916). A hero or merely a shell-shocked child?

10. William Avery 'Billy' Bishop, the Canadian fighter pilot who authenticated many of his own victories. Fearless and undoubtedly an excellent pilot, Bishop's VC was as much for propaganda purposes as his own courage.

11. Women Politicians at the House of
Commons: (from left to right) Miss
P. Hornsburgh, Mavis Tate, the
Duchess of Atholl, Thelma Cazalet
and Irene Ward, London, 5 December,
1935. After 1945, Ward fought a long
but unsuccessful campaign to award
Violette Szabo a posthumous VC.

12. Anglo-French wartime secret agent
Violette Szabo (1921–45) with her
husband Etienne Szabo, who was
killed early in the war. Szabo was
a successful and courageous agent
who was tortured and probably raped
before being executed at Ravensbrück
concentration camp in February 1945.
A clear and obvious candidate for the
VC by any standard, efforts to secure
her a posthumous VC were thwarted.

13. Winston Churchill shakes hands
with Wing Commander Johnny
Johnson on 30 July, 1944. Johnson,
a fighter pilot ace with thirty-four
kills, survived the war – but his form
of courage was not useful enough
to merit a VC.

14. Margot Turner: a nurse in the army
who demonstrated astonishing
courage at the hands of the Japanese
when taken prisoner following the
fall of Singapore in 1941. She was
not awarded the VC. Remarkably
enough, no-one saw fit to nominate
her – or any other exceptionally
brave woman – for the Cross,
despite women (and civilians) being
eligible since 1921.

15. Lance Corporal Johnson Beharry on 21 February, 2007. A politically useful VC in an unpopular war.

Many male soldiers had received the VC for much less. Yet even with this recommendation it was a struggle to get a GC for Odette. A letter from Gubbins dated 6 June 1946 revealed that he feared that Odette might be denied the GC unless 'we were able to produce concrete evidence that she refused to speak under torture. I am afraid that such evidence is impossible to obtain, for, as this torture was carried out in solitary confinement, the only witnesses would be the torturers themselves or the Gestapo interrogators. I hope and pray that these men have long since been shot.' The authorities had to make do with circumstantial evidence in the form of supporting statements from those with whom Odette worked in France, and the fact that the operatives for whose names she was tortured remained free from arrest.[61]

Ward realized that, with Odette having gained a grudging GC, her argument for a posthumous VC for Violette Szabo was always going to be a struggle.[62] The tall, dark-haired, striking Violette Reine Elizabeth Szabo was a highly professional, popular and courageous SOE agent. The daughter of a British father and a French mother, and the widow of a French legionnaire, Szabo joined SOE on 1 July 1943, even though she had a one-year-old daughter, Tania. Her first SOE interviewer, on 27 August 1943, recommended her for training:

A quiet physically tough, self-willed girl of average intelligence. Out for excitement and adventure but not entirely frivolous. Has plenty of confidence in herself and gets on well with others. Plucky and persistent in her endeavours. Not easily rattled. In a limited capacity not calling for too much intelligence and responsibility and not too boring she could probably do a useful job, possibly as courier.[63]

Later reports were ambivalent, that of 7 September 1943 stating: 'I seriously wonder whether this student is suitable for our purpose. She seems lacking in a sense of responsibility and although she works well in the company of others, does not appear to have any initiative or ideals. She speaks French with an English accent.' By 8 October the instructors seemed to have decided that Szabo was unsuitable:

> I have come to the conclusion that this student is temperamentally unsuitable for this work... when operating in the field she might endanger the lives of others working with her. It is very regrettable to have to come to such a decision when dealing with a student of this type, who during the whole course, has set an example to the whole party by her cheerfulness and eagerness to please.[64]

Yet despite such negative comments Szabo left for France on 7 June 1944, where her courage was questioned by none. The final paragraph of her GC recommendation, dated 10 July 1946, read:

> Although Szabo was continuously and atrociously tortured she never by word or deed gave away any of her acquaintances or told the enemy anything of any value. She showed great courage in exhorting other women prisoners to be of good cheer and walked proudly to the gas chamber,[65] knowing full well the fate that was in store for her. She gave a magnificent example of courage and steadfastness to all that had the honour of knowing her. She is very strongly recommended for the George Cross.

Prior to news of her death, Szabo had been recommended for a Civil Division MBE. It may seem incredible to modern readers, but as far as the army was concerned, Szabo was a civilian and she therefore merited a civil award. Szabo's file in the National Archive contains various reports from French sources who worked with her up to her arrest: one, dated 27 June 1945, described her:

> Jeune femme d'un courage extraordinaire. Elle a donne un très bel example de cran, et elle a été trés débrouillarde. Nous avons énormément d'admiration pour elle.

[Young woman of extraordinary courage. She showed lots of guts, and was very resourceful. We have enormous admiration for her.]

And under the section proposing a citation: 'Proposée pour la M.C. et pour une décoration française.'

Szabo's GC was gazetted on 17 December 1946, although inevitably her citation was largely fictitious: few of those who might have verified it were around to be consulted. Stories about her capture, including that she used a Sten gun to fend off her attackers, are now widely regarded as inventions or embellishments. But she was unquestionably valiant under extreme torture and abuse before she was wretchedly murdered: if the requirement of the VC, unspoken during the war itself, was that one had to perform some supererogatory act and also run the risk of almost certain death, Yeo-Thomas deserved the VC – and Szabo, who did die, even more so.

The award of the George, rather than the Victoria, Cross to Major Hugh Paul Seagrim is also difficult to explain. Seagrim was one of five brothers who joined the British, or British Indian, armies prior to the Second World War.[66] He had wanted to train as a doctor but the death of his father meant the family was too poor to send him to university. He tried to join the Royal Navy but was turned down on the grounds of colour blindness. Instead he went to Sandhurst, and because the pay was better in the British Indian army, he joined the 19th Hyderabad Regiment but was attached to the 1st Battalion, the Burma Rifles. In the 1930s he took three months' leave to travel in Japan. Clever, eccentric and popular, Seagrim frequently said he would sooner be a postman in Norfolk than a general in India.

When war against Japan broke out, the by now Major Hugh Seagrim was ordered to organize the Karen levies in Burma. Force 136, an organization established by SOE, dropped parachutists into the Karen Hills in 1942, and they joined up with Seagrim's force, which regularly passed on valuable intelligence by wireless. In January 1944 he was awarded the DSO for his 'determination, courage and devotion... of the highest order'. In March 1944 Japanese forces closed in on Seagrim, torturing and murdering Karen villagers to persuade them to betray Seagrim. He was finally tracked down to the village of Mewado, where the Japanese threatened to arrest all the inhabitants and burn down the village unless the headman pinpointed Seagrim's exact location. Seagrim, who by now had enormous affection for the Karen people, chose to surrender to the Japanese rather than permit this to happen. He was imprisoned close to Rangoon, along with several Karens; all were sentenced to death. Among his last words were: 'I do not mind what you do to me. But, I do ask you, if you are going to punish anyone, punish me. Do not punish these Karens. It is only because of me that all these Karens have got into trouble.'[67] Seagrim, along with seven Karens, was executed by firing squad on 14 September 1944 and, almost two years later, he was gazetted on 12 September 1946 with the George Cross.[68]

A decade after the end of the Second World War, Irene Ward published a history of the FANYs in which she tried to rationalize – perhaps to herself as much as for the reader – the unjust manner in which military decorations had been adjudicated during the war:

> The bestowal of Honours is always a matter for criticism – sometimes unjust criticism... to give the minimum decoration for the maximum effort is a deplorable way of acknowledging outstanding service. I can only assume – and this can be said about other awards also – that secrecy was so well maintained that those who recommended individuals for relatively minor recognition were unaware of the distinguished services rendered, or perhaps those who sifted the names had never heard of SOE.[69]

A hierarchy of committees must be navigated to gain the VC and unhelpfully their deliberation is kept well away from public scrutiny;

secrecy inevitably fosters distrust and suspicion. The VC's history is one of amorphous definitions of what constitutes conspicuous courage, sometimes stretched to accommodate fairly ordinary acts of military duty, occasionally shrunk to absurdly narrow limits, ruling out all acts save those that defy human imagination. For some individual women, who so clearly performed heroically under unimaginable pressure in occupied France during 1943–4, the pity is that they were not even considered for this prestigious honour.

As women increasingly come to be seen as capable of fulfilling combat roles – if they want them – it will be a vital question whether or not the VC really is open to them. In the Iraq and Afghanistan conflicts that dominated British military life during the first fifteen years of the twenty-first century, women were increasingly drawn into front-line combat roles. On 7 March 2008, Flight Lieutenant Michelle Goodman became the first woman to be awarded the Distinguished Flying Cross (DFC), equivalent to an MC. In 2007 she flew her Merlin helicopter, with a crew of three others, into the centre of Basra in Iraq to rescue a critically injured Rifleman, Stephen Vause, at night and under heavy mortar and small-arms fire. Vause survived. Certainly Goodman's exceptionally cool head and determination merited the DFC; but in the past, with a different gender, she might have been judged worthy of a VC. In the asymmetric wars that are now increasingly likely to set the pattern for future British military engagements, women will increasingly be drawn into 'facing' the enemy. The traditional response to women who might wish to serve in a combat role in the British army is that they are physically too weak to successfully complete the infantry combat physical fitness test – as are many men. But as warfare becomes more hi-tech and equipment becomes lighter, women's physical capacity will become less significant. The twenty-first-century soldier is much more likely to be supervising drones, far from the battlefield, as rushing to bayonet the enemy in a trench.

British women certainly have it 'in them', as Ethel Grimwood put it, to defy the enemy and show equal disregard for their own safety as any man, but the resistance to bestowing a VC, and the opportunity given by the GC to reduce pressure for granting the highest award to a courageous woman, is extremely deep-rooted. That no woman has ever gained a Victoria Cross is today an enormous psychological obstacle; who would dare to make the first female VC recommendation? The question of whether women will become more 'acceptable' as VC candidates, the more they inexorably become drawn into combat or near-combat roles with the British armed forces, is frankly otiose. The barriers are informal, neither written into the VC warrant nor ever committed to paper, and exist – like the informal 90 per cent risk-of-death requirement – only in the minds of senior military officers and perhaps some quarters of Whitehall. Denying women the VC – the 'gold' – will, however, steadily become more difficult – even with 'silver' and 'bronze' medals available in the form of the Conspicuous Gallantry Cross and the Military Cross – not least because greater numbers of women will either seek or be drawn into combat or quasi-combat roles. Gender equality in military affairs is increasingly being dictated by equal opportunities legislation, particularly in Western countries. In the US, legislation in 1975 mandated the right of women to enter the armed forces. As a result, the percentage of women serving in the US Army jumped from 1.6 per cent in 1973 to 8.5 per cent in 1980. From 2016 the US will permit women to serve in ground-combat roles in its armed forces; Britain cannot be far behind, although we are likely to see a female Medal of Honor earlier than a female VC. By January 2016 most branches of the US military will be forced by legislation to accept women in all roles. As Lieutenant-General (retired) Carol A. Mutter of the US Marines put it: 'Twenty years from now we're going to say, "Why didn't we have women in combat?" It's the same thing with African-Americans in World War II: "They're not smart enough to fly. They can't be pilots." Well, they proved that they could be.'[70]

After the end of the Second World War the government formed a committee, chaired by Major General John McCandlish, the Director of Personnel Administration at the War Office, to consider the function of the Women's Royal Army Corps (WRAC) in the face of the enemy, now that the WRAC was a corps within the regular army. The committee's deliberations were highly reminiscent of the 1918–20 committee set up to revise the VC warrant. Some members, including McCandlish, wanted weapons training for women; others were deeply opposed. One male member of the committee asserted:

> The fact that 'little Olga' [a sarcastic reference to women in the Red Army] is trained to kill and prides herself on the number of notches on her revolver butt is no reason we, too, should cry 'Annie get your gun'. It is still the soldier's duty to protect his womanfolk whatever they are wearing. Even in these days when war means total war let us at least retain that degree of chivalry.[71]

A government study, Women in the Armed Forces, was published by the UK Ministry of Defence in 2002. In the intervening five decades, only the language had changed: comments that openly belittled women soldiers had become unacceptable. The essence, however, was unaltered: the 2002 review upheld the ban on women serving in front-line combat roles in the army, although they were allowed to serve on fighting vessels in the Royal Navy and to fly fighter aircraft in the RAF. In 2002 the official reason for keeping women from combat roles in the army was that to include them would 'involve a risk with no gains in terms of combat effectiveness'.[72] This was reiterated in 2010, when a further report stated that 'there was no way of knowing whether mixed gender teams could function as well as all-male teams in a ground close-combat environment.[73] Female scholars, however, certainly attribute

– with strong if anecdotal evidence – the resistance of the army to including women in combat roles to a deeply misogynist culture, one that is difficult to eradicate despite the Ministry of Defence and the armed forces identifying themselves as 'equal opportunities employers'.[74] Since 1992 there has been a steady rise in the number of women in the British armed forces, from around 6 per cent in 1997 to almost 10 per cent by 2013; but by barring female soldiers from activities that are specifically seen as combat roles, old attitudes endure:

> British female officers are significantly disadvantaged in terms of promotion because of their exclusion from combat units and their under-representation in combat support units. Overwhelmingly, the senior ranks in the British Army are dominated by officers who are from these arms and it is very difficult to be promoted beyond one-star [General] rank from combat service support branches. This structural difficulty is compounded by the expectations of male officers, many of whom – particularly those born before the mid-1960s – operate with traditionalist assumptions of the feminine role.[75]

In other words: the British army is generally run on informally sexist lines.

Yet good soldiering is as much about mental as physical capability; the ability of women to fight in combat roles was proved long ago by women who served in the Soviet army, fighting against Nazi Germany. More than 800,000 women served in the Soviet Union's armed forces during the Second World War, and eighty-nine achieved the Hero of the Soviet Union, the USSR's highest decoration. In the Red Army, women served as snipers, tank drivers, machine-gunners, pilots, transport drivers, communications personnel, medics and political officers; Soviet women could be men's equals in the most testing of conditions. But perhaps the most insuperable barrier to a woman VC is the existence of the George Cross and the false belief that the GC is the equal of the VC. That equality exists only in the minds of those who wish to perpetuate an artificial distinction between male soldiers and female, and between the military and civilians – a distinction that was blown apart when the first bombs were dropped on London in 1940. In twenty-first-century warfare, where technological competence is at least as important as sheer brute force, the lines of gender separation in combat will increasingly dissolve. For the time being, in Britain, Admiral Everett's views still hold sway: let sleeping dogs lie.

Dame Irene Ward's campaign for belated justice on behalf of Violette Szabo deserves a fresh hearing. Bestowing a single retrospective VC on all women who served SOE behind enemy lines – the clever, the strong, the indomitable, as well as the fallible, the foolish and the feeble, for all suffered – would be an act of laudable humanity, analogous to the VC granted to America's Unknown Soldier in 1921. It would also be politically useful: if a posthumous VC was granted to all female SOE agents, the psychological barrier against future individual women gaining the VC would be less insurmountable. Dame Irene lost a campaign but lit a fuse that still burns; the final word should perhaps go to her:

> women themselves are often more far-sighted in appreciating what is fundamental in a struggle for life itself. Women would suffer equally with men in defeat – perhaps even more – and if they can contribute to victory they will accept any liability irrespective of its implications. This is the truth which called out so much spiritual strength from so many remarkable women.[76]

6

Bigger War

'I have never seen a brave man. All men are frightened. The more intelligent they are, the more they are frightened. The courageous man is the man who forces himself, in spite of his fear, to carry on.'

GENERAL GEORGE S. PATTON[1]

'The classic VC case would be that of Samson who in immolating himself destroyed the enemy – the Philistines.'

AIR FORCE MINISTRY OFFICIAL, SEPTEMBER 1942[2]

When war broke out in September 1939, the broad definition of what constituted a VC-winning action – 'conspicuous bravery or some daring or pre-eminent act of valour or self-sacrifice or extreme devotion to duty in the presence of the enemy' – left ample room for the armed forces to make their own interpretation of the new 1920 warrant. And, left to their own devices and with no public oversight, they tightened considerably the definition of 'conspicuous bravery'. In the Second World War there were to be no VCs for the kind of futile ineffective action, the dash forward for a 'glorious' death, as displayed by Lieutenant Freddy Roberts at Colenso during the Boer War.

The 1920 warrant was ushered forth in a context of cuts in Britain's military budget – from £766 million at the end of the First War to £102 million by 1932 – and the belief that the recently ended conflict had indeed been, as the US president Woodrow Wilson said, 'the war to end all wars'. The UK's armed forces had shrunk from more than 4.5 million in 1918 to less than half a million by 1921. In the army, conscripted officers and men were the first to go; regular officers who had risen to lieutenant colonels during the war considered themselves lucky to be captains once it was over. It became not just an honour to have the VC, but useful too. An equitable way had to be found to distribute 300 regular commissions in the infantry and cavalry after the end of the war. Age limits were imposed: under twenty-five for second lieutenants, under thirty for lieutenants, and under thirty-five for captains. A 'mark' scheme was created to allocate the scarce commissions, with five marks allotted per month of service overseas, fifteen per wound stripe, 250 for each six-month period in command of a battalion or similar-sized unit in a theatre of war, and 125 for the same period in command of the same-sized unit at home. Those with the highest marks were invited to accept regular commissions.[3] It was a brutal shake-out; but conspicuous courage had another value, beyond its £10 annuity – a VC holder automatically qualified for 250 marks.

The biggest change in the 1920 VC warrant was the inclusion of women and civilians, the smallest the standardization of the ribbon's colour to crimson for all services. The formalization of posthumous VCs was a significant step, the implications of which quickly became clear: half of the ten VCs awarded during the inter-war period were posthumous, and the first VC of the Second World War, awarded to Captain Bernard Warburton-Lee, was also posthumous. Captain of HMS Hardy, Warburton-Lee led a flotilla of five destroyers up a fjord towards Narvik, an ice-free harbour in German-occupied northern Norway. He took a German squadron of five destroyers by surprise and successfully attacked them, sinking two and damaging three others before withdrawing. A shell hit *Hardy*'s bridge and Warburton-Lee was fatally injured. His last signal was: 'Continue to engage the enemy.' Engaging the enemy, even though mortally wounded, had always been a mark of a worthy VC winner; it now became the benchmark by which all were judged.

In the whole Second World War, just 182 VCs were awarded: 30 per cent less than during the 1914–18 war. The level of expected courage was raised to incredible heights, far beyond the mild-sounding sentences of the warrant. The increased emphasis placed on leadership and example, not just bravery, was partly a response to the perceived degree of threat; as Churchill said in the House of Commons on 20 August 1940, 'The whole of the warring nations are engaged, not only soldiers, but the entire population, men, women and children. The fronts are everywhere.'[4] In the same debate, John Profumo – who in 1961, in his capacity as Secretary of State for War, would sign a revised VC warrant – made his maiden speech, depicting Nazi Germany as a 'Satanic power... menacing the whole of civilisation... day after day and hour after hour indescribable acts of gallantry and valour are being performed'. A comparison between the 182 Indian Mutiny VCs and the 182 of the Second World War reveals that, in the former, 101 went to privates and non-commissioned officers, seventy-seven to officers (and four to civilians), including one colonel, two lieutenant colonels, four majors, thirteen captains and the other fifty-seven to lieutenants. In the Second World War, eighty-six VCs went to privates and non-commissioned officers, ninety-six to officers; fifty-one to junior officers, and forty-five to senior officers – majors and above in the army, lieutenant commanders and higher in the Royal Navy, and squadron leaders and higher in the RAF. 'Leadership' – at least, as expressed by rank – had become more highly prized.

Some of the services during the Second War saw a remarkable

preponderance of officers over other ranks gain the VC – for example, fifteen of the nineteen VCs gained by Bomber Command went
to officers. No rear-gunner ever received a VC, despite the terribly
exposed and important position they occupied in the aircraft. Bomber
Command pilots were rewarded for initiative and determination – for
pressing home an attack – as much as for courage; on bombers all
crew members ran the same risk but only the pilot could choose to
increase the risk by, for example, continuing to fly a damaged aircraft
rather than ordering the crew to bale out. It was exceptional for crew
other than pilots to win a VC. One such exception was Flight Sergeant
Norman Jackson, a flight engineer on a Lancaster bomber.

On 26–27 April 1943, Jackson was flying his thirty-first mission
with 106 Squadron, a Lancaster squadron, to attack the ball-bearing
factories at Schweinfurt. On the return journey Jackson's Lancaster
was attacked by a night fighter and an engine caught fire. Jackson
was already wounded by shell splinters, but he put on a parachute,
grabbed a fire-extinguisher, and then climbed out onto the wing while
the Lancaster's speed was around 140 miles per hour. He clung on
by gripping the air-intake on the leading edge of the wing with one
hand while using the extinguisher with the other, but he was badly
burned on hands and face. The fighter returned for a fresh strafe of
the crippled Lancaster and Jackson was shot in the legs and fell from
the wing with his parachute smouldering, but it worked well enough
to save his life. The Lancaster's pilot ordered the crew to abandon the
plane; four of the crew survived but the pilot and rear-gunner were
presumed to have died in the wreck. Jackson was captured and spent
ten months recovering in hospital before being transferred to the
Stalag IX-C prisoner-of-war camp. He made two escape attempts,
the second successful, when he bumped into a unit of the US Third
Army. Jackson's astonishing exploit only became known when the
surviving crewmen of his bomber were released from German

captivity at the end of the war; his Victoria Cross was gazetted on 26 October 1945.

Flight Lieutenant William Reid, a Lancaster pilot who gained his VC on the night of 3 November 1943, later shrugged off any suggestions of heroism: 'I don't think I was a hero. I don't think of myself as a brave man. We were young. All we wanted was to get our tour over and done with.'[5] Reid, serving with the 61st Squadron, was headed for Düsseldorf when his aircraft was attacked by a Messerschmitt 110 night fighter as it crossed the Dutch coast. The windscreen was shattered; the cockpit and steering mechanism were badly shot up; Reid sustained serious injuries to his head, hands and shoulders. His aircraft dropped 200 feet before he managed to bring it back under control. Reid said nothing of his injuries to his crew but asked for a damage report, following which he proposed to continue the mission. His plane was attacked again; a Focke-Wulf 190 raked it from stem to stern, killing the navigator, fatally wounding the wireless operator, and injuring Reid's right arm. He pressed on with the mission, having memorized the course to his target, sustained by bottled oxygen from a portable supply administered by his flight engineer, Sergeant J. W. Norris. The plane reached the target and released its bombs. Reid then turned his aircraft for home, and – semi-conscious at times, freezing cold because of the smashed windscreen, and half-blinded by blood streaming from his head wound – he and Norris, also wounded, kept the plane in the air. As it crossed the North Sea, the four engines cut out and the plane went into a spin: Norris had forgotten to change over the petrol tanks to their reserve supply but he remembered in the nick of time. As they touched down at RAF Shipdham in Norfolk, the Lancaster's undercarriage collapsed and the bomber skidded along the runway before juddering to a halt.

Reid had another narrow escape. He joined 617 Squadron (the 'Dambuster' squadron) in January 1944. In July 1944 he was over a target in France and released his bombs at 12,000 feet. He then felt his aircraft shudder under the impact of being hit by a bomb dropped from 6,000 feet above, which plunged through the Lancaster's fuselage and severed the plane's controls. Reid ordered the crew to bail out, and as they did so, the aircraft nosedived, pinning him to his seat. He managed to release the overhead escape-hatch panel and parachute free, just as the Lancaster broke in two. He was captured and ended the war a prisoner.

The dividing line between Jackson's and Reid's VCs is paper-thin. The first seems more like an attempt at a rescue; the second might be said to represent the kind of spirited determination to press on regardless that, nominally at least, was preferred as good VC 'material'. Notes in archive files dismissing individual VC recommendations as 'not up to standard' often seem random; the truth is that many VCs went to those who demonstrably led and inspired, rather than for heroic rescue efforts – and that generally meant officers. Within that 'leadership' aspect of the VC, the class segmentation between officers and other ranks broke down into the more considered or thoughtful courage – determination against the odds – shown by officers and the more instinctive variety shown by a man who, perhaps in a blind rage, charged a machine-gun nest.

Neither blind rage nor thoughtful determination would get a VC for a woman or a civilian; they were ruled out partly by entrenched military opposition, while ignorance of the facts did not help either. In a House of Commons debate on 8 October 1940, some MPs, who might have been expected to be more *au fait* with the VC warrant, revealed a total lack of knowledge of what it actually said. Captain George Sampson Elliston, MP, who had served with the Royal Army Corps in the First War and gained an MC, asked Churchill whether 'in view of recent developments of modern warfare, he will advise revision of the Royal Warrant so that the Victoria Cross may be awarded to any subject of His

Majesty who displays supreme courage in countering enemy action?'
Henry Morris-Jones, MP, bluntly asked: 'Why should not civilians get
the Victoria Cross for heroism in the face of the enemy, just as did
soldiers in the Army in the last war? The whole standard ought to be
changed.' Rather than point out to Elliston and Morris-Jones that the
VC's terms *had* changed, Churchill gave a disingenuous reply, omitting
the fact that civilians had been eligible for the VC since 1920. Instead
he suggested that civilians now had their 'own' VC:

> For this honour, men and women in all walks of civil life will be eli-
> gible... There is no difference in merit between the Victoria Cross
> and the George Cross; the George Cross ranks equal with the Victoria
> Cross, and after it in priority only. The whole question has been most
> carefully reconsidered, and the very far-reaching scheme which has
> been announced and the new decorations [GC, GM] are the fruits of
> that reconsideration.[6]

Churchill's formulation, that the George Cross 'ranks equal' with the
VC, but comes after it 'in priority only', has given rise to no end of
confusion: what does it mean to be equal in ranking but second in
priority? There is no sensible answer, and many have been the efforts
to square this particular circle. In truth, the creation of the George
Cross was an unnecessary step at a moment of crisis, in an attempt to
whip up publicity and boost national morale. There were just too many
senior military figures that would have bristled at the thought of a VC
going to a woman or someone not in uniform. There was no official
announcement that, in this war, only astonishing acts of courage would
be sufficient to be even considered for a VC; and indeed, certain VCs
were granted when a lesser award would have been more plausible,
but for the intervention of that old, all-important influence – 'friends
at Court'. An unwritten rule generally prevailed: only the very bravest
need apply, and even then they needed to have been in uniform; and

their case would be considerably more persuasive if they happened to have died in the performance of their deed.

Although the British empire officially fought many more battles in 1939–45 than in 1914–18 – the official compilation, published in January 1956, listed 970 operations, compared to 167 for the First World War – there were far fewer casualties; almost 600,000 British empire armed forces personnel died in the Second World War, against some 1.05 million in the First.[7] This lower casualty rate ought to have had little or no bearing on the number of VCs distributed, if merit alone was to be the judge; in fact the 'pool' of acts of outstanding bravery was artificially limited by the imposition of a quota system. It is difficult to prove a negative; trying to assess the number of those who might have merited, but did not get, a VC is futile. But some overall numbers are suggestive. Bluntly, the chance of gaining a VC in the Second War was nearly twice as remote as in the First; the number of uniformed dead per VC in the Second War was almost 3,300, against 1,658 per VC in the First. Three-and-a-half times more VCs were distributed in the First World War than the Second; and posthumous VCs were more than 45 per cent of the total in the Second World War, against almost 30 per cent during the First.[8] The VC became more difficult to win, and more deadly.

Nothing in the VC statutes stipulated this: it all resulted from unstated and, it might be said, unjustified standards imposed by senior officers. This was not a case of senior officers interpreting the warrant; rather it was an unspoken and only occasionally written-down determination that only certain types of acts – ones that demonstrated absolute courage in the pressing home of an attack, for example – would be deemed VC-worthy. The VC was to be rationed, like all other gallantry awards. Conspicuous bravery became a necessary but not sufficient hoop to jump through; higher priority than ever before was to be given to actions that were demonstrably aggressive, rather than simply noble. Killing – publicly displayed, able to be seen by others and perhaps giving them inspiration – was in; kindness – in the form of helping to rescue the fallen or injured – was marginalized. When the struggle was so extreme, this new emphasis was perhaps understandable. German SS units notoriously shot uniformed prisoners, and word began to arrive of massacres, such as that at Wormhout in May 1940, on the retreat to Dunkirk, when almost ninety British soldiers were captured and killed by the Waffen-SS Liebstandarte Adolf Hitler regiment.[9] There was precious little battlefield chivalry and any failure was without honour; national defeat would have meant not a repeat of the humiliation wrought on Germany through the Versailles Treaty, but a form of totalitarian slavery. Determined leadership was required, pressing home the attack no matter what the odds. Helping the wounded was all very well – but that did not inspire others to kill.

It is almost as if the military establishment began to pay attention to late nineteenth-century warnings that the Cross was being given out too freely. The Broad Arrow said in 1879 that 'Beyond all question the Cross will be cheapened if it is to be conferred upon every man who puts his powers of physical endurance to their proper use, and carries through the particular service mainly by the natural conduct of a well-balanced act.'[10] By 1940 duty – even acts that moderately exceeded duty – was not enough; what was wanted was the unnatural pursuit of acts that would generally be described as unbalanced, even mad. In the build-up to D-Day, General Montgomery presented his plans for the Normandy invasion to George VI. Under the subheading 'morale', Montgomery succinctly stated that aggressive heroism was what he looked for:

> We shall have to send the soldiers in to this party 'seeing red'. We must get them completely on their toes; having absolute faith in the plan;

and embued [sic] with infectious optimism and offensive eagerness. Nothing must stop them. If we send them in to battle this way – then we shall succeed.[11]

For obvious reasons, serving officers were not prepared publicly to speak out against the Second World War's quota system, and the anomalies it created, for gallantry awards. According to a Second War major, once the war was over, 'many deserving acts have been unrewarded, and undeserving acts rewarded – to keep within the ration'.[12] Sir Martin Lindsay, an intrepid polar explorer in the years before the Second War, was a professional soldier who, after Sandhurst, joined the Royal Scots Fusiliers. He rejoined the army when war broke out and ended his military career commanding 1st Battalion, Gordon Highlanders in sixteen operations in north-west Europe during 1944–5. Lindsay was courageous; he was wounded in action, twice Mentioned in Despatches, and awarded the DSO. He retired from the army with the rank of lieutenant colonel and became a Conservative MP. In a 1978 article on gallantry awards, Lindsay considered the VC would always be fraught with difficulty, for two reasons:

The first is the impossibility of placing noble deeds in any satisfactory order of priority, bearing in mind the vastly differing standards of descriptive powers of those who wrote the citations and supporting statements. The second is the impossibility of reconciling two conflicting considerations: the desirability of keeping the VC a rare and coveted distinction on the one hand, and on the other the always larger number of recommendations than could be satisfied... every 'failed VC' among officers was awarded the DSO, and in the same way a 'failed DCM' normally got the MM.[13]

Lindsay cited his own experience of a brigade commander massaging a recommendation to give a soldier what he thought was deserved; the (unnamed) commander 'deliberately falsified the dates in the citation' to ensure that an officer commanding a battalion in Normandy, and who was killed in action, received the DSO, despite the ban on posthumous DSOs. Lindsay pointed out that the ration system for gallantry awards led to absurdities:

> For the [crossing of the] Rhine my Brigade (153) was in the lead and incurred 15% casualties. We were then informed that for the whole Brigade the awards would be limited to six, which worked out at 0.4% of those actively engaged... 21% of the aircrews in the Mohne Dam operation were decorated, and 7% of those who took part in the sinking of the Tirpitz... Having been told that only one award could be considered for a particular operation, the CO could hardly look beyond his leading Company or Squadron Commander if it had not been for whom his battle would not even have started.[14]

On becoming MP for Solihull after the war, Lindsay waged a campaign against 'the scandal of the difficulty we had experienced in obtaining decorations for our "rank and file". The Secretary of State for War [the Labour MP Jack Lawson]... denied that there had ever been any system of "rationing" of decorations. In the aftermath of war there were in the House plenty of ex-officers who knew from their own experience that this was totally untrue.'[15]

When individuals did something both outstanding *and* useful, then they were obvious candidates for the highest prize. On the ground, the European theatre was bookended by examples of classic VC-winning actions from the army. The British army's first VC went to Second Lieutenant Richard Annand of the 2nd Battalion, Durham Light Infantry,[16] who gained his for twice fighting off a German attack on a blown bridge across the Dyle River in Belgium on 15–16 May 1940. German troops tried to launch a bridging party across the river and, under mortar and machine-gun fire, Annand threw hand grenades onto the enemy from the top of the wrecked bridge, driving them back. Although wounded, Annand continued in command of his platoon. A second crossing attempt by German soldiers was again driven back by Annand, single-handedly and effectively wielding grenades. When the platoon was ordered to withdraw, Annand left with his platoon but noticed that his batman was missing; he went back to find him and carried him off in a snatched wheelbarrow, eventually collapsing from loss of blood. He was rescued, evacuated, and spent the rest of the war in Britain training other soldiers; his fighting days were over as a result of permanent damage to his hearing.

The last European theatre VC was that of Guardsman Edward Charlton of the 2nd Battalion, Irish Guards, who was a driver in a tank troop.[17] In the early hours of 21 April 1945 his troop, together with a platoon of infantry, took Wistedt, a small town some sixty kilometres south-west of Hamburg. A German counterattack by a battalion of Panzer Grenadiers, supported by several self-propelled guns, blew up the British tanks and threatened to overrun the British platoon. As the superior German force advanced, Charlton took the Browning machine gun from his disabled tank and fired it from the hip, halting the lead German company; under this covering fire the Guards reorganized and retired. Charlton was hit several times and his left arm rendered useless, but he mounted the Browning on a fence and continued firing until he collapsed from his injuries. He was captured and died shortly afterwards.[18]

The possibility that women or civilians might do something meriting a VC was put to rest by their *de facto* exclusion, the result of the creation of the George Cross and George Medal, which provided the military establishment with another means of slicing and dicing courage. The George Cross warrant, signed into being by Winston Churchill on 8 May 1940 at the behest of George VI, made no mention of whether the brave action was to be performed *not* in the presence of the enemy, but that was how it often came to be interpreted, as it still is today. That the distinction between being in the presence or not of the enemy was often razor-thin seemed to perturb no one; the military establishment was only prepared to recognize a uniformed male as worthy of a VC, and even then the George Cross might be given. Thus, demarcating the grounds for giving the George as opposed to the Victoria Cross would test the expertise of a medieval philosopher trained in the arcane art of distinguishing between individual angels. Today the George Cross usually goes to a person in the armed forces who has done something unusually courageous, but not in the presence of the enemy. But, rather like common law, it is all very fluid, and precedents can be made, broken, reset, all according to how much personal influence a much more senior officer might bring to bear on a particular case. If we take one case, that of Petty Officer Tommy Gould and First Lieutenant Peter Roberts, both of whom gained a VC while on patrol off Suva Bay, on the northern coast of Crete, it is evident that they should have been a perfect fit for the George rather than the Victoria Cross.

On 16 February 1942 Gould and Roberts were serving on the submarine *Thrasher*, which torpedoed and sank a 3,500-ton Axis supply ship. Five enemy anti-submarine escorts dropped some very accurately placed depth charges, but *Thrasher* miraculously survived.[19] The following evening, when the anti-submarine escorts had given up the hunt, *Thrasher* surfaced and an inspection for damage to its hull was conducted. An unexploded depth charge was found in the casing – the metal structure on top of the sub's main hull – in front of *Thrasher's* four-inch-gun mounting. Roberts and Gould volunteered to go on deck and remove the explosive, which might have blown not just them but the entire crew to smithereens. In darkness, they crawled along the narrow gap between the casing and the hull, located the bomb, and then hauled it twenty feet to the bow, where they gently eased it overboard. They then discovered lying on the hull another depth charge, which had penetrated the casing and was stuck firm. It was impossible to pull the depth charge back up through the hole in the casing, so the two men lowered themselves through a metal grille and wriggled on their stomachs towards it. Lying on his back, Gould gripped the depth charge while Roberts dragged him by his shoulders back towards the metal grille. They pulled the depth charge through the grille, wrapped it in a sack, and pushed this second bomb, weighing about 300 kilos, over the bow. The whole nail-biting exercise lasted around an hour. The two sailors had voluntarily put their lives at risk: from the depth charges, which might have exploded, and from possible drowning – Thrasher's commanding officer, Lieutenant Hugh Mackenzie, was constantly on watch for enemy surface vessels and aircraft, and would have dived had any been spotted. Gould and Roberts modestly dismissed what they had done, both at the time and subsequently, and Mackenzie's patrol report limited itself to praising their 'excellent conduct'.

That they deserved something was obvious; but what? A George Cross perhaps, as Thrasher was far from 'the presence of the enemy' when Roberts and Gould did their brave deed? On the other hand, they were uniformed, and the George Cross was widely (if mistakenly) regarded then as the civilian's VC. Perhaps an (officers only) Distinguished Service Cross to Roberts, and a Distinguished Service Medal (for naval ratings) to Gould? In the new era, when determined killing and/or inspirational leadership was required to gain the VC, surely not that? Yet on 9 June 1942 they were both gazetted with the VC, the citation helpfully quashing any lingering doubts about the enemy's proximity by stating that 'Thrasher's presence was known to the enemy; she was close to the enemy coast, and in waters where his patrols were known to be active day and night'.[20] Thrasher's presence might have been suspected by the enemy; her precise whereabouts were obviously a mystery. This was playing fast and loose and made a nonsense of the terms of the VC's statutes.

Immediately after Roberts' and Gould's VC citation in the *London Gazette* appeared a citation for George Patrick McDowell, acting yeoman of signals, and Leading Seaman Cyril Hambly, both of HMS *Kandahar*, a destroyer that hit a mine and was scuttled as it was sailing to Tripoli to intercept an Italian convoy. McDowell and Hambly swam across to a destroyer that came to the rescue. Unfortunately the rough seas prevented it closing right up next to *Kandahar*; Hambly and McDowell could have been rescued but chose to stay in the water to help others who were either drowning or in danger of it. According to their citation, they 'saved many men, until they lost all their strength and were drowned'. Hambly and McDowell received posthumous Albert Medals, a rarer but less acclaimed decoration than either the VC or the GC.

McDowell and Hambly lacked something that Gould and Roberts, unbeknown to them, possessed, the extra ingredient necessary for many VCs: a champion – in Gould and Roberts's case Admiral Sir Andrew Cunningham, commander-in-chief of the Mediterranean Fleet. In 1942 Cunningham was fifty-nine, had seen action as part of the Naval Brigade in the Second Anglo-Boer War, and gained the DSO and two bars during the First World War. He had a deserved reputation as an aggressive and successful senior naval officer. The Admiralty Board thought very highly of Cunningham, as did Churchill. Thus when Cunningham read Lieutenant Mackenzie's report of events on board *Thrasher* and digested the cool nerve shown by Roberts and Gould – as they moved the second depth charge, it kept making a disconcerting twanging sound – he did not hesitate to recommend both for the VC; he was confident that opposition, if raised, would be overcome. Removing two large enemy bombs from a submarine adjacent to the enemy's coastline in his view constituted more than enough enemy presence.[21] Cunningham got his way. Brave though they were, Gould and Roberts did no more than many bomb-disposal experts daily faced in Britain, for which some – if they were blown up and died – received a GC. In one respect Cunningham simply interpreted the VC and GC warrants more strictly than anyone else; after all, the third clause of the George Cross warrant simply said that it was 'intended primarily for civilians'.[22] Gould and Roberts were not civilians; they displayed considerable courage; *ergo* they deserved the VC.

Other submariners could do equally astonishing things, yet go almost unnoticed, or at least grudgingly rewarded. Twenty-one-year-old Lieutenant Henty Henty-Creer, an Australian of the Royal Naval Volunteer Reserve (RNVR), was the commanding officer of a group of six X-class midget submarines that were involved in 'Operation Source', in which the German battleships *Tirpitz*, *Scharnhorst* and *Lützow* were to be attacked in a Norwegian fjord on 22 September 1943. The midget subs were towed by conventional submarines close to the area; X-9 was lost with all hands when her tow snapped, while X-8 had to be scuttled when leaks in the explosives meant they had to be jettisoned. The remaining four midget subs travelled fifty miles up the fjord, through minefields and past patrol boats, to reach the German vessels; X-10 then abandoned the mission when it found that *Scharnhorst* was missing. Three – X-5, Henty-Creer's boat, X-6 and X-7 – were to place explosive charges underneath the *Tirpitz*, then lying at anchor in the heavily defended fjord. X-6 was commanded by Lieutenant Donald Cameron, RNVR, and X-7 by Lieutenant Godfrey Place, Royal Navy. Both successfully deposited their explosives, but they were spotted, attacked, and Cameron and Place captured. X-5 disappeared and was never seen again, possibly sunk by a shell from one of *Tirpitz*'s four-inch guns. At slightly after 8 a.m. the midget subs' charges exploded; *Tirpitz* was lifted out of the water and smashed back onto it, coming to rest with a slight list to port. Electronic and fire-control systems were seriously damaged, and all auxiliary machinery either thrown off its housings or damaged internally. *Tirpitz* was out of service for seven months, before being finally destroyed by a Lancaster bomber raid on 12 November 1944.

For this action Place and Cameron received Victoria Crosses, while three others gained the DSO and another the Conspicuous Gallantry Medal; even the commander of the X-8, which had to abort its mission, was appointed a Member of the British Empire. For Henty-Creer, who was never seen again, there was merely a Mention in Despatches. There is no conclusive evidence that Henty-Creer's X-5 laid its explosive charge and deliberately attacked Tirpitz; equally, in the confusion it is possible that one of the explosions resulted from the charge carried by X-5. According to the harsh standards usually implemented during the Second World War, VCs were only for demonstrable winners; merely to have shown courage by participating in, even leading, such a difficult mission to attack something of such vital importance as a German battleship was not enough. 'True' leadership was successful leadership; disappearing without trace was not leadership.

This necessity of setting an example was laid out in a memo distributed by a senior commander of the Canadian army. In April 1943 Guy Simonds was promoted to major general and appointed GOC (General Officer Commanding), 2nd Canadian Infantry Division. Although Simonds had never been under fire and would not be so until July 1943, he had enjoyed a meteoric rise from major to major general in three-and-a-half years. In the spring of 1943 Simonds, chief of staff of the First Canadian Army, clashed with Lieutenant General Andrew McNaughton, the army's GOC, over the army's organization, and was shunted off on attachment with the 8th Army in Tunisia, under the wing of the already upwardly mobile General Bernard Montgomery. Aggressive, prickly and determined – like his new mentor – at forty, Simonds was precisely the kind of young officer Montgomery prized. In 1944 Montgomery confided to his diary that the 'only really good general in the Canadian forces is Simmonds [sic]', a verdict he conveyed in a letter to Field Marshal Sir Alan Brooke on 14 July 1944:

> the Canadian senior commanders are not good. They have some good officers; but their top commanders are bad judges of men – and Harry Crerar is no exception, and does not know what a good soldier should be. The great exception is Simmonds [sic]; he is far and away the best general they have; he is the equal of any British Corps Commander.[23]

In October 1943 Simonds issued to the 1st Canadian Division, then fighting its way up the Italian peninsula, a directive that defined what was expected of soldiers if they were to be considered for honours and awards. This directive, which would have had Monty's approval, would 'provide the basis upon which I will scrutinise all recommendations when passing for consideration by higher authority'. In this document, apparently written without reference to the VC statutes, Simonds said that a 'proper' allocation of military decorations should:

> (a) give recognition to exceptional acts, or duties performed with outstanding ability, or recognition of exacting duties performed unfailingly during a difficult or long period;

> (b) encourage aggressiveness and skill and the offensive spirit;

> (c) discourage foolishness or the unnecessary and useless risk of lives and equipment. I look to every Commander and Commanding Officer to strictly discourage any forms of 'medal hunting';

To ram the point home, Simonds stated that

> except in the most extraordinary circumstances, acts of gallantry NOT directly contributing to damage to the enemy (such as rescuing of our own personnel, salvage of equipment, extricating a unit or sub-unit from a difficult position) will NOT be considered for these awards

even if performed in the presence of the enemy and under fire... In the case of the V.C. the act must be so outstanding as to provide an example to the Army for all time and its effect in damage to the enemy and furtherance of operations must be marked beyond question and of the first importance.[24]

This went far beyond anything stipulated in the VC warrant or indeed in regulations regarding lesser decorations. Noticeably, it made no mention of the elective peer principle. There was to be no tolerance of the kind of easy-come, easy-go attitudes of the past. Officers and men were clearly not to be trusted to exercise the 'right' kind of judgement; the idea that they might select representatives from their own number for a VC recommendation was ignored. Simonds, and above him, Monty, was the new Cerberus standing at the entrance; only the truly deserving would get past to secure a VC.

That the army, Royal Navy and RAF operated with different criteria in the recognition of supreme, VC-meriting gallantry during the Second World War is evident. Partly it was a matter of opportunity, partly a matter of assumptions about what the VC was for, and part a matter of perceived usefulness. If the definition of a VC-winning act was to be not only supererogatory courage but doing lasting damage to the enemy – and all that in front of your comrades in arms in order that they might be inspired by your example – then the navy and air force generally lacked the opportunity to perform such deeds, or to offer up candidates for the VC.

But puzzles remain. It is remarkable to recall that, for all the public fuss made at the time and since about the Battle of Britain, only one RAF fighter pilot gained a VC throughout the whole war. Of the twenty-two VCs that went to aircrew, nineteen went to Bomber Command, with two to members of Coastal Command. The single VC to a fighter pilot went to James Nicholson, a twenty-three-year-old flight lieutenant with 249 Squadron. On 16 August 1940 Nicholson's Hurricane was bounced by a Messerschmitt 110 over Southampton. Nicholson was injured in a foot and one eye, and his Hurricane's fuel tank was set alight. He struggled to bail out of his blazing aircraft, but he spotted another Messerschmitt, fired on it and shot it down, and then bailed out of his plane and landed safely. For all the many valiant RAF fighter pilots who in summer and autumn of 1940 flew innumerable missions to fend off the planned invasion of Britain, Nicholson remained the sole and, it must be said, rather odd VC. It was not that he did not deserve a VC, but the type of action he gained it for would become relatively commonplace as the war went on. That more fighter pilots were not awarded VCs reflects the balance of power at the highest level of the RAF, and the way the VC came to be massaged to fit the offensive spirit. By early 1942 Bomber Command was in the RAF driving seat, thanks in part to the dominating personality of Sir Arthur 'Bomber' Harris, who took over as commander-in-chief of Bomber Command on 22 February 1942. Of the nineteen Bomber Command VCs, twelve date from after Harris took over. Fighter pilots – even publicly acknowledged and acclaimed aces such as James 'Johnny' Johnson, who survived the war and ended with thirty-four confirmed kills – often displayed enormous courage over (in Johnson's case) years of combat, yet did not apparently merit a VC; Johnson gained a DSO and a DFC. 'Never in the field of human conflict was so much owed by so many to so few,' intoned Churchill in Parliament on 20 August 1940; and never was the VC so sparsely awarded as in the case of RAF Fighter Command between 1939 and 1945.

What was required in the RAF to qualify for VC consideration was an offensive coup of which great propaganda could be made – and to which the VC could be pinned – such as the 'Dambuster' raid of 16–17 May 1943, for which the undoubtedly brave and highly skilled Wing Commander Guy Gibson, who by that date had completed 170 sorties, received his VC. This raid was, however, enormously costly, and its strategic usefulness debatable; fifty-three of the 133 aircrew were killed, and by the end of June electricity generation in the region of Germany attacked by the RAF was back to full strength. Of the eighty survivors, thirty-four were decorated,[25] with five DSOs, ten DFCs and four bars, two CGMs and eleven DFMs and one bar. Ruthlessness, leadership and determination became the stepping stones towards a VC; the opportunity of a demonstrable propaganda success was not always necessary, but it could tip the balance in favour of the highest decoration.

John Nettleton's VC, awarded for a low-level daylight raid on the MAN diesel-engine factory at Augsburg, Bavaria, on 17 April 1942, illustrates the point. This raid was a formidable task, requiring the aircraft and their eighty-five-strong aircrew to fly 700 miles across France and Germany (and back) in broad daylight. It was predestined to be an expensive raid in terms of lives and aircraft. First into the attack was the squadron led by South African-born Acting Squadron Leader John Nettleton, of 44 (Rhodesia) Squadron. He led a formation of twelve Lancaster bombers, newly in service, in the attack; four were shot down on the way, but he continued and, amid fierce anti-aircraft fire (which brought down three more Lancasters), bombed the factory. Five aircraft, including Nettleton's, returned safely to Britain.[26] Churchill called the Augsburg raid 'an outstanding achievement of the RAF', even though Lord Selborne, Minister of Economic Warfare, complained that his ministry had not been consulted by Bomber Command and thought the attack would delay submarine production by three months at most. In a broadcast BBC interview on 19 April 1942, Nettleton provided just the kind of rallying tone required:

> We Lancaster crews believe that in the Lancaster we have got the answer for heavy bombing. We have tremendous confidence in

everything about the Lancasters and in the workers who are turning them out in such numbers. We know that we are only sent to attack the most worthwhile targets. We believe that the way to win the war is to have our own spring offensive before Hitler has his and in places not of his choice but of ours.[27]

The general public had been made aware of the Lancaster, depicted as a war-winning weapon, for the first time. Nettleton's action – and that of the rest of the Lancaster crews that day – was courageous, certainly; it was also useful propaganda, showing a will to take the fight to the enemy. Squadron Leader J. S. Sherwood DFC, who led 97 Squadron, which followed up 44 Squadron, was recommended for the VC but got nothing, even though he was killed in the action. The *Sunday Pictorial* of 19 April was in no doubt what should happen. 'Give Them All the VC', it declared in a subhead below the banner headline 'Most Daring Raid Of War':

> No greater story of personal daring and gallantry has ever been printed than that told on this page today... Heroism of this kind must be rewarded without delay. In the name of the people who today read with astonishment the story of their great deed, the *Sunday Pictorial* asks that these twelve pilots should be awarded the Victoria Cross. Just as no one will feel that justice has been done until every member of their crews has received the Distinguished Flying Medal.

Nine days after the raid Nettleton's VC was gazetted, along with lesser decorations for all the Augsburg survivors.[28] The dead may have been just as brave; but they received nothing.

The VC continued to serve two purposes: most obviously, the recognition of supreme courage; most pertinently (if less obviously), the rewarding of those who could be held up as examples to the nation and an inspiration to their fellow countrymen, such as Group Captain

Leonard Cheshire. No one could deny that his VC was deserved, for countless acts of determined bravery against considerable odds. As his citation said,[29] Cheshire gained it not for any particular action but for completing 100 missions over four years, for his 'cold and calculated acceptance of risks', for 'placing himself invariably in the forefront of the battle'. But much the same could have been said of the fighter pilot Squadron Leader 'Johnny' Johnson and his own hundreds of operational sorties. The difference between Cheshire and Johnson was not their level of courage, but of how useful they were as propaganda tools and how well their function served strategic aims: bombing Germany to dust had a higher priority, and a much higher public profile, than shooting down enemy aircraft.

In the case of the army, the British and colonial contingents of which took the lion's share of VCs during the Second World War – 137, almost 75 per cent of the total – there was a tendency early in the war to reward good service couched in terms of 'conspicuous gallantry', such as the VC awarded to Second Lieutenant Premindra Singh Bhagat, of the Corps of Indian Engineers. Bhagat had been recommended for an MC in 1940 in East Africa, but that had been downgraded to a Mention in Despatches. He gained his VC while serving in Ethiopia in January and February 1941. Over four days and for a distance of fifty-five miles, while mounted in a Bren carrier, he detected and supervised the clearance of fifteen minefields, twice having his carrier blown up and once being ambushed. Brave man, but his deeds were probably not particularly unusual.

As the war drew on and the Simonds's directive became more widely inculcated, what was demanded for VC eligibility was not only to remain coolly determined when under fire – the Cheshire VC, for example – but to demonstrate extreme anger in the most impossible circumstances; aggression, not moderation. In May 1945 Lachhiman Gurung, who was less than five feet tall, was with the 8th Gurkha

Rifles in the Burma jungle. One night the Gurkhas' position came under ferocious attack, and grenades flew into Gurung's trench. He picked up and threw back the first and then a second, but a third exploded, ripping off fingers and injuring his face and side. With just his left arm working he managed to reload and fire his rifle, keeping the attackers at bay. At regular intervals, nearby fellow Gurkhas heard him shout: 'Come and fight a Gurkha!' At the end of the battle thirty-one Japanese soldiers were found lying dead around his trench. He always spoke modestly about the night he gained his VC: 'I felt I was going to die anyway, so I might as well die standing on my feet. I'm glad that helped the other soldiers in my platoon, but they'd have all done the same thing.'[30]

Little wonder, therefore, that VCs became as rare as hen's teeth, even in the army. Only one man gained a bar to his VC in the Second World War – Captain Charles Upham, who fought in the 20th Battalion of the 2nd New Zealand Expeditionary Force.[31] The greater the hero, the bigger the modesty; Upham, a taciturn individual, simply said: 'The military honours bestowed on me are the property of the men of my unit.'[32] Upham won his first VC on Crete in May 1941 when in command of a platoon in the battle for Maleme airfield. During the course of an advance of 3,000 yards, his platoon was held up three times. Upham attacked a German machine-gun nest with grenades, killing eight paratroopers, destroyed another, and finally knocked out a Bofors anti-aircraft gun. The advance completed, he helped carry a wounded man to safety in full view of the enemy. Next day he was wounded in the shoulder by a mortar burst and hit in the foot by a bullet. He continued fighting, hobbling about in the open to draw enemy fire – the kind of reckless action that Simonds's directive tried to discourage – and lodging his rifle in the fork of a tree to kill approaching Germans. During the retreat from Crete, while still injured, he climbed a steep ravine and used a Bren gun on advancing Germans, killing twenty-two out of fifty at a range of 500 yards. Upham's VC prompted *The Times* to reflect in an editorial:

> In the Baghdad of the *Arabian Nights* it used to be ordered that the story of any notable achievement should be written down in letters of gold. Is gold good enough, we can but ask, for the achievements of the two New Zealanders who have been awarded the Victoria Cross for valour?... the men of Talavera and of Waterloo were heroically brave; but there may be some excuse for asking whether the nature of modern warfare has not raised the standard of courage to heights unknown before.[33]

Upham's second VC was awarded for his role during the defence of the Ruweisat Ridge at the Battle of El Alamein on 15 July 1942, when he ran through a position swept by machine-gun fire and lobbed grenades into a truck full of German soldiers. Later that day he took a Jeep on which a captured German machine gun had been mounted and drove it through the enemy position, at one point commandeering a bewildered group of Italian soldiers to push the Jeep out of the sand. By now wounded, Upham nevertheless led an attack on an enemy strong point, was shot in the elbow and captured, eventually being incarcerated in Colditz because he was such a difficult prisoner. His citation for the second VC read in part: 'his complete indifference to danger and his personal bravery have become a byword in the whole of the New Zealand Expeditionary Force.'[34] Upham fulfilled Simonds's strictures: not only incredibly brave, but an example for all time.

The most appreciated and feted Second War VC winners were the determined killers in the Upham mould and, unlike the nineteenth century, rogues were permitted so long as they fulfilled the brief of setting an outstanding example. John Kenneally would have had his VC stripped from him in the nineteenth century, for he was a deserter. In April 1943 Kenneally was with the 1st Battalion, Irish Guards, when he gained the VC for his part in the final assault on Tunis. Kenneally's VC citation stated that he had 'influenced the whole course of the battle' – a key wording – by twice in the course of a few days picking up his Bren gun and, from the ridge where his unit was situated, charging single-handed down the bare hillside towards German troops who were gathering to attack. On the second occasion, he was wounded but refused medical treatment, and remained in the front line until the end of the day. Prior to this, on his eighteenth birthday, Kenneally had joined the Territorial Reserve of the Royal Artillery. When war broke out, he was posted to an anti-aircraft battery in north London, which he found enormously dull. In 1941 some Irish labourers persuaded him to desert and he went with them to Glasgow, where they gave him the identity card of John Patrick Kenneally, a labourer who had returned to Ireland. He adopted this new identity and enlisted with the Irish Guards in Manchester. When he got his VC, Kenneally later recalled: 'It was the worst thing that could have happened to me. I thought I was bound to be rumbled.'[33] 'Rumbled' he was; but progress had been made, and petty wrongdoing was no bar against a useful, inspirational hero legitimately gaining the VC in 1943. Courage-and-inspiration examples were useful propaganda; courage-but-failure had no wider use and would be overlooked.

Many VCs were recommended but few passed Simonds's stringent tests; those who failed to get a VC were usually downgraded to the next decoration in the hierarchy. One illustrative case suggests that, even with a remarkable level of official support, a well-deserved VC could get turned down.[34] On the morning of 2 March 1945, C Company of the Lake Superior Regiment (Motor), part of Canada's 1st Army, was ordered to pass through positions held by A and B Companies in a gap to the south of the Hochwald Forest in Germany and to occupy a group of buildings. Acting Sergeant Charles Henry Byce, a twenty-four-year-old Métis, was part of C Company. The dawn attack was successful, but by early morning C Company was being shelled and mortared, and its three supporting tanks were knocked out; the company commander and all the other officers became casualties. Byce assumed command of his platoon. His task was to consolidate the left flank. The enemy were entrenched not more than seventy-five yards away and Byce's platoon came under continuous machine-gun fire. Byce organized and led an assault on the enemy dugouts to quell resistance, moving from post to post, directing the fire of his men and maintaining contact with the other platoons.

As the day went on, enemy tanks manoeuvred into position for a counterattack. Byce took up the only remaining PIAT and stalked the German tanks.[37] His first and second shots at the leading tank missed, thus giving away his position; the tanks then directed gunfire at him. He took aim again and knocked out the tank. A second German tank then appeared at a railway underpass; Byce realized that if he could destroy it in the underpass, it would block other tanks from attacking his position. He went forward with another soldier to a house which was a point of vantage, but found it occupied by the enemy. Sergeant Byce and his companion cleared the building with hand grenades, but by this time the tank was through and moving on to his position. He ordered his platoon to let the four enemy tanks go through them and then to open fire on the infantry following behind. This they did and the attack was broken up, the enemy infantry withdrawing. The tanks, however, remained and, with no further anti-tank weapons available, Byce realized that his platoon was no longer effective. He then extricated what remained of C Company. The Germans then called on Byce to surrender but he refused, instead ordering his men back across the bullet-swept ground to A Company lines. By now he had been in combat for almost twelve hours. For the rest of the afternoon he sniped at approaching enemy infantry on the railway embankment, killing seven and wounding eleven, before being relieved.

Byce's VC citation was signed up the chain of command by the commanding officer of the Lake Superior Regiment, Lieutenant Colonel Bob Keane; approved by the acting brigade commander, Lieutenant Colonel G. D. Wotherspoon; endorsed by the acting 4th Division commander, Brigadier R. E. Moncel; approved by the corps commander, Lieutenant General Guy Simonds and by the commander of the 1st Canadian Army, General Harry Crerar; last but not least it was approved by Field Marshal Bernard Montgomery. Yet Byce's award was downgraded to a Distinguished Conduct Medal, although the citation clearly suggests a VC:

> The magnificent courage and fighting spirit displayed by this Non Commissioned Officer when faced with almost insuperable odds are beyond all praise. His gallant stand, without adequate weapons and with a bare handful of men against hopeless odds will remain, for all time, an outstanding example to all ranks of the regiment.[38]

Byce's courageous action was obviously well written up, but lacked the almost unbelievable quality of, for example, that of Sergeant Thomas Derrick, an Australian who had already gained a DCM at El Alamein for destroying three machine-gun posts and two tanks and taking around 100 enemy prisoners. On 24 November 1943, the 26th Australian Brigade, in which Derrick was serving, was ordered to capture Sattelberg, a township in New Guinea sitting on a densely wooded and heavily defended hill that rose 1,000 metres. On 22 November, two of the Australian battalions had been pinned down some 600 metres from the top of the slope, and as night fell they were instructed to withdraw. Derrick refused, saying: 'Bugger the CO. Just give me 20 more minutes and we'll have this place. Tell him I'm pinned down and can't get out.'[39] What happened that night was truly remarkable. Derrick used one hand to clamber up the cliff and the other to lob grenades into machine-gun nests, clearing seven before returning to his platoon, gathering it up, and then personally assaulting and destroying three more, all at no more than eight metres' range. As *The Times* reported: 'Undoubtedly Sergeant Derrick's fine leadership and refusal to admit defeat in the face of a seemingly impossible situation resulted in the capture of Sattelberg. His outstanding gallantry, thoroughness and devotion to duty were an inspiration not only to his platoon and company but to the whole battalion.'[40]

Winston Churchill, who as a dashing youth had proved his gallantry on numerous occasions and probably deserved the VC, ended the Second World War with nothing more than campaign medals. It was wrong, felt General Douglas MacArthur, commander of the US forces in the Philippines. MacArthur reflected on the mammoth flights Churchill had taken in 1942, criss-crossing the Atlantic for a second meeting with Roosevelt, then flying to Cairo on a morale-boosting visit to the troops, then to Teheran to meet Stalin, and then back to London:

> If disposal of all the Allied decorations were today placed by Providence in my hands, my first act would be to award the Victoria Cross to Winston Churchill. Not one of who wears it deserves it more than he. A flight of 10,000 miles through hostile and foreign skies may be the duty of young pilots, but for a Statesman burdened with the world's cares it is an act of inspiring gallantry and valour.[41]

Buckingham Palace announced in December 1945 that King George VI, who had personally presented more than 44,000 decorations since the start of the war (and there were about 55,000 still to go), would henceforth send most decorations by post:

> [T]he King does not propose to delegate to others the authority to present these medals on his behalf, as he regards each award as his own personal gift... the King will, however, continue to hand to their

next-of-kin all decorations and medals, of whatever degree, awarded to those who fell in action before they could receive them at his hands.

On the select list of honours the king still intended to personally present, the VC was at the top.[42]

7

The Integrity of the System

'Sometimes one may feel that the utmost rot may be written
about the British army, as long as it is complimentary rot,
but that serious criticism... is somehow indecent.'
SPENCER FITZ-GIBBON[1]

'If courage were common there would be no purpose in this book.'
LORD MORAN[2]

'The system knows what to expect, and no one wants
to upset the integrity of the system.'
MINISTRY OF DEFENCE COLONEL

Total VCs distributed as of December 2014
1,357 to 1,354 individuals (three bars)

1856–1914	522
1914–20	634
1920–39	5
1939–46	182
1946–2014	14

In 1956, the centenary year of the VC, there were 385 living holders of the Victoria Cross; by 2013 there were just five.[3] The oldest, John Cruickshank, was ninety-four by the time this book was completed. In the Second World War Cruickshank was a flight lieutenant with 210 Squadron, which operated Catalina flying boats. On 17 July 1944 his aircraft was on patrol across the Atlantic when a German U-boat was spotted on the surface. The submarine may already have been in difficulties, or perhaps its commander felt confident to take on this lumbering aircraft; in any case it did not dive but prepared to fight. On the Catalina's first run, its depth charges did not release; Cruickshank went round for a second run and this time the depth charges fell and sank the U-boat. But the submarine's anti-aircraft guns were also on target and Cruickshank was severely injured, hit in seventy-two places, while Flight Sergeant Jack Garnett, the second pilot, was also wounded. The flight back to Sullum Voe, the Catalina's Shetland base, took five-and-a-half hours through the night, but Cruickshank, drifting in and out of consciousness, refused morphine as it would cloud his judgement. When Sullum Voe was in sight, Cruickshank took over the controls from Garnett; he considered the sea conditions too risky for a water landing, so he kept the plane aloft for an hour until the weather improved. The Catalina landed safely and Cruickshank was given an immediate blood transfusion, as the medical officer thought he was too close to death to be moved to hospital immediately. Garnett got the DFC. Cruickshank was so badly wounded that he never returned to flying but instead went back to his pre-war job as a banker. Of four VCs to Coastal Command during the war, Cruickshank's was the only one not to be awarded posthumously.

Cruickshank narrowly avoided death in 1944; VC winners of today and tomorrow are expected to run no less a risk than he did. This certainly keeps the VC exclusive, but by definition it condemns the ranks of the Cross to be filled largely with dead men. The 1961 VC warrant, like the preceding one of 1920, is silent, or at least not explicit, about the level of risk required in order to be considered for the VC; the imposition of a strong likelihood of death is entirely a construction of the military establishment, enthusiasts for keeping this decoration extremely exclusive. It is a very wide deviation from what Victoria and Albert originally proposed. The key, third clause of the 1961 warrant states that the VC shall 'only be awarded for most conspicuous bravery, or some daring or pre-eminent act of valour or self-sacrifice or extreme devotion to duty in the presence of the enemy'.

That senior officers who swear an oath of allegiance to 'the monarch and their heirs and successors' should manipulate what the sovereign has signed into being is very odd indeed. It might be thought that Christopher McDonald and Andrew Badsell merited at least consideration for the VC, when they were ambushed in Mosul in 2004 during the conflict in Iraq. Badsell was a Canadian civilian; McDonald was working for a private security firm during his final leave period from the Royal Irish Regiment. They were escorting a private contractor, heading for the city's power plant, when they were ambushed by hostile vehicles. They drove their car into the line of fire, protecting the one carrying the contractor, returned fire and died, enabling the contractor to escape. According to the coroner at McDonald's inquest, 'they died in their efforts in the most heroic manner'.[4] It is irrelevant what the VC warrant may say; allocation of the VC is entirely dependent on standards applied by the military, intent on safeguarding what it likes to call the 'integrity of the system' – a system that seems to resemble no more than an informal set of guidelines established by erratically applied custom and practice and implemented by a small group of senior officers according to opaque guidelines.

There is, however, a system – the statutes of the VC warrant – whose integrity ought to reside in their strict application. For the military, however, 'integrity' is interpreted very differently, and involves applying what are considered to be the highest possible standards, not permitting dubious awards to creep in (as in the past they certainly have) and thus devaluing the decoration. Saddled with an unnecessarily complicated scale of operational gallantry awards, with extremely difficult distinctions to be made between each award, senior officers of the armed forces have surreptitiously inserted, or at least tolerated the development of, the 90 per cent risk-of-death requirement, which today is used as a means of winnowing out VC claims and keeps the number of possible VC awards to an artificially low level.

That this has made the Victoria Cross a decoration synonymous not with heroism but with death, and completely contradicts the declared intention of the Cross's founders, appears not to bother the military establishment. It puts the cart (protecting the esteem of the VC) before the horse (recognizing conspicuous bravery). In any situation where the award of a VC is at issue, two questions are posed by the VC committee. The overt question is 'does this constitute a VC act?'; the covert one is 'what signals might we send to the wider world by giving a VC in this instance?' It is not the case that McDonald was considered for a VC and ruled out; no one even recommended him. Generations of generals, admirals and air marshals – never mind MoD civil servants – have become accustomed to the unwritten rules of the Cross. No women; no civilians.

Awarding sufficient numbers of VCs that the medal does not become impossibly remote, without distributing so many that it becomes devalued, calls for fine judgement. Unfortunately, human judgement is fallible. Since 1856 the process involved in making a recommendation for a VC has not altered, but 'the assumptions of the various people along the chain... have changed'.[5] In the almost seven decades since the Second World War, only fourteen VCs have been awarded – nine to members of the British army and five to the

Australian army – eight of them posthumous. Over the course of the twentieth century, those adjudicating VC awards have gradually narrowed the gateway through which recommendations must squeeze. Billy Bishop's and John Cornwell's VCs were prompted as much by political requirements as by anything to do with personal courage; they were propaganda Crosses. To call them that in no way undermines Bishop's or Cornwell's actions (after all, it was not them who judged they were worthy of a VC); but in the absence of a stable, shared definition of what supreme courage might be – beyond calling it a supererogatory act, which does not really help, as what is exceptional for a Cornwell might be perfectly normal for a Pollard – we are all floundering in the dark, expecting that senior officers handed the difficult task of deciding grades of courage will do so objectively and consistently, paying attention to what the VC warrant actually says, rather than relying on custom and practice.

What is inappropriate is to maintain the pretence that the VC is purely for exceptional personal courage, when plainly it is not. It would be much simpler if General Patton's instruction, that 'decorations are for the purpose of raising the fighting value of troops', was all there was to it.[6] Patton wanted to professionalize the medal-awarding process:

> It is vital to good morale that decorations get out promptly and on an equitable basis. There should be in every Army and Corps Staff one member of G-1 Section [dealing with personnel matters] whose duty it is to prod divisions and attached lower units to get citations out. He should further see that they are properly written.[7]

The Victoria Cross, however, has never simply been that kind of utilitarian vehicle. From its inception it has fulfilled a much greater, if unhelpfully intangible, function: the recognition of nobility. No one bothered to construct a compelling philosophical foundation for the VC. Yet, if asked the question 'what is the VC for?', the answer must surely involve an ideal of selfless dedication to others under the most severe conditions, in broadly defined military contexts. Because it is so precious, the VC needs to work effectively, and that means distributing it with as much integrity as possible. Not that the VC is irretrievably flawed. Just as there are numerous cases of VCs having been awarded on spurious grounds, serving either political or personal interests (and sometimes both), there are many outstanding examples of 'noble' VC winners, such as the Reverend John Weir Foote, a chaplain with the Royal Hamilton Light Infantry, part of the Canadian contingent that conducted the Dieppe Raid on 19 August 1942. Foote landed on the Dieppe beach under heavy fire. He immediately joined a first-aid post on the beach and for the next eight hours calmly went about the beach – which was under continual fire – helping the medical officer, ministering to the wounded, and carrying men back to receive medical attention. When landing craft arrived to ferry back the wounded, he carried injured soldiers and saw them off the beach. Foote refused the chance of evacuation, preferring to stick by the wounded men, and became a prisoner of war.[8] From Foote's nobility to Pollard's semi-sane killer drive; two extremes, both of which could be seen as justifying the VC, although the common ground between them is only that someone up the chain of command was impressed sufficiently to promote their cases.

The VC, as with all military and civilian honours, lives in two worlds: the official, with grandiloquently worded warrants and florid citations published in the London Gazette; and the closeted, where committees adjudicate recommendations behind closed doors. From its inception the monarchy has valued the VC so highly that it anxiously guarded it against disgrace. Bigamy, theft, drunkenness... all brought personal disgrace in Victorian society; if a VC holder behaved immorally, then by extension he tainted this new order of the über-hero and defiled the monarchy itself. After King George V's declared wish that a man might wear the Cross on the scaffold, moral oversight of the VC dissolved. Yet clearly it would not do to have someone of dubious personal standing receive the most prestigious decoration. From being governed by an overt moral code, the VC has steadily been enveloped by more subtle considerations, in the final stages of which – the decision to give the Cross or not – the process is remarkably opaque. This may be necessary in order to avoid public controversy, but lack of clarity in how the judgements of the VC committee are reached inevitably gives rise to suspicion.

John Keegan's anxiety that the Cross is approaching unattainable levels was prompted by the list of gallantry awards for the Iraq War covering 2003 to 2010, in which Private Johnson Beharry's was the only VC; prior to Beharry, the previous VC awarded to a surviving British serviceman was in 1966, to Rambahadur Limbu, a Gurkha who fought in Borneo. In the Iraq list alongside Beharry's Cross were fifteen Conspicuous Gallantry Crosses (CGCs) – all non-commissioned officers – and eighty-four MCs. A posthumous CGC was awarded to Sergeant Jon Hollingsworth of the Parachute Regiment, who was serving with the SAS. He died during a raid in Basra, where he single-handedly faced a group of insurgents, killing six. Another Iraq CGC went to Lance-Corporal Justin Thomas, who was awarded the medal for his actions when his unit was pinned down by intense fire. Thomas clambered aboard an open-top vehicle and for the next fifteen minutes or so fired a machine gun, enabling his twenty colleagues to move to better cover. A rocket-propelled grenade passed between him and another Para, Gary Lancaster, who had come to Thomas's assistance by feeding ammunition belts, and exploded behind them.[9]

The wording of the current MoD instructions for gallantry awards says the VC goes for 'gallantry of the highest order during active operations', while the CGC is for 'conspicuous gallantry during active operations'; 'conspicuous gallantry' is the phrase that opened VC citations during the First World War. This subtle – and difficult to define – move from 'conspicuous' to 'of the highest order' imposes doubt on all commanding officers when considering VC nominations. Is this act really gallantry of the 'highest' conceivable order? The person who performed it survived; so perhaps not. Such doubt helps preserve the VC's exclusivity and thus the esteem in which it is held, but there are degrees of exclusivity; the creation of the CGC has spelled the death not just of most VC candidates, but possibly of the decoration itself. The CGC is a medal that has little or no grip on the public imagination. While the awarding of a CGC is, of course, of considerable public interest and will gain media attention, the massive media fuss following the bestowal of a VC utterly overshadows the kind of attention a CGC would get. The VC quite simply is seen to be a public, even national, property, unlike any other award, either military or civil. That a VC went to a soldier who fought in Iraq was both justified and fits with the overall history of the decoration. Moreover, it was an intensely 'political' war which Prime Minister Tony Blair was determined to prosecute against considerable domestic opposition. The Prime Minister needed a very public hero, preferably from a humble background, someone who could be presented as 'of the people'. But it is remarkable that Private Beharry gained a VC while the lesser CGC went to Hollingsworth and Thomas, to pluck only two examples from the fifteen CGCs.

The decisions in this case sit oddly with the third clause of the still extant 1961 VC warrant, which stipulates that the Cross is 'for most conspicuous bravery, or some daring or pre-eminent act of valour or self-sacrifice or extreme devotion to duty in the presence of the enemy'.[10] Beharry, Thomas, Hollingsworth – all performed a supererogatory act, an undemanded ideal, the willingness to sacrifice self for others; it is confusing, to put it no more critically, that the MoD operates with one standard, while the VC warrant operates with a different one. Logic dictates that it is time for an updated VC warrant; or a revision and cleansing of the MoD's medals 'league table'.

Courage is a virtue, the demonstration of which can inspire others and encourage resilience in adversity; courage needs to be encouraged. Part of the current confusion surrounding the apparent need to defend the VC against possible dilution is that the establishment is anxious that creeping debasement of the decoration's national importance is a real threat – when it is no such thing. It is, of course, right to be afraid; language debasement has suffused contemporary society – more or less anything today can be deemed courageous. As the American thinker and professor of law, William I. Miller, puts it:

> Contemporary gender, sexual, and ethnic politics argues that all are entitled to their stories of courage, that no one is to be denied the virtue simply for having been relegated to powerlessness... Merely being all you can be need hardly involve courage; more likely it is a less glorious matter of plain hard work.[11]

For the military, the degree of courage displayed remains an ultimate test; the hero must remain an exclusive item. According to the philosopher J. O. Urmson, the heroic person 'does more than his superior officers would ever ask him to do'; he is 'the man to whom, often posthumously, the Victoria Cross is awarded'.[12] In 1856 it was enough to show simple courage while in danger to gain a VC. Today an act that far exceeds duty is required; and even that may not be enough. The definition of what it takes to win the VC has thus been shunted higher, without anyone in authority over the VC warrant specifying this, but where it lies today is far from clear; a settled, universally shared definition of military courage is no easier than it has ever been. The early years of the VC saw the authorities struggle to define the kind of act that qualified for the Cross, but many cases – which today seem aberrations – either crept in or were forced through by powerful senior officers. But because acts of courage stem from extreme situations in which an individual's subjective mental state is crucially relevant, any objective recognition of that act – by giving a medal, for example – enters the public domain, with inevitable questions. In what way is the courage of an Alfred Pollard 'equivalent' to that of a Jack Cornwell, or a Johnson Beharry? It is absurd to seek an answer; yet, once embarked on the path of giving decorations for individual courage, it was inevitable that stratification and the creation of subdivisions, together with the inevitable dissatisfaction, would follow. Saddled with the practice – for good or ill – of recognizing and rewarding individual courage, the authorities have understandably tried to impose a more systematic approach, creating a hierarchy of military decorations with the VC at the peak.

This 'scaling' of courage is our inheritance and perhaps very little can be done about it. Lieutenant General Stannus was unfortunately right: once started, the process of individualizing courage inevitably demands adjudication by authorities who are only human; the scope for error expands, particularly when those same authorities try to prevent the peak from becoming too easily accessible by imposing unbelievably high standards. The military gatekeepers of all gallantry awards have an invidious task, that of trying to maintain the integrity of the system they have been handed, and which they have expanded. Adjudicating between the different standards of courage in order to bestow the 'right' gallantry decoration is a thankless task; a seat on the VC committee is perhaps one of the most unwelcome positions a senior officer can occupy – there will always be someone to say they got it wrong in a particular case. We could, however, turn this situation on its head; from that different perspective we might conclude that maintaining the rigidities of the system – trying to follow as exactly as possible the grading of courage, even when it leads to absurdities – has imperceptibly become more important than guarding its integrity, which is all about justice, and being seen to be dealing with individuals justly.

Does it matter? For individuals, obviously it does, although most VC winners are, almost by definition, exceptionally modest when it comes to their VC-winning act, as Kipling said:

> I have met perhaps a dozen or so of V.C.'s, and in every case they explained that they did the first thing that came to their hand without worrying about alternatives. One man headed a charge into a mass of Afghans… and cut down five of them. All he said was: 'Well, they were there, and they couldn't go away. What was a man to do? Write 'em a note and, ask 'em to shift?'[13]

The Victoria Cross is much bigger than the individuals who win it, because for our society it represents courageous selflessness, and the highest possible devotion to the defence of our nation. Raising or lowering the price of heroism are equally risky, because that threatens to unsettle the overall moral quality of society. The paradox today is that, while everyone can be a hero for performing what once might have seemed relatively trivial acts of stoicism or endurance, the British military hero now normally needs to die in battle to obtain the VC. The critical problem threatening the clarity of what the VC once stood for is the military's determination to sustain rationing, a decision that paradoxically is rational yet results in irrational judgements. Imposing a quota (itself ill- or undefined) avoids the risk of devaluing the Cross; yet this can lead to excluding clearly meritorious cases. According to Lord Ashcroft, writing in the *Spectator*, 'The beauty of the V.C. is… the fact that it is awarded entirely on merit.'[14] That is clearly untrue; or 'merit' is being defined here in a very peculiar fashion.

The military prefer a (rarely acknowledged) quota system rather than a (difficult-to-administer) avowedly merit system of operational gallantry decorations, because rationing is seen as a bulwark against the VC, and other gallantry awards, becoming commonplace. Lieutenant Colonel 'X' (speaking on condition of anonymity), then Secretary of the Armed Forces Operations Awards Committee, explained this supply-and-demand defence against cheapening the VC. This committee is chaired by the Defence Services Secretary and includes the Secretaries for the Royal Navy, the Royal Air Force and the Army, and the Deputy Chief of Joint Operations.[15] 'X' described his role

> [as auditing] the system to keep it credible. The number of overall awards [including VCs] that will be distributed depends on various factors, partly on the number of troops engaged in an operation; the length of the conflict; the level of overall risk involved; the number of casualties... Our work must be guided to some extent by custom and practice. *The system knows what to expect, and no one wants to upset the integrity of the system* [my emphasis].

Step outside the military world for a moment and it is obvious that the moral 'system' in which the VC exists is far wider than the purely military, and that its 'integrity' depends as much on how well our society defends itself against surreptitious language debasement as on any perpetuation of artificially elevated requirements for VC eligibility. If anyone can be a 'hero', what price the 'heroism' of the VC?

During the Second World War the 'integrity of the system' began to be privileged above the recognition of individual supererogatory acts of military valour. The nineteenth century saw a lengthy tussle over the VC between War Office civil servants who tried (and sometimes failed) to implement strictly the terms of the VC warrant and senior officers who would do their best to ride roughshod over those scruples. Some nineteenth-century senior officers – Lord Roberts being a notable example – chose to distribute the VC generously, while their twentieth-century counterparts believed that the Cross

225

should be handed out on a much more restricted, but equally informal, basis. Today, we are living through a period in which control over the VC has been vested almost entirely in the hands of the military, and the policy they implement is one of extremely tight control over the numbers of VCs handed out – yet still with scant regard to the strict terms of the existing, 1961, VC warrant. Crudely speaking, throughout the VC's history the military has loosened or tightened the strings around the VC 'bag' as it sees fit, no matter what the warrant says. Currently, the military establishment gets extremely agitated whenever it believes the Cross may be given too easily. That may be right or wrong, but it is a matter of (possibly wayward) judgement, for which there would be no need if the VC Warrant were actually referred to, rather than ignored, in making recommendations. The establishment has painted itself unnecessarily into a corner; very few VCs are given because no one dare suggest giving more; the VC has become untouchable, and is placed on such an elevated pedestal that it is almost beyond reach. This is not how it started, and is not how it should be today.

The military's obsession with 'the system', which entails comparing and contrasting current and past VC recommendations, rather than 'integrity' – the judgement of individual cases on their merits – can be seen in the case of the four VCs that went to Australian troops during the Vietnam War. Australian regular soldiers joined a purpose-built unit created in 1962, the Australian Army Training Team Vietnam (AATTV), Australia's contribution to America's war against the Vietcong and the North Vietnamese regular army. The AATTV initially consisted of thirty officers and warrant officers, although by the time it was disbanded in 1972 around 1,000 men – mostly Australians but also a few New Zealanders – had served in its ranks. The 'advisory' role of the AATTV was a mask that rapidly slipped, and the unit was soon fighting alongside the South Vietnamese regular army. All the AATTV VCs were written up by senior Australian officers attached to the unit. Two of the VCs were posthumous, one of them witnessed by no senior officer. A complicating factor was that, between 1975 and October 1992, Australia ran two parallel systems for award-ing medals, its own and the Imperial (British and Commonwealth) system. Any recommendations for the Imperial VC were channelled via the Foreign Office to the Ministry of Defence (MoD) in London. Curiously, the VC committee in London lacked the authority either to judge Australian VC standards or to reject recommendations.

The MoD regarded four VCs as excessive, and there was suspicion that the Australians were cheapening the decoration. The MoD diplomatically waited four years before commissioning an internal study to consider – actually, to undermine – the four AATTV VCs.[16] That four VCs went to such a small contingent was only remarkable, however, if the analysis compared – as it did – what happened in Vietnam with the Korean War of 1950–3, when the same number of VCs (including two posthumous) was distributed among some 20,000 British and Commonwealth armed forces personnel, more than 1,000 of whom were killed in action. Thirty-three AATTV members were killed in action and 122 wounded during its ten-year existence. In Korea, the chance of winning a VC was one in 5,000; for members of the AATTV it was one in 250. Four VCs for the AATTV was only remarkable if the blinkers of a quota system were donned; if each action was judged purely on its own merit, then why not four, or five, or more?

The report took a dim view of the posthumous VC awarded to AATTV Warrant Officer Kevin Wheatley, although it tactfully added that 'it would be completely improper to make comment today on a standard that was not criticised at the time'. On 13 November 1965, Wheatley's platoon was surrounded while in action in Tra Bong Valley, in Quang Ngai province. Wheatley refused to leave his comrade,

Warrant Officer Swanton, who had been grievously injured, even though Wheatley knew Swanton was dying from a chest wound.[17] According to the original VC recommendation, Wheatley 'discarded his rifle and radio to enable him to half drag, half carry Warrant Officer Swanton, under heavy machine-gun fire and automatic rifle fire, out of the open rice paddies into the comparative safety of a wooded area some 200 metres away'. Wheatley was then seen to pull the pins from two hand grenades; shortly afterwards an explosion and gunfire were heard. The MoD report observed that Wheatley's VC recommendation had been massaged before it became a citation: 'the words "rifle and" [were removed] on the grounds that a soldier should never discard his weapons... The two bodies were found at first light the next morning after the fighting had ceased, with Warrant Officer Wheatley lying beside Warrant Officer Swanton. Both had died of gunshot wounds.' The report noted that this paragraph had drawn 'comment from the Palace... As the citation [actually, recommendation] stood it could have been a suicide pact.[18] In conjunction with the Australian Army Liaison Officer the words "Both died of gunshot wounds" were added.' It then concluded: 'It is questionable if this act is really to VC standard.'

An authoritative history of the Australian involvement in the Vietnam War provides an altogether more subtle context for Wheatley's tragic end:

> AATTV was an extraordinary unit, elite and unique... The normal role for team members was advising or leading forces of Vietnamese or Montagnards in combat or calling in artillery and air power for their support, with only one other Australian or American close at hand. Under these circumstances advisers developed a code of mateship... It was a kind of pact. Each looked after the other, and neither left the field of battle alone. Sometimes they died together.[19]

Desk officers at the MoD in London, almost 6,000 miles away from Vietnam, can have had only the faintest understanding of Wheatley's situation. It probably was suicide, the final defiant act of a man who in his last moments must have experienced a vast array of conflicting emotions – the most powerful, perhaps, that he would not desert his mate. To have denied Wheatley the Cross at the time it was awarded, on the basis that he deliberately chose to die while standing by a dying comrade, would have caused a serious diplomatic row between Canberra and London; even four years later it was impossible for the MoD's report author to state baldly that Wheatley's VC did not, in his opinion, meet VC requirements. But Wheatley's VC certainly fulfilled the critical term of the 1961 VC warrant: 'for most conspicuous bravery, or some daring or pre-eminent act of valour or self-sacrifice or extreme devotion to duty in the presence of the enemy'. Wheatley's VC citation, the sole entry in a supplement to the *London Gazette* on 13 December 1966, stated that 'the Queen has been graciously pleased on the advice of Her Majesty's Australian Ministers to approve' Wheatley's VC; it omitted that he discarded his rifle and bluntly asserted that he and Swanton died 'of gunshot wounds', even though the precise cause of death would have been impossible to ascertain, given the two grenades that exploded. The VC was deserved; the citation was massaged to fit required form; and the MoD belatedly and in private undermined Wheatley's claim to receive it. Such is the muddle that results from an over-protective desire to preserve the fictions and myths surrounding the VC, rather than relax and – as is within their right under VC statutes – let the men and officers on the ground actually choose for themselves.

In 1992 the *British Army Review* published a pseudonymous article by 'Sustainer', who claimed to be a recently retired General Officer Commanding. He advised how to maximize the chances of getting a gallantry decoration: 'First you have to be in the somewhat unattractive situation of having your life endangered. Then you have to do something damned irrational and what's more be seen doing it by a cove with a flair with the old pen and who can cobble together a passable citation.'[20] Sustainer's irreverence disguised a serious point. A good write-up by an officer is today almost de rigueur for the VC, the first stage of an onerous process, comprising not just comparisons with past 'standards' but an assessment of how any VC awarded might fit a wide political, media and personal arena.[21]

The write-up issue was considered by the MoD report regarding the VC awarded to AATTV Warrant Officer Ray Simpson.[22] Simpson, who had already won a DCM while in Vietnam, gained his VC for actions on two separate occasions: he was in action in Kon Tum province, near the border with Laos, when, on 6 May 1967, he rescued a wounded fellow warrant officer and unsuccessfully attacked an enemy position; on 11 May he fought alone against heavy odds to cover the evacuation of some wounded. The report judged that the recommendation for Simpson represented 'A good VC badly told. There are too many clichés and a great lack of detail. "Disregarding the danger involved... at great personal risk... complete disregard for personal safety... at the risk of almost certain death." It is a pity the author of the citation was not able to describe the detail of the dangers involved in short and clear sentences.' Overall, concluded the report: 'In each of these four citations it seems as though the person writing the report knew that if he had all the "correct" phrases his citation must succeed. This theme of poor expressive capability... is the cause of comment on the standards of the current Australian awards.' The fact that 'poor expressive capability' in the initial write-up of a VC recommendation might swing the balance between getting and not getting the Cross might be thought to cast doubt over the 'integrity of the system'. According to Lieutenant Colonel 'X':

A well-written recommendation is more likely to be approved than one that is poorly written. For a VC we would normally expect two eyewitness accounts, but there is a degree of fluidity about this. There's not much experience around as to what constitutes gallantry. For a VC recommendation there has got to be a major punch-up somewhere.

In the case of 'operational honours', the theatre commander initially judges each recommendation, weighing the degree of courage displayed. If endorsed at this level, the recommendation then passes up to the operational commander for further comment and comparison, until a higher committee of senior officers gives its judgement and the recommendation is passed up to government, with the fig leaf of royal assent, for final approval. A further step is necessary in the case of the VC and the George Cross. A VC or GC recommendation alerts the chiefs of staff, and they then invoke the VC committee, chaired by the Chief of the Defence Staff and comprising the Permanent Under-Secretary at the MoD and the chiefs of staff of the various services, representatives from the Armed Forces Operations Awards Committee, and others. At every step this process has scope for subjectivity, for factors other than the act itself to enter into the discussion. The process may also be blighted by groupthink. Intent on preserving standards, the VC committee will naturally incline towards conservatism: challenging the system in such a setting would require exceptional – perhaps VC standard – courage. That the integrity of the system is questionable inevitably follows from a situation where officers wrestle with an informal policy requiring almost certain death in order to merit a VC, while simultaneously considering a plethora of alternative possible decorations.

That the judgement of Solomon is called for is illustrated by the recent campaign in Afghanistan.[23] It is invidious to select an individual example, but the VC is, after all, an individual award. Lance-Corporal

Matthew Croucher, a former regular soldier with the Royal Marines who later joined the Royal Marines Reserve, was awarded the George Cross in July 2008. On 9 February 2008 Croucher was part of a four-man night-time reconnaissance patrol in Helmand province. As the patrol moved through a compound, he felt his leg touch a trip-wire that released a grenade which would, within seconds, blast shrapnel and probably kill or severely injure not only him but other members of the four-man team. The quick-thinking Croucher immediately threw himself onto the grenade, pinning it to the ground under an enormous rucksack on his back and tucking up his legs to make himself as small as possible. 'Then there was the loudest bang I have ever heard, a flash of light and I was flying through the air.'[24] The explosion ripped the rucksack from him and sent metal splinters into his body armour and helmet. Of the other three troops, the rear man managed to take cover behind a building, the patrol commander threw himself to the ground, and the final one remained standing. The rucksack took most of the blast and Croucher – stunned, deafened, disoriented and with blood coming from his nose – was luckily relatively unscathed. He then insisted, against the advice of a medic who was quickly on the scene, on staying to fight off a Taliban ambush, during which he shot one insurgent. Croucher's instinctive reaction saved his life and that of at least one other soldier. He later recalled thinking, 'I've set the bloody thing off and I'm going to do whatever it takes to save the others.' Croucher received the GC and not the VC because his selfless bravery was 'not in the presence of the enemy'. There have of course been numerous VC precedents for actions similar to Croucher's. Charles Lucas was a midshipman on HMS *Hecla* when, on 21 June 1854, he gained his VC for picking up an enemy shell that had just landed on *Hecla* with its fuse fizzing; Lucas threw the shell overboard, where it exploded. Without this quick-wittedness, many lives might have been lost.[25]

The VC–GC distinction hinges on the single word 'not': the VC is 'for gallantry of the highest order during active operations'; the GC is 'for gallantry of the highest order not in active operations'. Sergeant Olaf Schmid, gazetted with a posthumous GC on 19 March 2010, is another anomalous case arising from the creation of the George Cross. Schmid was with 11 Explosive Ordnance Disposal Regiment, Royal Logistics Corps, and in June 2009 he arrived in Afghanistan. Between then and his death on Saturday, 31 October 2009, he dealt with more seventy improvised explosive devices (IEDs). That day he had already tackled three IEDs before a fourth exploded and killed him. Schmid was due to leave the field that same day and be back in the UK one week later. Lieutenant Colonel Robert Thomson, commander of 2nd Rifles Battle Group, said Schmid was 'simply the bravest and most courageous man I have ever met. . . Superlatives do not do this man justice. Better than the best of the best.' His *London Gazette* citation read (in part): 'his selfless gallantry, his devotion to duty, and his indefatigable courage displayed time and time again saved countless military and civilian lives and is worthy of the highest recognition.'[26] There is an absurd quality to such hair-splitting: one moment Croucher was 'not in active operations', the next he was; once the Taliban fire-fight was over, was he once again 'not in active operations'?[27] To award Schmid the GC was a fine and justified recognition, and the GC has enormous esteem; but to deem that a soldier is not in the 'presence' of the enemy when he was killed in action by an explosive device, laid by an enemy that surrounded him, seems inappropriate.

Preservation of the VC's scarcity means that, when one is bestowed, it can be a match to a tinderbox: the winner's life is altered forever, amid relentless and continual publicity. As Lieutenant Colonel 'X' put it, the VC committee asks itself: 'Can someone "carry" the VC? Is it fair to give someone such a burden? I don't want to see the VC becoming something which is unattainable; but ultimately it's the politicians who call the shots – and they are all above the system. The military are ultra-conservative in not wanting to abuse the system.' Nor is the pressure associated with the VC purely personal. Lieutenant Colonel 'X' acknowledged that gallantry decorations are occasionally subject to political pressure, interference even: 'regrettable, but human nature', as he put it. When I asked for an example, he suggested that Margaret Thatcher may have taken a hand in the VC awards for the 1982 Falklands War, and she would have been within her constitutional right to make a direct recommendation to the sovereign on a particular medal issue. According to him, the list of recommendations for Falklands military decorations was sent to 10 Downing Street for approval, and the list was returned with a note from the prime minister, asking: 'Where are the Victoria Crosses?' Lieutenant Colonel 'X' offered no evidence to support this, however; he may indeed have sought to distract attention from the fact that the Special Honours Committee, formed by the three armed services to consider the Falklands gallantry decorations, appears to have been in some disarray at the time. For while two posthumous VCs were approved, for Lieutenant Colonel Herbert Jones and Sergeant Ian McKay, both of the Parachute Regiment, a third member of the regiment, Private Stephen Illingsworth, had his posthumous VC recommendation downgraded to a Distinguished Conduct Medal.[28] The Jones VC was controversial and remains so; if awarded for recklessly suicidal courage, then perhaps it was thoroughly deserved; but if it was for Jones's leadership, then it is highly questionable.[29] By contrast, Illingsworth's recommendation appeared to tick all the right boxes.

Illingsworth had been in the regiment for almost two years when, on 28 May 1982, he was with 5 Platoon, near the Darwin and Goose Green settlements. His platoon was ordered to provide covering fire for an advance section of B Company of 2nd Battalion. As dawn came up, Illingsworth's platoon found itself on an exposed slope that soon came under intense Argentine machine-gun and rifle fire. As the platoon withdrew back over a crest, a Private Hall was hit in the back. Illingsworth had already reached safety but, together with another private, returned to tend to the wounded Hall. The two rescuers removed Hall's webbing to give him first aid and left Hall's gear, including spare ammunition, as they stumbled back to cover, miraculously avoiding being shot. As the fire-fight intensified, 5 Platoon started to run short of ammunition. Illingsworth again left the safety of cover to retrieve Hall's ammunition, but he was shot and killed. Illingsworth was strongly recommended for a posthumous VC by Lieutenant General Sir Richard Trant, Land Deputy Commander in the Falklands, and Admiral John Fieldhouse, commander of the Falklands Task Force, who in his note on the recommendation form said: 'Private Illingsworth's heroic acts of total disregard for his own safety were in the highest traditions of his regiment. He was an inspiration to others and is strongly recommended for the posthumous award of the Victoria Cross.' Trant commented: 'In these two acts of supreme courage Private Illingsworth showed a complete disregard for his own safety, and a total dedication to others... a display of coolly calculated courage and heroism of the very highest order.'

At what point does 'heroism of the highest order' fail to qualify for a VC? Illingsworth was twice a casualty, first of the Argentine army's sniper and second of the British army's rationing of gallantry decorations. Clearly Illingsworth's recommendation never reached Mrs Thatcher's desk, but the greater pity is that individual senior officers were alarmed that too many VCs were being recommended – and especially too many for the Parachute Regiment. The Military Secretary at the time of the Falklands campaign was Lieutenant General Sir Roland Guy. He advised the VC committee:

> It is not for the VC Committee to make any judgement on what would be the appropriate number of VCs to award for this campaign

in comparison with the numbers that have been awarded in past campaigns. However there will inevitably be great public interest over whether the award is in any way being cheapened if an excessive number are awarded.[30]

General Guy's carefully phrased final sentence was enough.

The inherent arbitrariness of the system is further highlighted by the decision to award a Military Cross to Captain Gavin John Hamilton of the Green Howards, who was on attachment with the SAS during the Falklands conflict. His citation, published in the *London Gazette* on 8 October 1982,[31] said Hamilton survived two helicopter crashes 'in appalling weather conditions' in South Georgia and then, two days later, led the advance elements of the forces that captured the main enemy positions in Grytviken, thereby securing the surrender of all Argentine forces on South Georgia. Ten days later Hamilton led his troop on the 'successful and brilliantly executed' raid on Pebble Island in the Falklands, destroying eleven enemy aircraft on the ground. The litany of achievements of Hamilton and his small team continues until finally, on 10 June 1982, he and a four-man troop were in an observation post near Port Howard, the biggest settlement on West Falkland, when they were surrounded by Argentine troops. Two of the patrol escaped; Hamilton and his signaller, Sergeant Fosenka, were pinned down. Shot in the back, Hamilton ordered Fosenka to make his escape under covering fire. Shortly after, Hamilton was hit again and died. His citation states he 'showed supreme courage and sense of duty by his conscious decision to sacrifice himself on behalf of his signaller'. Why did Jones and McKay get the VC and Hamilton an MC? The official explanation is that no senior officer witnessed Hamilton's courage, but this, as Lieutenant Colonel 'X' acknowledged, is not a formal requirement. Moreover, there was ample testimony from Argentine officers who were present – and enemy testimony has in the past been sufficient supporting evidence for a VC.[32]

While no one doubts Colonel H. Jones's bravery, John Geddes, a corporal in 2 Para who fought at Goose Green, was amongst those who later questioned his leadership. When Colonel Jones ordered A Company to follow him in a frontal attack on a well-established Argentine position, they refused because they 'had watched the futile loss of three men's lives... [they] knew what was waiting for them up there in the Gorse Gully and they were going to sort it out in their own way and that didn't include charging into machine guns First World War style.'[33] Jones charged recklessly to his death, followed only by his personal bodyguard, who were obliged to follow him in any conditions. That the regiment's commanding officer rushed to attack a bunker, when he should have directed the attack from further back, was both heroic and foolish. The futility of Jones's charge and death was a thoroughly nineteenth-century act. His second-in-command, Major Chris Keeble, recalled that 'he was a man straight out of Boys' Own... he was a guy who ruled by a bullwhip rather than a conductor of an orchestra'[34] – and, had he survived, his reckless behaviour may have been more rigorously probed.

Almost immediately after Colonel Jones was killed, there was another example of remarkable courage, one that actually did turn the battle. Corporal David 'Pig' Abols of the 2nd Battalion of the Parachute Regiment was, according to Geddes, 'the man who broke the enemy at the Gorse Gully with a fantastic piece of heroism. He's the soldier that the 2 Para Toms [privates] think should have got the VC.' The Goose Green situation was deadlocked; Abols was lying exposed, armed with a light anti-tank rocket. Geddes recalled events:

> Pig jumped to his feet in the middle of a howling gale of machine-gun fire, lifted the rocket to his shoulder, lined it up on the bunker

opposite, breathed out and squeezed down the rubber trigger on the top of the tube... In the space of twenty minutes two of our comrades, H and Pig, had carried out attacks that were so brave they would put the fear of God into any enemy. But they were very different in their nature. I believe H's death-or-glory dash... was lion-hearted but ill-conceived and futile. It didn't make a difference to the battle... [It was Abols's action,] the culmination of a lot of nerve, balls and superb field craft, which broke the Argies, not H's emotional charge into the Valley of Death.[35]

Some get the VC, some get lesser awards, some get nothing at all: perhaps it has always been thus and there is nothing to be done to prevent perceived inequities. 'No medals policy will ever keep everyone happy' was the opening remark of Sir John Holmes's government-sponsored military medals review, published in July 2012. That luck plays a part is, perhaps, palatable; but the pretence that merit alone dictates, or that the system's integrity functions well, is not. Hamilton may well have been deemed more worthy of an MC than a VC because he was serving with the SAS, from which a higher level of courage and grit is usually expected. The SAS is also intensely secretive; a VC for an SAS member would have provoked uncomfortably intense media interest. Then again, Jones and McKay died during high-profile battles, Goose Green and Mount Longdon respectively, both regarded as crucial steps towards final recovery of the Falklands; Hamilton's fight, important and tough as it was, may have been seen as a sideshow. Illingsworth may simply have lacked 'friends at Court'. We simply do not know.[36]

There is always a risk that, through excessive largesse, military gallantry awards are cheapened and thus lose esteem among the troops for whom they are intended to be an encouragement. After the 2003 Iraq War, the US Air Force handed out more than 69,000 medals, commendations and other awards, while the US Army gave out some 40,000, with officers the main beneficiaries of the higher awards: 'A list of medals granted to the American brigade which captured Baghdad shows that of twenty-six Silver Stars, four went to colonels, eleven to captains, and only eleven to non-commissioned officers. Private soldiers did not receive any.'[37] In 2000, 185 US Air Force personnel were awarded the Bronze Star, America's fourth-highest combat award, for the air campaign against Yugoslavia, NATO's first all-out military campaign; 90 per cent of those were given to personnel who never approached the combat zone, which President Clinton defined as Yugoslavia, Albania, the Adriatic Sea and the northern Ionian Sea, and the airspace above those areas. One Bronze Star went to a civil-engineering squadron commander for building what the citation called a 'miraculous' tent city at the Aviano air base in Italy. This reckless distribution of military decorations might have pleased General Patton; but it renders the identification and individuation of courage laughable.

American veterans who have already seen their decorations thus cheapened were deeply angered in February 2013 by an initiative of the US Defense Secretary, Leon Panetta, who announced the creation of a new medal specifically for drone pilots, the 'Distinguished Warfare Medal'. This medal would have been the first combat-related award created by the US military since the Bronze Star in 1944. It was to rank higher than the Purple Heart (awarded to wounded troops), slightly higher than the Bronze Star, but lower than the Silver Star. According to Panetta: 'The contribution they [drone pilots] make does contribute to the success of combat operations... even if those actions are physically removed from the fight.' The US military is at the forefront of embracing technological change, and now possesses miniature drones that, from a base thousands of miles distant, can crawl, hover, inspect, report back – and finally kill through a variety of means. Pilots who once flew F-16 fighters in aerial combat now sit in front of computer screens watching 'insurgents' before killing them. Drone technology changes not just the conduct of war but also what might constitute the demonstration of courage and, by extension, the awarding of military decorations.[38] US veterans found it insulting that an armchair pilot whose greatest danger might come from a cup of hot spilled coffee could be eligible for an award that ranked higher than that given for being wounded in combat; underlying those complaints was the further factor that, in the US, grades of medal (commendation, merit, distinguished) play a wider role – each medal grade gives the recipient a certain number of the points needed for promotion. The drone warfare medal was rapidly aborted by the new Defense Secretary, Chuck Hagel, in March 2013; drone pilots will instead be eligible for existing medals and have a 'distinguishing device' attached to them. As long-distance slaughter becomes more dominant on the battlefield, close combat will become increasingly rare. Robots, too, threaten the VC's survival.

Politicians and the general public are only interested in the VC when there is a war on. In the case of unpopular wars (such as those in Iraq) or wars that have very obscure antecedents and whose original purpose was largely lost sight of (such as the war in Afghanistan), a medal serves the useful purpose of buying good media coverage at a very economical rate, while deflecting awkward questions, such as: why did so many British service personnel lose their lives overseas in a conflict that was utterly remote from British interests? The dilemma for the guardians of the VC – trying to balance too liberal a distribution, thus devaluing the award, against a policy that restricts its award so tightly that the bar to gaining it is set impossibly high – has been at the heart of the award since shortly after its inception. Today, when the contingent of surviving VC winners is just a handful, there should be a publicly transparent debate about who determines when a VC is awarded, and why. The criteria according to which it should be granted have become far too stringent. For politicians and the military hierarchy, the bestowal of gallantry awards serves different but equally useful purposes: for the former, it can deflect uncomfortable public criticism of the way in which a war has been conducted; for the latter, it helps preserve public esteem and demonstrates the vitality of the military's contribution to the general social good. And for the general public, it answers the yearning to know that we still live in a time when genuine heroes can be found – although the heroes have become scarcer, and the pressure on those identified as such by being awarded the VC have become ever greater.

It is the task of a Patton or a Napoleon to persuade soldiers that bits of ribbon are intrinsically valuable. The historian's job, in part, is to spot contradictions and unravel obfuscations, and the history of the VC is steeped in both. The assiduous nurturing of the image of the VC has surrounded the medal with the greatest prestige, an iconic status that it was never originally intended to possess. By the time the last British troops leave Afghanistan, and the final assessment of Operation Enduring Freedom is made, the conflict will have lasted at least six years longer than the Second World War.[39] History will judge that Enduring Freedom – and Operation Herrick, as the British contribution was called – was a political mistake, and that NATO's armed forces were handed an impossible task, as should have been evident from the outset if only politicians and generals read a bit more history. Enduring Freedom has endured for much longer than anyone initially expected, but has resulted in far fewer casualties than the Second World War: 453 British armed forces personnel have died in Afghanistan (as of October 2014) against almost 600,000 British and Commonwealth military fatalities/missing and presumed dead during the 1939–45 conflict. But there is little difference in mortality rates: slightly more than 5 per cent of those serving in the British forces in

1939–45 were killed in action, while of the approximately 9,500 British troops who have served in Afghanistan 5 per cent have died. The Falklands War against Argentina in 1982 lasted just seventy-four days and saw 255 service personnel killed in action out of a total of 28,000 who sailed in the task force – a mortality rate of less than 1 per cent. Two Falklands VCs, two Afghanistan VCs: is the balance right? In the Falklands, the chance of winning a VC was thirty times greater than in the Second World War; even in the Afghanistan struggle, serving personnel were ten times more likely to win a VC than their predecessors in the Second World War. For the Crimean War, the ratio of combat deaths to VCs was approximately seventy-seven to one. If the same ratio of combat deaths to VC awards had been applied in the 1914–18 war, there would have been almost 13,000 VCs. The chance of winning a VC is not dependent on the nature of the individual act performed, but when that act happened.

The burden of being declared a hero by the media, only to find subsequently that mundane life goes on, cannot be underestimated. In Iraq in 2004, Private Johnson Beharry saved the lives of several wounded comrades, suffering severe head injuries. His VC award occupied the whole of the front page of The Sun in its 18 March 2005 edition, with the headline 'For Valour' superimposed over an illustration of the VC.[40] In September 2006 he confessed to a different newspaper the pressure of being a hero. Although he was proud of his VC, 'you don't get something like this for free. You get it and survive with the pain – or you get it and die... Everyone thinks that because I receive the Victoria Cross, I receive a wall of money. They expect me to give them whatever they ask for. But the Victoria Cross is just a medal.'[41] By September 2010 Beharry, who had been headed for invalidity retirement from the army prior to his VC being announced, was unhappily working in army recruitment; he said that he 'didn't join the Army to sit behind a desk. I joined to serve in the infantry. I have been told that I will never serve in combat again... I am willing to take the risk but I suppose the Ministry of Defence doesn't want a VC holder being killed in action.' A personal burden has always been part of the VC, but in its early, more liberal days, when more VC winners were around, a return to relative obscurity and, in some cases, poverty was more of a problem than the spotlight of public attention. In 1979 the author John Winton identified an unusually high rate of suicide among early VC winners:

> [The] Victoria Cross has always had its sombre side, when paradoxi-
> cally too much was demanded of its recipients, and then not enough
> attention paid to them... Of the 1,349 men who have won the VC to
> date, 19 committed suicide and at least as many more died in circum-
> stances where it was charitable to return an open verdict.[42]

The professionals of Britain's armed forces are trained to be courageous, but to become a hero depends on public acclaim, and being a
hero is a mixed blessing.

Michael De-la-Noy, in his book The Honours System, wrote that 'Those who hold the Victoria Cross are a classless band of the elite, in whose dwindling presence other individuals, regardless of their general opinions on war or honours, do well to give way and keep their peace.' True enough. Less accurate is the statement that follows immediately after: 'There is no conceivable way in which a Victoria Cross can be canvassed for, purchased or in any other way debased.' The VC has in the past often been canvassed for, and is at risk not of debasement but of decline through ossification. When the medal first appeared, the network of social ties that bound the monarchy and the armed forces was vigorous and unquestioned; those ties have decayed, as the monarchy has retrenched in power and diminished in esteem. Remarkably, however, the VC remains one of the few British institutions that is untarnished by accusations of corruption, scandal, political intrigue or manipulation. The fact that the VC is not necessarily or simply

awarded purely for a heroic deed, or that heroic military deeds that are deserving of a VC go unnoticed – that the history of the medal, right up to the present day, is peppered with anomalies, contradictions, prejudice and favouritism – is discomforting. But voicing doubts ought not to be taken as implying any denigration of past VC winners, who after all are usually passive actors in this interesting ritual, individuals plucked from obscurity, as the bar to be considered for a VC has risen, fallen and risen again. But a soldier who risked his life in the Crimea in 1855 is in no different position from one doing precisely the same thing in Afghanistan in 2010. Yet the fact that the VC has become more difficult to win is obviously partly related to the changing nature of combat. The kind of close encounters that once dominated a battle-field are today few and far between, so the opportunities to show the kind of courage that might merit a VC are rarer than previously. On the other hand, Lieutenant General Stannus wanted to do away altogether with honours for military services, as 'the best officers in the Army do not value them, knowing, as they do, that they are not distributed with any regard to fairness'.[43] He may have been correct, but his advice was impractical. Rather than dismantle a flawed system, it ought to be possible to remove the flaws. The expiring Cross could be revived by a fresh revision of the VC warrant – one that reiterated the necessity of outstandingly noble courage in military operations while eliminating the informal 90 per cent risk-of-death requirement; at the same time it could slim down the number of operational gallantry decorations, so reducing the chance of anomalies. For Victoria and Albert, the VC's diffident appearance was itself a defiance of the norm, and helped promote a bigger ostentatiousness; the VC's strength, its incalculable intangible value, is that – unlike other military decorations – it has very wide social recognition. At its simplest the VC was a useful recruit-ment device; at its most complex it represents an ethical response by an eternally grateful British society.[44]

The imminent withering of the Victoria Cross would be a national loss, which could be avoided if more VCs were to be distributed. Colonel H. Jones's VC was controversial because – for all the intense scrutiny behind closed doors – it was tainted with the suspicion of arbitrariness; similar (and different) controversy could be mitigated if the current quota system was dropped and, instead, the type of rationing system suggested by Prince Albert – which was included in the very first VC warrant and remained in the 1961 warrant – was reasserted.[45] Had this elective peer system been invoked, Colonel Jones might still have been chosen by fellow officers; Abols may have been nominated by his comrades; and Illingsworth, Hamilton and many others may have been remembered rather more than they are.

As it is, a collective amnesia appears to have infected Britain's military, which has turned a blind eye to elected VCs. The ballot process was used again in the Second Anglo-Boer War; possibly by the army during the Gallipoli landings in April 1915, when six VCs were awarded, and one formerly gazetted DCM, which went to Sergeant John Grimshaw, was raised to a VC almost two years later;[46] and on three occasions by the Royal Navy, twice in 1917 and once more – the final occasion to date – for a combined naval and marines assault on Zeebrugge on 22–23 April 1918, when casualties were exceptionally heavy (of 1,700 men involved at Zeebrugge, more than 300 were wounded and some 200 killed). The Royal Navy Zeebrugge balloted VCs illustrate how it was done, and could be done again. Captain Gordon Campbell of the HMS *Pargust* conducted a ballot following his ship's clash with a submarine on 7 June 1917. On 15 August 1918 the special committee formed to consider the revision of the VC warrant received a memo from Campbell, prefaced by the statement that 'a representation was made to His Majesty The King that the gallantry of all officers and men was such that it was desirable an officer and man should be selected by ballot of the V.C., under Clause 13 of the statutes'. Campbell wrote:

I read out the reward to the officers and men and gave 24 hours' notice of the ballot. I got an officer from C. in C's Office (Plymouth) to super-intend the ballot. Each officer wrote the name of an officer on a chit and each rating wrote the name of a rating on a chit – personally I took no part in the voting beyond writing down the name of an officer and man, which were only to be used in the event of an even draw (neither were necessary). The ballot officer only gave out the name of the selected ones, so that no one should know how near he might have been. Of course, as Captain of the ship I made it clear I was not to be included in the voting – the position would be impossible, and I did not consider it Their Lordships' intention.[47]

The eight VCs given for Zeebrugge followed two separate ballots, one for the sailors and the other for the marines. In August 1918 the inter-services committee established to draw up what became the 1920 VC warrant considered the balloting process. Frederick Ponsonby asked Admiral Everett, the Naval Secretary, to comment on the awarding of VCs by ballot. Everett may have had misogynist tendencies, but his instincts on the election system were sound. He was keen to ensure that the warrant should specify a secret ballot, as the men might feel duty-bound to vote for the senior officer: 'In fact you know the blue jackets – and probably the Army are the same – will always say "We had better give it to the top bloke." Therefore I think the ballot ought to be a secret ballot.' Colonel Graham, the army representative on the committee, added: 'I think it all comes back to this that if people can see what is going on they can do their best to see that the best men are selected.' The ballot system remained in place. It would be a positive move if all VC recommendations could in future come from the officers and men – and women – themselves, put to the theatre or campaign GOC for approval, and then forwarded, with the GOC's endorsement, to the inter-services VC committee.

In his 2012 review of military medals,[48] Sir John Holmes wrote:

> [The] British system of awarding campaign medals over the last century or so has been characterised by a deliberately parsimonious approach: a British military campaign medal should be something which has been hard-earned, recognising service where life is at risk and conditions are tough... there is a degree of disdain among the military in this country for other countries which have gone down different routes and awarded medals less sparingly.

The military has long trod a finely balanced path between frugality and miserliness when it comes to the most prestigious military medal, the VC. In defending the first, it has occasionally lapsed into the second, as Rudyard Kipling, chief literary spokesman for the empire and defender of the fading myths of chivalry, identified:

> Any rank of the English Army, Navy, Reserve or Volunteer forces, from a duke to a negro, can wear on his left breast the little ugly bronze Maltese cross with the crowned lion atop and the inscription 'For Valour' below... every V.C. of the Great War I have spoken to has been rather careful to explain that he won his Cross because what he did happened to be done when and where some one could notice it. Thousands of men they said did just the same, but in places where there were no observers.[49]

By now it ought to be clear that there is no lasting or stable definition of ultimate military courage nor should we expect to be able to formulate one that will cover all circumstances. The belief that levels of courage can be finely segmented, and that closeted committees can allocate appropriate military decorations accordingly, is reminiscent of Jonathan Swift's fictional island of Laputa, in Gulliver's Travels, where society is preoccupied with abstruse calculations and ignores the fact that its houses are shoddily constructed. We should trust our soldiers, sailors, airmen and women, and let them choose for themselves. Mistakes will be made – they always have been – but at least they will be mistakes for which the troops actually in combat, who face death with courage and distinction, will be responsible.

Current Military Decorations

(source: Ministry of Defence)

A summary of state awards available to the armed forces for gallantry and meritorious service:

Operational gallantry

1 Victoria Cross – Level 1: post-nominal, VC
   For gallantry of the highest order during active operations

2 Distinguished Service Order – Level 2: post-nominal, DSO
   For highly successful command and leadership during active operations

3 Conspicuous Gallantry Cross – Level 2: post-nominal, CGC
   For conspicuous gallantry during active operations
   (The CGC replaced the Distinguished Conduct Medal and the Conspicuous Gallantry Medal in 1993)

4a Distinguished Service Cross – Level 3: post-nominal, DSC
   For exemplary gallantry during active operations at sea

4b Military Cross – Level 3: post-nominal, MC
   For exemplary gallantry during active operations on land

4c Distinguished Flying Cross – Level 3: post-nominal, DFC
   For exemplary gallantry during active operations in the air

5 Mention in Despatches – Level 4: post-nominal, none
   For an act (or acts) of bravery during active operations

Non-operational gallantry

6 George Cross – Level 1: post-nominal, GC
For gallantry of the highest order not in active operations against the enemy

7 George Medal – Level 2: post-nominal, GM
For conspicuous gallantry not in active operations against the enemy

8 Queen's Gallantry Medal – Level 3: post-nominal, QGM
For an act (or acts) of exemplary gallantry not in active operations against the enemy

9 Queen's Commendation for Bravery – Level 4: post-nominal, none
For an act (or acts) of bravery not in active operations against the enemy

10 Air Force Cross – Level 3: post-nominal, AFC
For exemplary gallantry while flying – not in active operations against the enemy

11 Queen's Commendation for Bravery in the Air – Level 4: post-nominal, none
For an act (or acts) of bravery while flying – not in active operations against the enemy

Meritorious service awards

12 Appointment as Commander, Officer or Member of the Order of the British Empire – Level 2/3 (rank-related): post-nominals, CBE/OBE/MBE
For meritorious service in an operational theatre (also awarded for meritorious service outside operational theatres in the Half-yearly Lists)

13 Royal Red Cross – Level 2/3 (rank-related): post-nominals, RRC/ARRC
Available to the Nursing Services only for meritorious service

14 Queen's Volunteer Reserves Medal: no level, post-nominal, QVRM
For meritorious service in the Reserves

15 Queen's Commendation for Valuable Service – Level 4, no post-nominal
For meritorious service in an operational theatre

Select Bibliography

Much of the research derives from the National Archives, henceforth referred to in the notes as 'NA', with the relevant file number following, e.g. NA WO 98/10.

Books

'A Soldier', *The Army, the Horse-Guards and the People*, part of the Knowsley Pamphlet Collection (University of Liverpool, 1860)

Bailey, Roderick, *Forgotten Voices of the Victoria Cross* (Ebury Press, 2010)

Beeton, S. O., *Our Soldiers and the Victoria Cross* (Ward, Lock and Tyler, 1867)

Bennett, Daphne, *King Without a Crown* (Heinemann, 1977)

Bidwell, Shelford, *Modern Warfare* (Allen Lane, 1973)

Binney, Marcus, *The Women Who Lived For Danger* (Hodder & Stoughton, 2002)

Bishop, W. A., *Winged Warfare* (Hodder & Stoughton, 1918)

Brooks, Stephen (ed.), *Montgomery and the Battle of Normandy* (Army Records Society, 2008)

Brownlow, Field Marshal Sir Charles H., *Stray Notes on Military Training and Khaki Warfare* (Women's Printing Society, 1912)

Buzzell, Nora, *The Register of the Victoria Cross* (This England Books, 1981)

Callwell, Colonel Charles Edward, *Small Wars: Their Principles and Practice* (HMSO, 1906)

Crook, M. J., *The Evolution of the Victoria Cross* (Midas Books, 1975)

Eyles-Thomas, Mark, *Sod That For a Game of Soldiers* (Kenton Publishing, 2007)

Fitz-Gibbon, Spencer, *Not Mentioned in Despatches: The History and Mythology of the Battle of Goose Green* (Lutterworth Press, 2001 reprint)

Foot, M. R. D, *SOE in France* (HMSO, 1966)

Geddes, John, *Spearhead Assault* (Century, 2007)

Gilbert, Martin, *Churchill: A Life* (William Heinemann, 1991)

Glanfield, John, *Bravest of the Brave: The Story of the Victoria Cross* (Sutton Publishing, 2005)

Gliddon, Gerald, *VCs of the Somme: A Biographical Portrait* (Gliddon Books, 1991)

Halliday, Hugh A., *Valour Reconsidered* (Robin Brass Studio, Toronto, 2006)

Hamilton, General Sir Ian, *The Soul and Body of an Army* (Edward Arnold, 1921)

Helm, Sarah, *A Life in Secrets: The Story of Vera Atkins* (Abacus, 2010 reprint)

Illustrated Handbook of the Victoria Cross and George Cross (Imperial War Museum, 1970)

Hyde, H. Montgomery and Falkiner Nuttall, G. R., *Air Defence and the Civil Population* (Cresset Press, 1937)

Kavanagh, Thomas Henry, *How I Won the Victoria Cross* (Ward & Lock, 1860)

Laffin, John, *British VCs of World War 2* (Budding Books, 2000)

Mayo, John Horsley, *Medals and Decorations of the British Army and Navy*, vol. ii (Archibald Constable and Co., 1897)

McMoran, C. W. [Lord Moran], *The Anatomy of Courage* (Constable & Robinson, 2007 edition)

Miller, William Ian, *The Mystery of Courage* (Harvard University Press, 2000)

Noakes, Lucy, *Women in the British Army: War and the Gentle Sex, 1907–1948* (Routledge, 2006)

Percival, John, *For Valour* (Methuen, 1985)

Pollard, Captain A. O., *Fire-Eater: The Memoirs of a V.C.* (reprinted by Naval & Military Press, 2005)

Ponsonby, Sir Frederick, *Recollections of Three Reigns* (Eyre & Spottiswoode, 1951)

Reid, Douglas Arthur, *Memories of the Crimean War* (St Catherine Press, 1911)

Rhodes James, Robert, *A Spirit Undaunted* (Little, Brown & Co., 1998)

Smith, Melvin Charles, *Awarded for Valour: A History of the Victoria Cross and the Evolution of British Heroism* (Palgrave Macmillan, 2008)

Smith-Dorrien, General H., *Memories of Forty-Eight Years' Service* (Leonaur edn, 2009)

Smyth, Brigadier Sir John, *The Story of the Victoria Cross* (Frederick Muller, 1963)

Stannus, Lieutenant General H. J., *Curiosities of the Victoria Cross* (William Ridgway, 1881)

Stannus, Lieutenant General H. J., *My Reasons for Leaving the British Army* (William Ridgway, 1881)

Strachan, Hew, *The Politics of the British Army* (Oxford University Press, 1997)

Toomey, T. E., *Victoria Cross and How Won, 1854–1889* (Alfred Boot and Son, 1889)

Turner, E. S., *Dear Old Blighty* (Michael Joseph, 1980)

Walton, Douglas N., *Courage: A Philosophical Investigation* (University of California Press, 1986)

Ward, Irene, *F.A.N.Y. Invicta* (Hutchinson, 1955)

Watson, Janet S. K., *Fighting Different Wars* (Cambridge University Press, 2004)

Wessels, André (ed.), *Lord Roberts and the War in South Africa, 1899–1902* (Army Records Society, 2000)

Articles

[no author], 'Precedency of His Royal Highness Prince Albert, King-Consort, de jure, of Great Britain and Ireland' (John Mortimer, 1840)

'Old Soldier', 'The War Medal: An Address to the British Nation' (London, 1849)

Arnstein, Walter L., 'The Warrior Queen: Reflections on Victoria and Her World', *Albion: A Quarterly Journal Concerned with British Studies*, vol. 30, no. 1 (spring 1998), pp. 1–28

Bashow, Lieutenant Colonel David, 'The Incomparable Billy Bishop: The Man and the Myths', *Canadian Military Journal*, autumn 2002, pp. 55–60

Cannon, John, 'The Survival of the British Monarchy', Prothero Lecture, *Transactions of the Royal Historical Society*, 5th series, vol. 36 (1986), pp. 143–64

Clarke, Major R., 'Medals, Decorations and Anomalies', *British Army Review*, August 1969

Gooch, Brison D., 'Recent Literature on Queen Victoria's Little Wars', *Victorian Studies*, vol. 17, no. 2 (December 1973), pp. 217–24

Greenhous, Brereton, 'Billy Bishop: Brave Flyer, Bold Liar', *Canadian Military Journal*, autumn 2002, pp. 61–4

Hamilton, C. I., 'Naval Hagiography and the Victorian Hero', *Historical Journal*, vol. 23, no. 2 (June 1980), pp. 381–98

Hichberger, Joany, 'Democratising Glory? The Victoria Cross Paintings of Louis Desanges', *Oxford Art Journal*, vol. 7, no. 2 (1984), pp. 42–51

Jackson, Michael W., 'Justice and Heroism', *Polity*, vol. 16, no. 2 (winter 1983), pp. 201–13

Jones, Edgar, 'The Psychology of Killing: The Combat Experiences of British Soldiers during the First World War', *Journal of Contemporary History*, vol. 41, no. 2 (April 2006), pp. 229–46

King, Anthony, 'Women in Combat', *RUSI Journal*, vol. 158, no. 1 (February/March 2013), pp. 4–11

Lalumia, Matthew, 'Realism and Anti-Aristocratic Sentiment in Victorian Depictions of the Crimean War', *Victorian Studies*, vol. 27, no. 1 (autumn 1983), pp. 25–51

Lieven, Michael, 'Heroism, Heroics and the Making of Heroes: The Anglo-Zulu War of 1879', *Albion: A Quarterly Journal Concerned with British Studies*, vol. 30, no. 3 (autumn 1998), pp. 419–38

Markesinis, B. S., 'The Royal Prerogative Re-Visited', *Cambridge Law Journal*, vol. 32, no. 2 (November 1973), pp. 287–309

Markovits, Stefanie, 'Rushing into Print: "Participatory Journalism" during the Crimean War', *Victorian Studies*, vol. 50, no. 4 (summer 2008), pp. 559–86

Rachman, Stanley J., 'Fear and Courage: A Psychological Perspective', *Social Research*, vol. 71, no. 1 (spring 2004), pp. 149–76

Sweetman, John, '"Ad Hoc" Support Services during the Crimean War, 1854–6: Temporary, Ill-Planned and Largely Unsuccessful', *Military Affairs*, vol. 52, no. 3 (June 1988), pp. 135–40

Notes

Preface

1. *Curiosities of the Victoria Cross* (William Ridgway, 1881), p. 34.
2. The *New York Times Saturday Review of Books* calculated in its edition of 7 January 1909 that 'in the intervening half century [since the establishment of the VC] something like 55,000 books of fiction have been published in the United Kingdom and colonies, and in 8 percent of these the hero, or some other chap, is the envied possessor of the VC'.
3. This arcane dispute seems to have been cleared up by an absorbing account from what is likely to be a definitive source, the curator of the Royal Artillery Museum (see www.westernfrontassociation.com/video/1252-wfa-agm-2010-presentations.html). Hancocks, the London jeweller given the job of making the first VCs (a task it still has today), has no record of where the original metal came from. The first few hundred VCs were thus probably made from metal held in stock. When in 1914 that ran out, the War Office called for the Royal Arsenal to choose some old guns as a metal source. The Arsenal selected two Chinese cannon, from which the cascabels (each weighing about sixty-four kilograms) were cut. These cannons, on display at the Royal Arsenal in Woolwich, have plenty of metal left. In 2005 John Glanfield estimated that 360 pounds of metal 'from all sources' had been used to manufacture the 1,352 VCs, three bars, and replacement or duplicate VCs that had been made up to that date. See Glanfield, *Bravest of the Brave: The Story of the Victoria Cross* (Sutton Publishing, 2005), p. 35. Two

books stand against the 'blood-and-guts' tide that passes for history vis-à-vis the VC: M. J. Crook, *The Evolution of the Victoria Cross* (Midas Books, 1975) and Melvin Charles Smith, *Awarded for Valour* (Palgrave Macmillan, 2008).

4. In January 1922 the London and North Western Railway decided that three of their Claughton locomotives were to carry nameplates dedicated to the three employees who had won the VC: Lance Corporal J. A. Christie, Private E. Sykes and Private W. Wood. Edward VII wanted a bunker in the shape of the VC to be constructed for the golf course in the private park at Windsor; the VC even had a cameo role in Walt Disney's 1967 version of *The Jungle Book*.

5. The idea of a Military Covenant feels as though it should be positively ancient but it was only invented in 2000. Nevertheless there is a new spirit abroad regarding the relationship between society and soldiery, in which the military is held today in higher regard than for many years – partly because there is a general sense that the wars in Iraq and Afghanistan were disastrous mistakes, started by politicians and handled badly by politicians. As distrust of conventional politics has slumped, respect for and trust of the military has risen. See Sarah Ingham, *The Military Covenant – Its Impact on Civil–Military Relations in Britain*, (Ashgate, 2014).

CHAPTER 1 The Price of Courage

1. William I. Miller, *The Mystery of Courage* (Harvard University Press, 2000).
2. Max Hastings, *The Spectator*, 16 April 2005.
3. Although it might have been a scarf, hand-crocheted by Queen Victoria during the Second Boer War. Nine inches wide by five feet long, these khaki-coloured scarves had the royal cipher VRI, *Victoria Regina Et Imperatrix*, woven into them. Only eight are thought to have been finished and they became highly prized The recipients had to be selected by a vote of the NCOs and men of each unit, and approved by Lord Roberts, commander-in-chief, who stipulated that 'gallant conduct in the field was to be considered the primary qualification'.

Four scarves awarded to British army regular soldiers went to men of the 2nd Brigade, 1st Division: Sergeant Henry George Clay, DCM, 2nd Battalion, the East Surrey Regiment; Sergeant William Colclough, 2nd Battalion, the Devonshire Regiment; Sergeant Thomas Ferrett, DCM, 2nd Battalion, the Queen's (Royal West Surrey) Regiment; and Sergeant Frank Kingsley, DCM, 2nd Battalion, the West Yorkshire Regiment. In 1902 the New Zealand government requested that the title 'Queen's Scarf' be used in the Army List and other official documents, but this was refused by London. The question of precedence cropped up again in 1956, when a descendant of one of the holders of a scarf requested permission to attend the VC centenary celebrations. The official reply laid to rest the 'VC competitor' myth: 'While the Queen's Scarf is regarded as a unique and most distinguished award, relatives of those who received it are not being included in the present ceremony as it does not carry equal status with the Victoria Cross.'

4. Miller, op. cit., p. 12.

5. Posthumous awards for all levels of military decoration were not introduced until 1977.

6. They do things differently elsewhere. On 18 March 2014, following an initiative from Congress, President Barack Obama awarded retrospective Medals of Honor to twenty-four US Army veterans who had fought in the Second World War, the Korean War and the Vietnam War, and who had been denied the award on the basis of their ethnicity. On the other hand, skin colour or religion has never been used to deny the VC; at least, not explicitly.

7. Colonel H. C. B. Cook, 'British Battle Honours', *Journal of the Society for Army Historical Research*, vol. 57, no. 231, autumn 1979, pp. 154–66. Battle honours have long been distributed without any apparent methodology. According to Cook, 'the whole system of awarding these much prized distinctions has been rather haphazard and sometimes quite illogical... Deserving cases may go unrecognized while others receive acknowledgement they have not really merited.'

8. The inquiry, *Unresolved Recognition for Past Acts of Naval and Military Gallantry and Valour*, received 166 submissions put forward by the Australian

government relating to the thirteen names, and another 174 nominating an additional 140 individuals and groups.

9. A copy of the report can be found here: http://defence-honours-tribunal. gov.au/inquiries/completed-inquiries/valour.

10. Spencer Fitz-Gibbon, *Not Mentioned in Despatches: The History and Mythology of the Battle of Goose Green* (Lutterworth Press, 2001), p. 130.

11. S. O. Beeton, *Our Soldiers and the Victoria Cross* (Ward, Lock and Tyler, 1867), pp. iii–iv. Samuel Beeton was the husband of the more famous Isabella, the author of domestic handbooks.

12. Macdonald Hastings, *Men of Glory* (Hulton Press, 1959). Worth a glance, not least for the no doubt inadvertent humour of passages such as this, from chapter 2, 'The VC I Went To School With', which features Captain H. M. Ervine Andrews, who won his VC at Dunkirk: 'The reason that I know the story is because I was at the same school, too. "Bummy" Andrews, as we used to call him, and I were in the same class at Stonyhurst together. I suppose we called him "Bummy" because he was well built around the middle. But we might easily have called him "Carrots" because he had a thick thatch of curly red hair.'

13. Beeton, op. cit., pp. 7–8.

14. John Keegan, *Daily Telegraph*, 13 February 2002.

15. The requirement that a person recommended for the VC should have barely escaped with their life has spread to those Commonwealth countries that now give their own version of the VC. The New Zealand military press kit accompanying the announcement of the VC awarded to Corporal Bill (Willy) Apiata of the NZ Special Air Service in July 2007 stated: 'Nominations which do not involve risk to the nominee's life are not usually successful.'

16. NA WO 98/10.

17. One British soldier managed to win both the VC *and* an Iron Cross – the only person to have this peculiar distinction. William George Nicholas Manley, an assistant surgeon in the Royal Artillery, gained the VC on 29 April 1864 for risking his life in an attempt to save a Royal Navy commander, during the Maori Wars in New Zealand. In the Franco-Prussian War of 1870 he was awarded an Iron Cross, 2nd class, for

tending to Prussian soldiers when he was part of the British Ambulance Corps.

18. As recently as the 1960s, VCs could be bought for considerably less than £1,000. By the 1970s the benchmark price had more than doubled. See *Journal of the Victoria Cross Society*, March 2004, pp. 23–4.

19. The annuity is increased each year in line with other pension increases and in 2014 was £2,129.

20. When Gunner James Collis, sixty-two, died a pauper on 28 June 1918, his sister appealed to George V to restore his name, and the king granted her wish. George V supposedly decreed, as expressed in a letter from Lord Stamfordham, his private secretary, that: 'The King feels so strongly that, no matter the crime committed by anyone on whom the VC has been conferred, the decoration should not be forfeited. Even were a VC to be sentenced to be hanged for murder, he should be allowed to wear the VC on the scaffold.' The source of this is M. J. Crook's book, *The Evolution of the Victoria Cross* (p. 64). Crook cites a 1956 issue of *Soldier* magazine as his source, which in turn cited the VC Register. But the original is missing. The last example of a VC recipient being forced out of the VC Register was that of Private George Ravenhill of the Royal Scots Fusiliers. He won his medal at the Battle of Colenso on 15 December 1899. In 1908 he was found guilty of stealing some iron and could not afford to pay the ten shillings fine. He died in poverty at the age of forty-nine.

21. The record price for an individual VC is believed to be £1.5 million paid to St Peter's College, Oxford, in a private sale in November 2009, for the VC and bar – one of only three – of Captain Noel Chavasse, a medic who died of wounds on 4 August 1917. This Cross and bar is in the Ashcroft Gallery at the Imperial War Museum.

22. Shout was the most highly decorated soldier to serve with the Australian Imperial Force (AIF) at Gallipoli, gaining a Military Cross and promoted to captain after leading a bayonet charge against Turkish machine guns on 8 April 1915. During a subsequent charge against Turkish lines at Lone Pine he was fatally wounded. His VC and other medals were sold by his grandson.

23. The *Daily Telegraph* of 1 May 2004 reported that Jackson's surviving family planned to give his VC and other medals to the RAF Museum at Hendon but were prevented from doing so by the terms of the will of Jackson's wife, Alma. The report quoted Jackson's son David as saying: 'The whole thing is shameful and should never have happened. We intended to give them to the museum but our solicitor's advice was we could not do this.'

24. Michael Ashcroft, *Victoria Cross Heroes* (Headline Review, 2006), p. 26. According to the gallery's website, Ashcroft's collection numbers more than 160 VCs, which puts the total estimated value at 'some £30 million'. Ashcroft – 'an international businessman and a philanthropist', according to the website – has *loaned*, not donated, the collection, which remains in the hands of a trust, the ultimate beneficiaries of which remain, by definition, a closely guarded secret.

25. Byrne's VC was stolen in South Africa when the Anglo-Boer broke out in 1899; it has never been traced. Byrne died in 1944.

26. Quoted in the *Journal of the Victoria Cross Society*, October 2003, p. 51.

27. A company called H. L. I. Lordship Industries produced the Medal of Honor. In 1996 the company pleaded guilty to illegally manufacturing and selling at least 300 Medals of Honor between 1991 and 1994.

28. *The Times*, Saturday, 30 March 1895.

29. A much repeated myth is that Rorke's Drift saw the highest number of VCs won on a single day or for a single action. At the Battle of Inkerman on 5 November 1854, sixteen were awarded; for the Second Relief of Lucknow, 14–22 November 1857, during the Indian Mutiny, twenty-eight VCs were awarded.

30. NA: DEFE 13/789.

31. On restriction of use of the George Cross, see www.justiceservices.gov. mt/DownloadDocument.aspx?app=lom&itemid=8651.

32. *Hansard*, 4 March 1993.

33. More than 115,000 Military Medals and over 37,000 Military Crosses were awarded during the First World War.

34. The Conspicuous Gallantry Cross replaced the Distinguished Conduct Medal (Army) and the Conspicuous Gallantry Medal (Air Force and

Navy), which had been the second-level award to other ranks and ratings. It also substituted for the Distinguished Service Order, which hitherto had been awarded solely to officers for gallantry. The DSO was retained as an award for 'outstanding leadership'. The CGC is awarded 'in recognition of an act or acts of conspicuous gallantry during active operations against the enemy', and all ranks of the army, air force, navy and marines are eligible. In 2012, during Operation 'Herrick', Sergeant Deacon Cutterham of The Rifles was on patrol with his unit when a grenade, thrown at them over a high wall by Taliban forces, landed in a ditch full of water. He threw it back over the wall moments before it exploded. In the nineteenth century, Cutterham could justifiably have expected a VC.

35. Major R. Clark, 'Medals, Decorations and Anomalies', *British Army Review*, August 1969.

36. Miller, op. cit., p. 9.

37. Frank Richards, *Old Soldiers Never Die* (Faber & Faber, 1933), p. 323.

38. Sylvester's VC is held by the Army Medical Services Museum at Mytchett, Surrey.

39. Rescuing a comrade seems to be the current standard set for winning an MC. Private Alex Robert Kennedy of the Mercian Regiment was gazetted on 19 March 2010 with the MC for running to the rescue of his injured platoon commander while under intense and close-range fire from Taliban insurgents in Helmand province in June 2009.

40. www.thisiscornwall.co.uk/news/HERO-KATE-MC/article-1558296-detail/article.html.

41. That same day, Lance Corporal Colin Spooner, of the 2nd Battalion, the Princess of Wales's Royal Regiment, also received the MC at the hands of Prince Charles. Spooner's contingent had been engaged in a gun battle with Taliban fighters in October 2008, during which the fighting was so intensely noisy that it became impossible to hear orders being communicated over the radio. Spooner took it upon himself to dash to and fro between various members of his unit, carrying instructions until eventually he was hit by a shell, thirty-two pieces of which lodged in his body. But he continued to issue orders

and refused to be carried off on a stretcher because, he said: 'It would have taken four blokes to carry me out but I knew we were still engaged so I walked. That's what did most of the damage, but I'd do the same again.'

42. *Daily Telegraph*, Saturday, 6 November 2010.
43. Crook, *The Evolution of the Victoria Cross*, op. cit., pp. 100–101.
44. *Bury & Norwich Post*, Wednesday 13 February 1856.

CHAPTER 2 A Most Grand, Gratifying Day

1. Quoted in Norman Dixon, *On the Psychology of Military Incompetence*, (Pimlico, 1994), p. 325.
2. *Lloyd's Weekly*, 1 March 1857.
3. *The Times*, 29 June 1857, p. 12.
4. Victoria's journal entry, 26 June 1857, Royal Archive, Windsor Castle.
5. *The Times*, 27 June 1857, p. 9.
6. *Illustrated London News*, 4 July 1857. In the entry for her journal for this day Victoria mistakenly put the number at forty-seven, not sixty-two.
7. The whereabouts of Lucas's original VC is a mystery. He left his medals, including his Victoria Cross, on a train and they were never recovered. His duplicate medals are on display at the National Maritime Museum in Greenwich, London.
8. Stanlack was evidently brave – he also gained the DCM – but a bit of a black sheep. He was later jailed for being drunk on duty, and later still for assault, and compulsorily discharged in 1863. His VC is in the hands of the Coldstream Guards in the Wellington Barracks, London.
9. The actual medal was legally the property of the recipient and so could not be forfeited.
10. Eight men suffered this humiliation. Midshipman Edward St John Daniel, a Crimean VC, rose to the rank of lieutenant, but in September 1861 was convicted of desertion and evading court martial. Sergeant James McGuire of the 1st Bengal European Fusiliers won his VC during the Indian Mutiny and forfeited it in 1862, after being convicted of stealing a cow. Private Valentine Bambrick was in the 60th Rifles when he

won his VC during the Indian Mutiny. After his discharge in 1863 he was accused of stealing another man's medals, found guilty and sentenced to a prison term. Deeply depressed and protesting his innocence, Bambrick hanged himself in Pentonville prison on 1 April 1864. Private Michael Murphy, of the 2nd Battalion Military Train, gained his VC during the Indian Mutiny; he forfeited it as a result of being found guilty of theft and was sentenced to nine months hard labour. Private Thomas Lane of the 67th Regiment won his VC at the Taku Forts, China, on 21 August 1860; he was convicted of theft in 1881. Private Frederick Corbett of the King's Own Rifle Corps was awarded his VC on 5 August 1882 for tending an officer during the Anglo-Egyptian War, but a conviction for embezzlement in July 1884 saw him stripped of his VC status. Gunner James Collis of the Royal Horse Artillery gained his VC during the Second Anglo-Afghan War, but was convicted of bigamy in 1895. Private George Ravenhill of the 1st Battalion Royal Scots Fusiliers gained his VC during the Second Boer War. He was convicted of theft in 1908, could not afford the fine and was sent to prison. He lost his VC pension, died in poverty aged forty-nine and is buried in an unmarked grave at Witton cemetery in Birmingham.

11. Crook, op. cit., p. 69.

12. NA WO 32/7300, letter dated April 1856.

13. Queen Victoria in A. C. Benson and Viscount Esher (eds), *The Letters of Queen Victoria* (John Murray, 1907), vol. iii, p. 72.

14. Theodore Martin, *Life of the Prince Consort*, (Smith, Elder, & Co, 1879), chapter lxiii.

15. NA E9/29: Private William McGuire of the 33rd Regiment of Foot. Taken prisoner by two Russian soldiers, he took advantage of their inattention and seized one of their rifles, shooting one and beating the other to death. He then donned a Russian uniform and made his way back to his own line. The French awarded him a Médaille Militaire, but Victoria judiciously thought the action undeserving of a VC because it might lead to the putting to death of all prisoners.

16. Up to 1871 all officers of the British army up to and including the rank of colonel usually held their rank by purchase. If an officer was

deemed to have disgraced the service, he could be cashiered – i.e. stripped of his commission without being reimbursed for the money he had paid for it. The 7th Earl of Cardigan, James Brudenell, who led the charge of the Light Brigade at the Crimea, paid more than £30,000 for his commission. A recording of a British trumpeter who sounded the charge at Balaclava can be heard here: http://archive.org/details/EDIS-SWDPC-01-04

17. *The Army, the Horse-Guards and the People*: 'A Soldier': published by the University of Liverpool, part of the Knowsley Pamphlet Collection (1860), p. 29.

18. www.london-gazette.co.uk/issues/21909/pages/2699

19. Sir Frederick Ponsonby, *Recollections of Three Reigns* (Eyre & Spottiswoode, 1951), p. 178.

20. Both the DCM and the CGM were cancelled in 1993, replaced by the Conspicuous Gallantry Cross, which can be awarded for all ranks across all services. Since 1993 the Distinguished Service Order (DSO) has been restricted solely to distinguished service, i.e. leadership and command by any rank, although in the recent conflict in Afghanistan only commissioned officers have been granted a DSO – which shows how enduring is the long-standing convention that 'orders' are for officers and 'medals' for other ranks. According to the Ministry of Defence: 'Although theoretically available to all ranks, the DSO, now awarded for distinguished leadership during active operations against the enemy, is likely to be awarded only to the more senior officer ranks.' (www.mod.uk/DefenceInternet/DefenceFor/Veterans/Medals/DistinguishedServiceOrder.htm)

21. If a man were promoted and became an officer, he would lose the £10 annuity. The fact that the VC annuity was £10 a year less than that of the DCM was a little odd; the Treasury, however, was always keen to limit expenditure.

22. *Hansard*, 23 January 1855, vol. 136, cc 899–910.

23. Royal Archives, Windsor Castle, 20 January 1855; Vic/Main/B/16/45.

24. Manuscripts and Special Collections, University of Nottingham; NeC9, 701/2 and 701/3. This memo also includes some acerbic comments on

the Légion d'Honneur: 'I would advise no reference to the Legion of Honour, the distribution of which is entirely arbitrary and guided by no principles, which is given indiscriminately to Soldiers and Civilians, and has long been made a tool for corruption in the hands of the French Govt the Number of whose members extends to 40,000 & which has almost become a necessary appendage to the French dress.'

25. *Hansard*, 29 January 1855, vol. 136, cc 1064–5.

26. *Liverpool Mercury*, Friday, 8 February 1856.

27. According to Daphne Bennett (*King Without a Crown*, Heinemann, 1977, p. 259), Albert's 'first sketch of the cross itself was made while commuting in an unheated train between Windsor and London during the freezing winter of 1854–5'. She gives no source for her claim, however.

28. Royal Archives, E6 69–71, December 1855.

29. Another document in the Royal Archives [EG 70] confirms Albert's influence. This is a letter dated 30 December 1855 – shortly after the revisions were made – from Lord Panmure to Prince Albert, in which he writes: 'Her Majesty & Your Royal Highness have greatly improved this reward for military subjects by changing its character from an "order" to a "decoration".'

30. Royal Archives, E6 71.

31. Royal Archives, G 44–30.

32. The warrant was of course later altered such that putting out a fire in a powder magazine, if not 'at home' then certainly far away from the enemy, did qualify for the VC.

33. *The Times*, 26 February 1857, p. 8.

34. The media have always lavished attention on 'heroes' yet the ordinary soldier is always shabbily treated when out of the spotlight. John Geddes (*Spearhead Assault*, Century, 2007, p. 31), a paratrooper corporal in the Falklands in 1982, wrote of his family's last night together in barracks before he headed off, 'in a damp, cold dump of a flat with no mushrooms in the fridge but plenty on the wall next to the peeling wallpaper... some of the 2 Para heroes who were destined to die on the Falklands spent the last night they would ever have with their loved

ones in these communal shitholes, with draughty crumbling window frames, disintegrating plaster on the walls, leaking plumbing and toilets that didn't work properly. What a disgrace.'

35. A.V. Dicey, An Introduction to the Study of the Law of the Constitution (10th edn, 1967), p. 424.

36. Victoria's role in government generally was much more than merely symbolic. In her final days, when she was too ill to work, Arthur Balfour, the prime minister at the time, was 'astounded' at the number of boxes that had quickly piled up containing business that required the sovereign's attention: 'Judges, for instance, could not function without a warrant signed by her: all sorts of appointments could not be made without her sanction' (Ponsonby, op. cit., p. 82).

37. The 62nd suffered 50 per cent casualties among its officers and non-commissioned officers.

38. NA WO 98/2.

39. Michael Hargreave Mawson (ed.), Eyewitness in the Crimea (Greenhill Books, 2001), p. 165.

40. For her services, the Queen 'decorated' Nightingale with a medallion of white enamel with diamonds, on which was the St George's Cross and the Royal Cypher and the words 'blessed are the merciful' and 'Crimea'.

41. http://hansard.millbanksystems.com/lords/1854/jun/19/the-war-with-russia-the-german-powers.

42. Elizabeth Longford, Victoria R. I. (Orion, 1998 edn), p. 241.

43. Benson and Viscount Esher (eds), op. cit., p. 15.

44. General Sir Ian Hamilton, The Soul and Body of an Army (Edward Arnold, 1921), pp. 86–8.

45. Mawson, op. cit., p. 57.

46. Ibid., p. 71.

47. The Times, 25 January 1855, p. 6.

48. Colonel Alex M. Tulloch, The Crimean Commission and the Chelsea Board (London, 1857). The French army initially coped much better with the local conditions. Nevertheless, out of a total of more than 300,000 French troops in the Crimea, around 200,000 required medical treatment at some point; only a quarter of those were wounded in action.

49. Their report heavily censured Lord Lucan (who had been in command of a regiment); Lord Cardigan, Inspector of Cavalry; Sir Richard Airey, Quartermaster-General; and Colonel Gordon, Deputy Quartermaster-General. Tulloch and McNeill were offered by the government £1,000 each for their work, which they declined on principle – it was a different era. They spent fifty-five days on their investigation and examined 200 witnesses in the Crimea, each of whom was given a copy of what would be included in the report and asked to sign it.

50. *The Times*, 29 December 1854, p. 5.

51. Mawson, op. cit., p. 88. Raglan died from disease in the Crimea. Queen Victoria insisted that Raglan's widow be voted by Parliament a pension of £1,000 a year, with a further £2,000 a year for his eldest son and successor in the title.

52. *Lloyd's Weekly Newspaper*, 11 February 1855, p. 7.

53. Orlando Figes, *Crimea: The Last Crusade* (Allen Lane, 2010), p. 147.

54. *Punch*, 14 April 1855.

55. Trevor Royle, *The Great Crimean War, 1854–1856* (Macmillan, 2004), p. 179.

56. Figes, op. cit., p. 468.

57. 'As one of those who went out to the Crimea in the first winter, when things were at their worst, when the Army was rotting away through the mismanagement of the war by the authorities at home, I can say from my own personal observation and knowledge that it was the letters of the *Times* correspondent and others, but chiefly the *Times*, that brought about a change for the better.' Douglas Reid, *Memories of The Crimean War* (St Catharine Press, 1911), p. 152.

58. *Aberdeen Journal*, 11 March 1857.

59. 'Every officer, for the discharge of his duty, holds a Royal Sign Manual [i.e. a document signed by the reigning monarch] commission under the counter-sign of a Secretary of State.' Charles M. Clode, *The Military Forces of the Crown: Their Administration and Government* (London, 1869), vol. ii, p. 65.

60. Before the Crimean War the *Morning Advertiser* accused Albert of treason and, absurdly enough, called for his execution. Victoria threatened to abdicate and was only slightly mollified by government ministers

promising to admonish leading editors, who (naturally) refused to change their ways.

61. Reid, op. cit. On this occasion *Punch* was pithier. It published a cartoon on 24 March 1885, depicting Raglan snoozing in his hut, through the window of which can be seen soldiers and horses dying in the snow. The caption was: 'The General Fast (Asleep). Humiliating – Very.'

62. Sir George Douglas and Sir George Dalhousie Ramsay (eds), *The Panmure Papers*, (Hodder and Stoughton, 1908),vol. i, p. 253.

63. The MGSM owed its existence to Charles Gordon-Lennox, 5th Duke of Richmond, who fought in the Peninsular Wars and promoted the idea of a campaign medal in Parliament. The Army (or Peninsular) Gold Medal was distributed only to officers who had been in command of a battalion or of higher rank. This latter medal came in three styles: a large and a small medal, and the third a pattée-style cross – precisely the same style later adopted for the VC. When the military Order of the Bath was created, the Army Gold Medal was discontinued.

64. After the Battle of Dunbar on 3 September 1650, when an army led by Oliver Cromwell defeated Scottish royalist forces under General David Leslie, the House of Commons granted medals to all those who fought. Officers got small gold medals, ordinary troopers a slightly bigger silver medal. Generals occasionally distributed their own medals. After the Battle of the Nile (1 August 1798), Alexander Davidson, Nelson's prize agent, organized at his own expense the creation and distribution of medals for all those who had fought but been given nothing – gold medals for senior officers, silver for more junior, bronze-gilt for petty officers, and bronze for ordinary seamen and marines.

65. Christopher Hibbert, *George IV: Regent and King, 1811–1830* (Prentice Hall Press, 1972), p. 310.

66. *The Times*, 7 February 1856, p. 6.

67. Figes, op. cit., p. 352.

68. In the Crimean War, Hugh Drummond of the Scots Guards wrote to his mother that he had for her a large silver cross: 'it came off a Russian Colonel's neck we killed, and, poor fellow, it was next to his skin'; *Letters from the Crimea* (London, 1855), p. 50. Stealing from the slain is

always with us. John Geddes, a British paratrooper who fought in the 1982 Falklands War, mentions a 'battlefield raven from our own ranks picking over the corpses of the Argy dead'; he used secateurs to snip off fingers to steal gold rings (*Spearhead Assault*, p. 247). After Waterloo everything was stripped from the thousands of corpses littering the field, including dentures which for many years afterwards were known as 'Waterloo teeth'.

69. The Cruisers and Convoys Act of 1708 formalized the practice of looting captured enemy naval vessels by decreeing a structured distribution of prize money, a practice that lasted until 1918.

70. Calculated via the website http://www.measuringworth.com/ppoweruk/

71. *The Battle of Waterloo*, printed for John Booth (bookseller) and T. Egerton (Military Library, Whitehall, 1817), p. 163, no author.

72. Waterloo Medals are surprisingly cheap compared to VCs. The latest to be auctioned, in March 2013, went for a mere £7,500 (www.bbc.co.uk/news/uk-england-suffolk-21878827).

73. Hew Strachan, *The Politics of the British Army* (Oxford University Press, 1997), p. 27.

74. Theodore Martin, *The Life of His Royal Highness the Prince Consort* (London, 1875–6), vol. ii, p. 262.

75. Clode, op. cit., vol. i, p. 97. Hardinge was speaking in Parliament in 1834.

76. Clode, op. cit., vol. ii, p. 36.

77. Sidney Lee, *Queen Victoria* (Smith, Elder & Co., rev. edn, 1904), p. 17.

78. Douglas and Ramsay (eds), *The Panmure Papers*, op. cit., p. 200.

79. *The Times*, 27 June 1857.

80. *Hull Packet and East Riding Times*, Friday, 3 July 1857.

81. *New York Times*, 7 March 1856.

82. *Reynolds's Newspaper*, Sunday, 10 February 1856. The Simpson was General Sir James; the Dundas was Admiral Sir James.

83. *Tinsley's Magazine*, 3 August 1879.

84. *Cheshire Observer*, 23 May 1857.

85. The paintings were a popular hit but a commercial flop. In 1900 they were presented to Wantage Town Council by Brigadier General Robert Loyd-Lindsay, who won his own VC at the Battle of the Alma. Lord

Wantage, as he became, a seminal person in the establishment of the British Red Cross, paid around £1,000 for forty-six of the collection of fifty-six paintings; some had already been sold. The collection was then open to the public until 1941 in the community room of the Wantage Corn Exchange. The Ministry of Food requisitioned the hall in 1941 and the paintings were put into storage. In 1951 they were rediscovered and some were found to be in very poor condition. Those that survived were then dispersed among many regimental museums.

86. Michael De-la-Noy, *The Honours System* (Allison & Busby, 1986), p. 78.

87. Sir O'Moore Creagh and E. M. Humphris (eds), *The Victoria Cross, 1856–1920* (J. B. Hayward & Son, Polstead, Suffolk, 1985), p. 20.

88. *The Times*, 6 March 1857, p. 3.

89. Victoria laid the foundation stone of the Royal Victoria Hospital on 19 May 1856, beneath which was laid the first Victoria Cross, now in the hands of the Army Services Museum at Aldershot. Victoria arrived at the hospital by the royal yacht. Artillery fired a royal salute; unfortunately one gun fired prematurely, killing two soldiers and injuring several others.

90. James Lees-Milne, *The Enigmatic Edward* (Sidgwick and Jackson, 1986), pp. 116–17; from Reginald Brett's journal, 16 May 1898.

91. Senior officers were now naturally eligible for the Order of the Bath as well as the VC. Commissioned officers pressed for their own, officers-only, medal, which led to the introduction of the Distinguished Service Order (DSO) in 1886. The word 'order' was seen as elevating this award, as it echoed the 'order' in Order of the Bath.

CHAPTER 3   Small Wars

1. Lieutenant General H. J. Stannus, *Curiosities of the Victoria Cross* (William Ridgway, 1881).

2. Quoted in C. I. Hamilton, 'Naval Hagiography and the Victorian Hero', *Historical Journal*, vol. 23, no. 2, June 1980, pp. 381–98.

3. Colonel Charles Edward Callwell, *Small Wars: The Principles and Practice* (HMSO, 1906), p. 21.

4. From 1858 to 1881 the VC could also be won for acts of bravery not in the presence of the enemy. Despite the creation of the Albert Medal on 7 March 1866, awarded for the saving of life, six such VCs were granted: Private Timothy O'Hea, Rifle Brigade, for suppressing a fire in a railway truck containing ammunition in Quebec on 19 June 1866; and Assistant-Surgeon Campbell Millis Douglas, Private Thomas Murphy, Private James Cooper, Private David Bell and Private William Griffiths, all of the 2nd Battalion, 24th Regiment, for saving the lives of comrades in a storm at sea at the Andaman Islands on 7 May 1867. It was also the period when both the youngest and the oldest VC winners were gazetted: Thomas Flinn was believed to be fifteen when he received his VC as a drummer boy with the 64th Regiment during the Indian Mutiny of 1857; William Raynor was sixty-two when, as a lieutenant with the Bengal army during the Indian Mutiny, he gained the VC for being one of nine who defended the arsenal during the siege of Delhi. Two others survived – John Buckley and George Forrest – and they too gained the VC.

5. http://hansard.millbanksystems.com/lords/1859/feb/03/the-queens-speech.

6. Walter L. Arnstein, 'The Warrior Queen', Albion, vol. xxx, no. 1 (spring 1998), pp. 1–28.

7. NA WO/32/7317.

8. The Times, 8 January 1859, p. 12.

9. In a letter to the Daily News published on 22 November 1858, 'One of the Defenders of Lucknow' crossly wrote: 'The Victoria Cross has not been awarded to any member of the Lucknow garrison because it is said that their numbers were large, and that they all behaved equally nobly. But how is that a reason why they should remain unrewarded and undistinguished?'

10. During the Mutiny, Outram led a volunteer force of cavalry, which voted to recommend him for the Victoria Cross, but he declined on the basis that he did not deserve it more than they did.

11. The Times, 11 July 1859.

12. He was right. His VC helped Wood's own career and he ultimately held

the highest rank in the British army, that of field marshal, from which position he wielded considerable power over the careers of future senior officers, such as Sir Douglas Haig.

13. NA WO 32/7307.

14. NA WO 98/2.

15. Pennington transferred to the War Office from the Colonial Office as Clerk on 5 December 1854. He was one of those obscure but key civil servants who oiled the wheels of empire, exercising considerable power by providing policy advice and recommendations. His main job when he first arrived at the War Office was to monitor recommendations for the Order of the Bath, but after 1856 his desk quickly became the sole conduit for VC recommendations.

16. Brigadier Stuart Ryder, 'The British Gallantry System', RUSI Journal (August 2000). According to Ryder, finding Spence's relatives almost five decades after he died was a major task. It was known that Spence was born in the parish of Dumfries, Scotland. The Black Watch could not provide further information regarding next of kin and the Under Secretary for Scotland was asked for help, along with local police and newspapers. Months later a Mr Richard Lynn of Hawick claimed the VC and finally the Provost of Hawick produced a family tree proving that Lynn's father's mother was Isabelle Ogilvie, Spence's nearest relative. Mr Lynn received Spence's medal, which is now in the Regimental Museum of the Black Watch in Balhousie Castle, Perth.

17. Crook, op. cit., p. 89.

18. *Saturday Review*, 15 October 1859.

19. *Glasgow Herald*, Friday, 24 August 1860.

20. George Macdonald Fraser, *Flashman in the Great Game* (HarperCollins, 2006, paperback edn), pp. 286–7. Of course Flashman gets his VC by the end of the novel.

21. Thomas Henry Kavanagh, *How I Won the Victoria Cross* (Ward & Lock, 1860), pp. vi–vii.

22. £2,000 was then a substantial sum, equivalent to some £170,000 in 2014 values.

23. *The Times*, 14 August 1859, p. 7.

24. Frederick Roberts and Countess Roberts (ed.), *Letters Written during the Indian Mutiny* (Macmillan, 1924).

25. Glanville J. Davies: 'The Wreck of the S.S. *Sarah Sands*: The Victoria Cross Warrant of 1858': *The Mariner's Mirror*, Vol. 61, Issue 1, 1975, pp. 61–71.

26. http://hansard.millbanksystems.com/commons/1858/jul/30/observations #S3Vo151Po_18580730_HOC_62.

27. Victoria Cross Register, vol. ii, p. 103.

28. Crook, op. cit., pp. 143–5.

29. Colonel Bowland Moffat, the commander of the regiment, had disgraced himself by taking to the lifeboats, along with his wife and daughters, and thus had been relieved of his command.

30. NA WO 32/7345.

31. www.london-gazette.co.uk/issues/23204/pages/22.

32. NA WO/327370.

33. *The Times*, 13 October 1881, p. 8.

34. Heaphy's VC is in the Auckland War Memorial Museum.

35. Stannus, *Curiosities of the Victoria Cross*, op. cit., p. 5.

36. Lieutenant General H. J. Stannus, *My Reasons for Leaving the British Army* (William Ridgway, 1881), p. 32.

37. Stannus is also a vital reminder of the dangers of relying on 'authentic' source materials. In a letter, for example, to *Broad Arrow*, a military affairs journal, published on 8 January 1881, Stannus corrected the assertion that only one general had died in action since Waterloo and drew attention to:

> the 'Illustrated London News' of 27 February, 1849, a correct representation of the death of General Cureton... in which that distinguished officer is depicted slashing and hacking at his numerous opponents in a manner that would have satisfied the most ardent aspirations for military glory. When General Cureton was shot by a stray bullet, he was moving at a walk at the head of the cavalry brigade. He dismounted and caught hold of his stirrup leather. I went up to him as he fell back dead. There was no enemy within 300 yards of the spot where he fell. I do not write with the view of impugning the accuracy of the illustrated representation,

which I believe is quite as nearly allied to fact as most other statements connected with military warfare and military matters generally.

38. Stannus, *My Reasons for Leaving the British Army*, op. cit., pp. 2–5.
39. Stannus, *Curiosities of the Victoria Cross*, op. cit., p. 5.
40. Ibid., p. 11.
41. Ibid., pp. 9–10.
42. Ibid., pp. 13–14.
43. This and the following quote are from *Hansard*, 30 July 1859.
44. Colliss later had his VC status removed after being convicted of bigamy. Despite being almost sixty, Collis joined the Suffolk Regiment when the First World War broke out, and died of a heart attack in June 1918. He is buried in an unmarked pauper's grave in Wandsworth Cemetery.
45. Stannus, *Curiosities of the Victoria Cross*, op. cit., pp. 17–18.
46. Immediately before the Collis case, in the definitive guide to VC citations and biographies by Sir O'Moore Creagh and E. M. Humphris (*The Victoria Cross, 1856–1920*), is an even flimsier case, that of Sergeant Patrick Mullane, also of the Royal Horse Artillery, who was awarded his Cross for an action the day before Collis's. Mullane's citation reads:

> For conspicuous bravery during the action of Maiwand, on the 27th July, 1880, in endeavouring to save the life of Driver Pickwell Istead. This non-commissioned officer, when the battery to which he belonged was on the point of retiring, and the enemy were within ten or fifteen yards, unhesitatingly ran back about two yards and picked up Driver Istead, placed him on the limber, where, unfortunately, he died almost immediately. Again, during the retreat, Sergt Mullane volunteered to procure water for the wounded, and succeeded in doing so by going into one of the villages in which so many men lost their lives.

47. *London Gazette* on 26 August 1881.
48. Stannus, *Curiosities of the Victoria Cross*, op. cit., pp. 22–3.
49. T. E. Toomey, *Victoria Cross and How Won, 1854–1889* (Alfred Boot and Son, 1889).
50. *London Standard*, 4 November 1886.

51. *The Victoria Cross: An Official Chronicle of the Deeds of Personal Valour* (no author, 1865), p. viii.
52. On 16 July 1879, the *Derby Mercury* in its 'Local News' column reported that 'Captain Allen Gardner, V.C., of the Hussars, (formerly the Derbyshire Yeomanry) arrived at Plymouth, from Cape Town, on Monday, in the *Durban*.' A case of rumour going in advance of the fact.
53. Chard's VC is yet another example of the Cross being cloaked in rumour and veiled allegations – as so often – about money. The actor Stanley Baker played Chard in the 1964 film *Zulu*. Chard's VC and another of his medals were auctioned in 1972; the VC was then described as a 'cast copy', to the shock of his family who had put them up for sale. Baker bought the VC for £2,700, a high price for a copy. When Baker's family put the Chard 'copy' VC up for sale after Stanley Baker's death in 1976, it sold for £5,000. It was then authenticated as the genuine VC and subsequently has become part of the Ashcroft Gallery collection. How much might a Rorke's Drift VC fetch at auction today? Think of a number and add several zeros.
54. Adrian Greaves, *Rorke's Drift* (Cassell Military Paperbacks, 2002), pp. 178–9.
55. *Morning Post*, 3 March 1879, p. 4.
56. The question of posthumous VCs had been debated within the War Office since at least 1902, when Mrs Atkinson wrote to the Office regarding her late son, Sergeant Alfred Atkinson, 1st Battalion, Yorkshire Regiment. Kitchener, then commander in South Africa, had recommended Atkinson for the Cross in February 1901, when, under heavy fire, he left his shelter seven times to get water for the wounded, was himself wounded, and died a few days later. The Military Secretary of the commander-in-chief, Lord Roberts, strictly adhered to the prevailing rules and explained that Alfred's death meant that his VC recommendation was invalid. Atkinson was gazetted with the VC on 8 August 1902. Roberts, however, who was always more generous in his distribution of the VC, overruled all opposition.
57. Adrian Preston (ed.), *Sir Garnet Wolseley's South African Journal, 1879–1880* (Balkema, Cape Town, 1973), p. 70. Wolseley was equally unimpressed

with the VCs bestowed on the defenders of Rorke's Drift: 'It is monstrous making heroes of those who shut up in buildings at Rorke's Drift, could not bolt, and fought like rats for their lives which they could not otherwise save.'

58. General Horace Lockwood Smith-Dorrien, *Memories of Forty-Eight Years' Service* (Leonaur, 2009 edn), p. 31. Smith-Dorrien deserved his own VC for his courage at Isandlwana, but in his fine memoir displayed his customary modesty:

> I would like my boys to know that on the evidence of eye-witnesses I was recommended for the V.C. for two separate acts on that day. These recommendations drew laudatory letters from the War Office, with a regret that as the proper channels for correspondence had not been observed, the Statutes of the Victoria Cross did not admit of my receiving that distinction, and having no friends at Court the matter dropped. In view of my latest experiences I am sure that decision was right, for any trivial act of good Samaritanism I may have performed that day would not have earned a M.C., much less a V.C., amidst the deeds of real heroism performed during the Great War 1914–18.

59. Michael Lieven, 'Heroism, Heroics and the Making of Heroes: The Anglo-Zulu War of 1879', *Albion: A Quarterly Journal Concerned with British Studies*, vol. 30, no. 3 (1998), pp. 419–38.

60. Captain A. K. Ffrench of the 53rd Regiment, who won his VC on 16 November 1857, was elected by his fellow officers, simply for being 'among the first to enter' the Secundra Bagh, at Lucknow, during the Indian Mutiny. Lieutenant H. E. Harrington of the Bengal Artillery, who was present at Lucknow in 1857, was elected by the officers of his battery. Lieutenant A. S. Heathcote, of the 60th Regiment, was elected to a VC by the officers of his regiment for his actions at the siege of Delhi.

61. Douglas S. Russell, *Winston Churchill: Soldier* (Conway, 2006), p. 172.

62. Winston Churchill, *My Early Life* (Reprint Society, 1944 edn), p. 192.

63. This rescue had its farcical elements, and was the kind of individual action that Stannus (and later Douglas Haig) so deprecated.

Montmorency's horse fled; he in turn then had to be rescued by a fellow
21st Lancer, Captain Paul Kenna, who gained his own VC for rescuing
Montmorency. Corporal Swabrick, also of the 21st Lancers, accompanied Kenna on his rescue mission; he got the DCM. An example of
surreptitious class distinction?

64. Churchill, op. cit., p. 257.

65. Quoted in Russell, op. cit., p. 258.

66. Martin Gilbert, *Churchill: A Life* (William Heinemann, 1991), p. 111.

67. Quoted in Russell, op. cit., p. 261.

68. Churchill, op. cit., p. 174.

69. Churchill (op. cit., p. 188) recalled his first encounter with Kitchener:
'The heavy moustaches, the queer rolling look of the eyes, the sunburnt
and almost purple cheeks and jowl, made a vivid manifestation upon
the senses.'

70. Hamilton, *The Soul and Body of an Arm*, op. cit., p. 47.

71. Churchill, op. cit., p. 241.

72. For his military services in South Africa, Churchill received, along with
176,999 others, the Queen's South Africa Medal with six clasps, one for
each battle in which he was involved. Cheated of the VC he so richly
deserved, he was nevertheless loyal to those who helped him – and he
had a long memory. In May 1910, when Home Secretary, he ensured that
the driver of the train, Charles Wagner, received the Albert Medal, First
Class, and the fireman, Alexander James Stewart, the Albert Medal,
Second Class.

73. In a letter to Lord Lansdowne, Secretary of State for War, on 8 December
1899, Roberts put himself up for overall command in South Africa. He
wrote of General Buller that 'he seems to be overwhelmed by the magnitude of the task imposed upon him' and that 'nothing but the gravity of
the situation and the strongest sense of duty would induce me to do
it, or to offer – as I now do – to place my services and my experience at
the disposal of the government. The difficulty of making this offer is
greatly increased by the fact that, if it is accepted, I must necessarily be
placed in supreme command...' Queen Victoria thought Roberts was
rather old for the post and she was irked that he was appointed without

her being consulted; see André Wessels (ed.), *Lord Roberts and the War in South Africa, 1899–1902* (Army Records Society, 2000), pp. 14–19. On his return from South Africa, Roberts was voted the astonishing sum of £100,000 (more than £36 million in 2014 terms) by Parliament.

74. www.london-gazette.co.uk/issues/27157/pages/506.

75. Warren was formerly Metropolitan Police Commissioner in charge of finding Jack the Ripper. Unfairly pilloried for the police's failure to find the murderer, he resigned in November 1888.

76. Reported in *The Times*, 15 November 1900, p. 8.

77. *The Times*, 26 November 1900, p. 15.

78. *Spokane Daily Chronicle*, 2 January 1901, front page.

79. The three elected were Gunner Isaac Hodge, Driver Horace Henry Glasock and Sergeant Charles Edward Haydon.

80. NA WO/32 7878.

81. Rather cheekily, the Assistant Adjutant General of the Royal Horse Artillery, Colonel Edward Owen Hay, requested in 1901 that the VCs granted at Sanna's Post should be accepted as a collective award and that all current and future members of the RHA should be allowed to wear a permanent badge on their uniform in recognition of this deed. This was denied. NA WO/32 7474.

82. Ponsonby, op. cit., pp. 75–9.

CHAPTER 4 Big War

1. Brigadier General F. P. Crozier, *A Brass Hat in No Man's Land* (Jonathan Cape, 1930), pp. 187–8.

2. De-la-Noy, *The Honours System*, op. cit., p. 37.

3. *The Times*, 6 August 1902, p. 10.

4. Sir Neville Bowles Chamberlain, 1820–1902, promoted to field marshal in 1900.

5. Field Marshal Sir Charles H. Brownlow, *Stray Notes on Military Training and Khaki Warfare* (Women's Printing Society, 1912), pp. 105–7.

6. *The Times* 3 September 1902.

7. www.london-gazette.co.uk/issues/30228/supplements/8211.

8. Brereton Greenhous, 'Billy Bishop: Brave Flyer, Bold Liar', *Canadian Military Journal*, autumn 2002, pp. 61–4.

9. Lieutenant Colonel David Bashow, 'The Incomparable Billy Bishop: The Man and the Myth', *Canadian Military Journal*, autumn 2002. Woken by Bishop at 3.00 a.m., Fry turned over and went back to sleep, according to Bashow.

10. The publicity machine brought to bear on Bishop's case had a deeper motivation. Lieutenant General Sir Richard Turner, who had gained his VC during the Boer War, and Sir George Perley, US-born but the Canadian High Commissioner in London and Minister of the Overseas Military Forces between 31 October 1916 and 11 October 1917, wanted a separate Canadian air force. The idea of splitting the RFC along national lines was anathema to the British government, not least because almost a third of RFC aircrew were Canadian. The devil creates work for incompetent (if not idle) hands: Turner had been relieved of command of the Canadian 2nd Division in December 1916, following a disastrous outcome of the Battle of St Eloi in September 1916, when badly handled communications saw 1,600 Canadian casualties, the result of being shelled by their own artillery. Turner managed to retain the support of the Canadian government and thus was handed the sinecure of command of the Canadian forces in London.

11. W. A. Bishop, *Winged Warfare* (Hodder and Stoughton, 1918), pp. 299–300.

12. According to Lieutenant Colonel David Bashow (op. cit., p. 58), on 12 September 1956, two days after Bishop's death, the *Globe & Mail* newspaper published an interview with him in which he said: 'It is so terrible that I cannot read it today. It turns my stomach. It was headline stuff, whoop-de-doop, red hot, hurray-for-our-side stuff. Yet the public loved it.'

13. Greenhous (op. cit.) incorrectly asserts that 'the award of the VC has always been, except in this one unique case, based on irreproachable evidence from two or more witnesses'.

14. www.nfb.ca/film/the-kid-who-couldnt-miss.

15. Commander (later Rear Admiral) Edward Bingham, in charge of a group of destroyers, led his own, HMS *Nestor*, to close to within 3,000

yards of German cruisers, bringing his torpedoes in range; Nestor was sunk but Bingham survived. The other two VCs were posthumous: Major Francis Harvey of the Royal Marines was a gunnery officer on HMS Lion and, although mortally wounded, ordered and supervised the flooding of Q turret, preventing tons of cordite from exploding and thus saving the ship and many lives; HMS Shark was badly damaged and its commanding officer, Commander Loftus Jones, lost a leg but continued to direct fire from the last gun in action. Shark was torpedoed and sank; Jones's body was later found on a beach in Sweden.

16. The Times, 11 July 1916.

17. The Times, 31 July 1916.

18. Alice Cornwell's remaining days overflowed with grief. Her husband Eli, who was with the Royal Defence Corps, garrisoned by men too old or ill to serve at the front, died shortly before she received Jack's VC at Buckingham Palace; her stepson Arthur was killed in action in France in August 1918; and she ran out of money and died in poverty at the age of forty-eight in October 1919. Cornwell's sister, Alice Payne, survived to witness the loan of his VC to the Imperial War Museum in 1968.

19. www.london-gazette.co.uk/issues/29752/supplements/9085.

20. George Coppard, With a Machine Gun to Cambrai (Imperial War Museum, revised edn, 1980), pp. 172–3.

21. Captain A. O. Pollard, VC, MC, DCM, Fire-Eater: The Memoirs of a V.C. (reprinted by the Naval & Military Press, 2005).

22. Siegfried Sassoon, Sherston's Progress (Penguin Books, 1948), pp. 124–36.

23. Pollard, op. cit., p. 143.

24. Ibid., p. 200.

25. Ibid., pp. 235–6.

26. General George S. Patton, War As I Knew It (Bantam Books, 1980), p. 322.

27. Miller, op. cit., p. 168.

28. John Percival, For Valour (Methuen, 1985), p. 82.

29. Michael Ashcroft (Victoria Cross Heroes, p. 150) puts the total number of First War VCs at 626. The Victoria Cross Centenary Exhibition Catalogue, published in 1956, gives a figure of 633, including two bars: one to Surgeon Captain Martin Leake, who gained his first VC in South

Africa in February 1902 and the bar in 1914; the other to Captain Noel Godfrey Chavasse, who won his first VC at Guillemont in August 1916 and his second at Wieltje in August 1917.

30. NA WO 32/5653. Minute dated 18 July 1924.

31. Sir Martin Lindsay, 'Gallantry Awards', British Army Review, 59, pp. 30–2.

32. Hamilton, The Soul and Body of an Army, op. cit., p. 175.

33. Byron Farwell, Mr. Kipling's Army (W. W. Norton, 1987, paperback edn), p. 110.

34. Lord Southborough (chairman), Report of the War Office Committee of Enquiry into 'Shell-Shock', (HMSO, 1922).

35. Winston Churchill, The World Crisis, 1911–18 (Macmillan, abridged edn), pp. 296–7.

36. Gary Sheffield, Forgotten Victory (Headline, 2001), p. 111.

37. The London Gazette had on 15 January 1907 unexpectedly announced that Edward VII had finally relented on the posthumous issue, agreeing that it could be sent to surviving relatives of those who had formerly been simply gazetted as 'would have been recommended' had they survived. He did so after receiving a letter dated 1 December 1906 from Sarah Melvill, wife of the late Teignmouth Melvill, pleading for the Cross.

38. There were thus four Albert Medals in all: Sea First and Second Class, and Land First and Second Class. On 28 August 1917 the titles changed to Albert Medal in Gold and Albert Medal, replacing the old First and Second Class.

39. The Edward Medal, initially to recognize bravery and self-sacrifice when rescuing mineworkers and later extended to industry generally, was established in 1907. The Albert and Edward Medals were discontinued in 1971, and all living recipients were deemed to be holders of the George Cross; holders of the two were asked to return them and receive in exchange a GC. Some people declined to do so. This change absurdly led to an unearned 'promotion' of those individuals who exchanged their Albert/Edward Medals for the GC, since the GC was supposedly on a par with the VC, while the Albert and Edward Medals were always second-order decorations. Although lesser in status, the Albert Medal is much rarer than the VC; in the 105 years of its existence

only sixty-nine of the gold (first class) versions were awarded and 491 of the bronze (second class). Yet Gold Albert Medals sold at auction in 2013 for between £15,000 and £20,000, far below the price of a VC. Scarcity alone is not enough to push up prices; publicity is needed too.

40. Lord Sydenham chaired the Central Appeal Tribunal, which administered conscription. In his later years he subscribed to the idea that there was an international Jewish conspiracy, and espoused fascism – the descent into madness probably completely unrelated to his chairing a royal commission on venereal disease from 1913 to 1916.

41. *Hansard*, 8 March 1916, vol. 21, cc 304–12.

42. NA WO 32/7452. Recommended by the GOC (General Officer Commanding), 2nd Corps, on 26 September 1914; Elliott did not get the VC.

43. Frank Richards [real name Francis Philip Woodruff], *Old Soldiers Never Die* (Faber & Faber, 1933), pp. 53–5.

44. Field Punishment Number One: a humiliating and sometimes painful ordeal in which a soldier was fixed to an upright post or gun wheel for two hours a day for a maximum of twenty-one days.

45. 'Mark VII' [pseudonym of Max Plowman], *A Subaltern on the Somme in 1916* (Dutton, 1928), p. 90.

46. Douglas Haig, *War Diaries & Letters, 1914–1918*, ed. Gary Sheffield and John Bourne (Weidenfeld & Nicolson, 2005), p. 84.

47. NA WO 32/7463. Letter from Kitchener, 26 June 1901.

48. Gary Mead, *The Good Soldier* (Atlantic Books, 2008), p. 109.

49. In the Battle of Atbara on 8 April 1898, a decisive defeat of the Dervishes in the Second Sudan War, Acting Major Haig had galloped to rescue a fallen Egyptian army soldier from possible capture – the kind of spirited effort that had gained the VC on other occasions. When the subject cropped up in later life, his wife Doris would insist that he should have got the VC for risking his life at Atbara. Haig maintained a dignified silence about the incident. (Mead, op. cit., p. 94.)

50. It was not gazetted until 8 September 1916, the two-month interlude implying some deliberation back at the War Office; www.london-gazette.co.uk/issues/29740/supplements/8869.

51. Cather was not the only VC awarded on the first day of the Somme for rescuing wounded. Captain John Leslie Green, of the 1/5 Sherwood Foresters, who attacked near Gommecourt, went to the assistance of Captain Frank Robinson, a fellow Sherwood Foresters officer, who was wounded and entangled in barbed wire. Green was shot in the head and died; Robinson died two days later.

52. *London Gazette*, 13 September 1918; www.london-gazette.co.uk/issues/30901/supplements/10877.

53. The combined British and Dominions forces totalled 8.7 million by November 1918. The approximate chance of gaining a military gallantry decoration – excluding the VC but including the MC, MM and DCM – was thus one in fifty. By the same crude calculation the chance of winning a VC was about one in 13,765.

54. Ponsonby,, op. cit., p. 311.

55. Invented in 1901, the DSC was originally called the Conspicuous Service Cross and was for warrant and junior officers. It was renamed in October 1914 and eligibility then extended to all naval officers below the rank of lieutenant commander.

56. Ponsonby, op. cit., p. 311

57. Ponsonby, *Recollections of Three Reigns*, op. cit., p. 312.

58. Ibid., pp. 312–3.

59. Ibid. The other ranks who became eligible for the Military Medal did not much like it because it carried no gratuity – unlike the £20 annual gratuity that went with the Distinguished Conduct medal. Little wonder perhaps that the numbers of DCMs handed out slowly fell, while those of the MM rose strongly.

60. Gerald Gliddon, VCs *of the Somme: A Biographical Portrait* (Gliddon Books, 1991), p. vii.

61. www.london-gazette.co.uk/issues/29740/supplements/8871.
    Immediately prior to McFadzean's entry in the London Gazette was another, that of Private William Jackson of the Australian Infantry, who also would have been ruled out by Haig's thumbs-down for the rescue of fallen comrades. Jackson was part of a group returning from a raid when several of the group were injured by shellfire. Jackson got back

safely and handed over a prisoner and then returned to retrieve one of the injured. He returned once more, with a sergeant, and his arm was blown off. He returned, got assistance, and then went out once more, looking for two wounded comrades. Jackson may have been rewarded for bravery on more than this occasion. The citation concludes: 'He set a splendid example of pluck and determination. His work has always been marked by the greatest coolness and bravery.'

62. *Illustrated London News*, 25 November 1916, p. 621.

63. H. Montgomery Hyde and G. R. Falkiner Nuttall, *Air Defence and the Civil Population* (Cresset Press, 1937), pp. 44–5.

64. The Most Excellent Order of the British Empire was from the start distributed with indiscriminate haste and in such vast quantities that it was instantly mocked. The first list of names for the new order (24 August 1917) occupied four densely packed small-print pages of the *London Gazette* (www.london-gazette.co.uk/issues/30250/supplements/8791). In the first list, dignitaries such as Edmund Sebag Montefiore (Secretary of the Civilian Internment Camps Committee at the Home Office, created CBE) could be found alongside Lady Sophie Beatrix Mary Scott (Head of Gifts Department Stores, British Red Cross Society, also CBE). E. S. Turner wrote in *Dear Old Blighty* (Michael Joseph, 1980), p. 223:

> While men won medals for working on at the bench with broken thumbs, soldiers with legs and arms blown off were forced to recognise that valour is its own reward. To stay at one's post in the Ypres Salient was the least that could be expected of a man; to stay at a switchboard during a Zeppelin raid on London merited a decoration.

65. The Medal of the Order of the British Empire was invented at the same time. In 1922 it was split into two: the Medal of the Order of the British Empire for Gallantry, usually known as the Empire Gallantry Medal (EGM); and the Medal of the Order of the British Empire for Meritorious Service, usually called the British Empire Medal. The EGM was awarded for acts of gallantry that failed to reach the standard required for the Albert and Edward Medals. In 1940 it was replaced by the George Cross.

66. NA WO 32/3443. The merchant navy's case for being eligible for the VC focused on the merchant ship SS *Otaki*, a 'Q' ship, a disguised, heavily armed merchant vessel designed to lure submarines to the surface and then attack them. Lieutenant Archibald Bisset Smith of the Royal Naval Reserve was in command of the *Otaki* on 10 March 1917 when he sighted a German raider, the *Moewe*. The *Moewe* called on *Otaki* to stop, which Smith refused to do. There then ensued a duel at 2,000 yards, lasting for about twenty minutes. The *Otaki* scored several hits, but she was no match for the superior firepower of the German vessel and soon was ablaze and sinking. Lieutenant Smith ordered the lifeboats to be lowered but went down with the *Otaki* when she sank. Smith was not eligible for the VC at the time of his death, although, according to Admiral Everett at the 8 August 1918 meeting,

> everybody agreed at the Admiralty that it was a case for the V.C. but at that particular time one hesitated about taking any action in view of what the Germans might do by regarding everybody as combatants and shooting them at sight. However, as you will see by these papers next you, Sir, that situation now is quite clear and the Germans do regard everybody as a foe, however they are dressed or whatever they are doing.

Everett pointed out to Ponsonby that the king had not yet approved the VC for the merchant navy. Ponsonby replied: 'the King said he approved of all decorations which could be given by the Navy, that is the V.C, the C.B, the D.S.O, in fact all of them being given to the Mercantile Marine. This debate on the merchant navy narrowly avoided a blunder that would have had future consequences: Ponsonby had proposed that the revised warrant should read 'it is Our will and pleasure that the officers and men of Our mercantile Marine shall during the present war be eligible' for the VC, but fortunately Everett suggested leaving out '"during the present war" because we may have a future one'. Smith's gallant action took place on 10 March 1917; he was finally gazetted VC more than two years later, on 24 April 1919.

67. The discussion that follows is based on National Archives file WO 32/3443.

68. Everett was subsequently appointed commander-in-chief, China Station, in November 1924, but he suffered a breakdown in April 1925 and was relieved of his command.

69. None of the committee possessed a VC; the highest gallantry award between them was a Military Cross. The other committee members were Colonel M. D. Graham, Military Secretary at the War Office, representing the army; Colonel More spoke for the Air Ministry; S. D. Gordon for the India Office; Everett represented the navy; Lieutenant Colonel A. E. Beatie and Mr H. C. M. Lambert represented the Colonial Office. Mr R. U. Morgan of the War Office acted as Secretary; minutes of the meeting were taken by a civilian clerk.

70. Melvin Charles Smith, *Awarded for Valour* (Palgrave Macmillan, 2008), pp. 138, 160–1.

71. Lord Southborough, *The Living Age*, 14 October 1922. The two-year-long inquiry cost the grand total of £1,113 17s 1d. The committee's full report is available in an edition from the Imperial War Museum, 2004.

72. *Daily Telegraph*, Monday, 28 June 1920.

73. *Daily Telegraph*, ibid.

74. Probyn's VC was bought at auction in 2005 by an anonymous bidder for £160,000. Myth has it that Probyn's long white beard hid the VC on his left breast, but contemporary cinema footage shows this to be untrue.

75. www.london-gazette.co.uk/issues/30400/supplements/12329.

CHAPTER 5 Go Home and Sit Still

1. Hew Strachan, *The Politics of the British Army* (Oxford University Press, 1997), p. 1.

2. Anthony Eden, *Another World, 1897–1917* (Allen Lane, 1976), pp. 131–2.

3. Lucy Noakes, *Women in the British Army* (Routledge, 2006), p. 81. One Englishwoman did officially serve in uniform in a combat role during the 1914–18 war, with a rank equivalent to sergeant major, but in the Serbian, not the British, army. Flora Sandes, who died in 1956, was born in Yorkshire. When the war started she joined a St John Ambulance unit that travelled to Serbia, where she joined up, and was wounded by a

grenade in close combat. She received Serbia's highest military decoration, the Order of the Star of Karađorđe.

4. *The Times*, 4 May 1891, p. 5.

5. *The Times*, 15 April 1891, p. 5.

6. *The Times*, 8 June 1891, p. 9.

7. Queen Victoria had instituted the Royal Red Cross in 1883, the first British military order solely for women. Ethel was also awarded a life pension of £140 by the government, with an additional £1,000 for 'exceptional services' – this on top of her regular Bengal civil service pension and compensation for the property she had lost in the destruction of the residency. She later remarried unhappily and died, insolvent, in an American sanatorium, from 'toxic psychosis'.

8. *The Times*, 12 June 1891, p. 10.

9. *The Times*, 29 April 1891, p. 10.

10. As late as 1894 Ethel was still fighting to quash these rumours. In *The Graphic* on 10 February 1894 she promised a reward for information enabling her to take proceedings against the originators of 'certain false and slanderous reports'.

11. On 31 March, Grant captured Thobal, about fifteen miles from Manipur, where he dug in. Next day, around 1,000 Manipuri troops attacked Thobal; for the next nine days Grant's tiny force repulsed repeated attacks. On 9 April he received orders to withdraw towards a British force, then advancing towards Manipur. Twice wounded, Lieutenant Grant joined the large British force which entered Manipur on 26 April and put down the rebellion. All seventy-nine survivors of Grant's force received the Indian Order of Merit, then the highest possible decoration for native members of the British Indian Army. There is no question that Grant deserved his VC.

12. In Manipur, the anniversary of the execution of Tikendrajit and his general Thangal, 13 August, is celebrated as Patriots' Day.

13. Ethel Grimwood (1867–1928) published in November 1891 *My Three Years in Manipur* (Richard Bentley & Son, 1891); it became an immediate bestseller. In its review, *The Times* (16 November 1891) called it a 'melancholy tale [which] notwithstanding the heroism incidentally displayed,

notably by Mrs Grimwood herself, reflects but little credit on those who were responsible for the policy pursued... her husband and the other victims of the disaster were sacrificed to a series of blunders'. A day before the mutiny, Ethel had been in despair over the death of a goat she had been fattening up; cattle were sacred and the Grimwoods grew weary of ducks and other game:

> There on the ground lay the goat, breathing his last, and with his departing spirit went all my dreams of legs of mutton, chops and cutlets. I sent to the house for bottles of hot beer and quarts of brandy, and I poured gallons of liquid down the creature's throat; but all to no purpose, and after giving one last heartrending groan, he expired at my feet. I could have wept. The pains that had been taken with that goat to make it fat and well-favoured... we could not help seeing the funny side of the affair, and ended by laughing very heartily over the sad end to my mutton scheme.

14. Noakes, op. cit., p. 62.
15. Leah Leneman, 'Medical Women in the First World War: Ranking Nowhere', British Medical Journal, vol. 307, no. 6,919, (18–25 December 1993), pp. 1592–4. Inglis did not sit still but formed the Scottish Women's Suffrage Societies, which sent all-women medical units to various fronts.
16. Noakes, op. cit., p. 5.
17. Janet S. K. Watson, Fighting Different Wars (Cambridge University Press, 2004), p. 56.
18. Leneman, op. cit. Churchill wrote: 'the grant of Commissions to medical Women cannot be entertained nor can they be demobilised with commissioned Rank in order to provide a precedent should any future emergency necessitate their employment.'
19. www.london-gazette.co.uk/issues/29535/supplements/3647 and www.london-gazette.co.uk/issues/29641/pages/6343.
20. The Times, 28 June 1916.
21. The supplementary warrant granting women eligibility for the MM was not signed by Lloyd George, who was a long-standing supporter of women's suffrage and took over as Secretary of State for War on

Kitchener's death, but by Andrew Bonar Law, former Conservative prime minister and then serving as Secretary to the Colonies in the coalition government under Asquith, who, although a Liberal, opposed female suffrage.

22. The first five women to receive the MM were Dorothie Feilding, Mabel Mary Tunley, Ethel Hutchinson, Jean Strachan Whyte, Nora Easeby and Beatrice Alice Allsop.

23. Irene Ward, DBE, MP, *F.A.N.Y. Invicta* (Hutchinson, 1995), p. 69.

24. Since it was created, the George Cross has been awarded 153 times (as of August 2013), often in circumstances that would have merited a VC in the First War. The George Medal has been awarded on more than 2,000 occasions. The GC is replete with its own peculiarities, being awarded to everything from a nation (Malta), female operatives in Special Operations Executive (SOE), a police force (the Royal Ulster Constabulary), and bomb-disposal experts – who, it might justifiably be thought, are 'in the presence of the enemy' more directly than most. At one point the GC was even considered for Stalingrad, but the king turned that suggestion down flat – thus avoiding future embarrassment.

25. Robert Rhodes James, biographer of King George VI, asserted that 'not only were [the GC and GM] the King's idea, he also designed them himself' (*A Spirit Undaunted*, Little, Brown & Co., 1998, p. 216). George VI was in fact as little artistically inclined as his predecessors; the design for both was by Percy Metcalfe.

26. *The Times*, 24 September 1940.

27. See *Debrett's*, www.debretts.com/people/honours/crown-honours-.aspx.

28. *The Times*, 26 September 1940.

29. Clement Attlee, deputy prime minister, was asked in September 1940 who served on this committee. He replied that it was chaired by the Permanent Secretary to the Treasury, Sir Horace Wilson. The other members were the Permanent Heads of the Admiralty, Air Ministry, Colonial Office, Dominions Office, Foreign Office, India Office and War Office, together with the Private Secretary to the King, the Prime Minister's Private Secretary, the Secretary of the Central Chancery of the Orders of Knighthood, the Naval Secretary to the First Lord of the

Admiralty, the Military Secretary to the Secretary of State for War, the Member of the Air Council for Personnel, and the Secretary, Military Department, India Office. The Secretary to the Committee was an Officer of the Treasury. http://hansard.millbanksystems.com/commons/ 1940/sep/18/war-honours-decorations-and-medals. A. N. Wilson in his *Hitler* reported a snippet of a 1968 interview of Sir Horace Wilson, then in his 80s, by the journalist Colin Cross. Sir Horace, who had been an appeaser of Nazi Germany in the late 1930s, purportedly said he understood Hitler's feelings about the Jews and asked Cross: 'Have you ever met a Jew you liked?'

30. Rhodes James, op. cit., p. 216.
31. In 1949 the QAIMNS became a corps in the British army and was renamed Queen Alexandra's Royal Army Nursing Corps.
32. Obituary in *The Independent*, 21 October 1993. Her biography, *The Will to Live* (Cassell, 1970) was written by John Smyth.
33. Hugh Dalton, *The Fateful Years: Memoirs, 1931–1945* (Frederick Muller, 1957), p. 366.
34. M. R. D. Foot, *SOE in France* (HMSO, 1966), p. 47.
35. Germany signed the Geneva Conventions in 1929 and ratified them in 1934.
36. Foot, op. cit., p. 47.
37. Noakes, op. cit., pp. 119–20.
38. Noakes, op. cit., p. 131.
39. 'Incessantly during these courses agents had it dinned into them that their task was aggressive, that they must make aggression part of their characters, eat with it, sleep with it, live with it, absorb it into themselves entirely.' Foot, op. cit., p. 58.
40. *How To Be A Spy: The World War II SOE Training Manual*, introduction by Denis Rigden (Dundurn Group, Toronto, 2001), p. 2. Available online at http://ironwolfoo8.files.wordpress.com/2010/07/the-wwii-soe-training-manual-rigden.pdf.
41. Marcus Binney, *The Women Who Lived For Danger* (Hodder &Stoughton, 2002), pp. 47–8.
42. The women of SOE F Section who were captured were Yvonne Rudellat,

Yvonne Baseden, Odette Sansom, Violette Szabo, Denise Bloch, Cecily Lefort, Lilian Rolfe, Vera Leigh, Diana Rowden, Andrée Borrell, Madeleine Dammerment, Yolande Beekman, Noor Inayat Khan, Elianne Plewman and Eileen Nearne. Yvonne Baseden, Eileen Nearne and Odette Sansom survived, the rest were executed or died at Natzweiler-Struthof, Ravensbrück, Bergen-Belsen and Dachau concentration camps.

43. Foot, op. cit., p. 48. She was later given a military MBE by the Air Ministry.

44. www.london-gazette.co.uk/issues/37181/supplements/3676.

45. *Hansard*, 18 January 1944, vol. 396, c 3030. Viscountess Astor asked Churchill a supplementary question: 'Would it be too much to ask my Right Hon. Friend to make a speech some day telling us what he really does think about women's services in the war?' To which Churchill replied: 'I addressed a meeting at the Albert Hall on this subject and I gathered that there was some criticism.'

46. Ward, op. cit., p. 218.

47. Ibid., p. 219.

48. According to Christine Hamilton in *The Book of British Battleaxes* (Robson Books, 1997, p. 169), Ward was part of a parliamentary delegation to Nazi Germany in 1936. During tea at Ribbentrop's villa she could be heard informing Adolf Hitler in a loud voice that he was 'talking absolute bosh'.

49. Foot, op. cit., p. 431.

50. Father of the poet Thom Gunn, Herbert Gunn is today best known for inventing in 1943 the headline 'It's That Man Again', a satirical reference to Hitler which later became the title of a popular radio show.

51. www.london-gazette.co.uk/issues/37468/supplements/961/page.pdf.

52. www.london-gazette.co.uk/issues/38578/supplements/1703.

53. Noor Inayat Khan was recommended for the GM, which was reduced to an MBE and then a Mention in Despatches. That she was finally granted a GC was thanks to the determination of Vera Atkins, Buckmaster's head of intelligence, who in 1947 interrogated Hans Josef Keiffer, head of German counter-intelligence in Paris. His testimony of Noor's

bravery after capture and her refusal to give any information was the basis for her GC – yet another example of it not always being necessary for a senior (British) officer to have witnessed the courageous act.

54. Delving into the history of SOE – about which conspiracy theories abound – is hampered by several facts: a fire in its Baker Street HQ in 1946 reportedly destroyed 85 per cent of its records; Buckmaster did not keep full records; and immediately after the war, when SOE was closed down in 1946, there was plentiful 'weeding'.

55. Jerrard Tickell, *Odette: The Story of a British Agent* (Chapman and Hall, 1949).

56. NA WO 32/20708. Ward was indefatigable in her efforts to get SOE agents who had gained the GC retrospectively awarded the VC. On 30 July 1963 she asked the prime minister, Harold Macmillan, 'whether he will consider the desirability of amending the conditions for the award of the Victoria Cross, in the light of modern circumstances, in such a way as to make it possible for a posthumous award to be made to those qualified for the award in the course of secret activities in enemy occupied territories during the war, for which they could not be decorated at the time. In an extremely unhelpful and somewhat strange written reply, the PM said: 'No. This would not in my view be a suitable amendment to the conditions of award and the George Cross was instituted in 1940.'

57. Although not related to the more famous Winston, Peter Churchill and Odette claimed to be married when they were captured, and used the surname to help ensure captors treated them with a degree of wary consideration. After the war, her marriage to Roy Sansom was dissolved; she married Churchill in 1947 and they divorced in 1956.

58. In her Ph.D. thesis ('The Women Agents of the Special Operations Executive F Section: Wartime Realities and Post-war Representations', submitted to Leeds University in September 2011), Kate Vigurs quotes M. R. D. Foot in an interview given on 14 January 2003 as the source of her assertion that 'Odette was frequently seen dining out in Marseilles and speaking English' (p. 72).

59. NA TS58/1160.

60. Ibid.

61. The War Office went to enormous lengths to corroborate Odette's story in order to validate the recommendation for her George Cross – far more extreme than many inquiries into the grounds for awarding VCs – and elicited some peculiar supporting evidence. Her lover, Peter Churchill, wrote to Colonel Perkins at the War Office on 23 May 1946. Perkins had requested some witness reports and medical certificates to back up Odette's story. In his reply, Churchill wrote that Odette's toe nails grew back, but that while she was in Ravensbrück concentration camp 'two or more of these fell off and she managed to keep them. If medical science can prove that these nails fell off because the original ones were pulled out then these can be seen at any time for that purpose.'

62. Szabo's SOE record is available at NA HS 9/1435.

63. NA HS 9/1435

64. Ibid.

65. She was actually shot in the back of the head or neck, possibly after being raped, although this was not known at the time of the citation.

66. One of his elder brothers was Lieutenant Colonel Derek Seagrim, who gained a VC in Tunisia on 20/21 March 1943. He died of his wounds fifteen days later.

67. www.britishmilitaryhistory.co.uk/documents.php?aid=125&nid=16& start=15.

68. www.london-gazette.co.uk/issues/37720/supplements/4573.

69. Ward, op. cit., p. 217.

70. *GQ Magazine*, May 2013.

71. Noakes, op. cit., p. 150.

72. *Women in the Armed Forces: Summary* (MoD, 2002), p. 6.

73. *Report on the Review of the Exclusion of Women from Ground Close-Combat Roles.* www.gov.uk/government/uploads/system/uploads/attachment_data/file/ 27403/Report_review_excl_woman_combat_pr.pdf.

74. Noakes, op. cit., p. xii.

75. Anthony King, 'Women in Combat', RUSI Journal, February/March 2013, vol. 158, no. 1, pp. 4–11.

76. Ward, op. cit., p. 229.

CHAPTER 6 Bigger War

1. George S. Patton, *War As I Knew It* (Bantam Books, 1980), p. 322.
2. NA Air 2/4890.
3. This mark scheme was laid out by Winston Churchill in the House of Commons on 10 August 1920. See *Hansard*, vol. 133, cc 239–41.
4. http://hansard.millbanksystems.com/commons/1940/aug/20/war-situation#S5CV0364P0_19400820_HOC_279.
5. *Daily Telegraph*, obituary, 29 November 2001.
6. *Hansard*, 8 October 1940, vol. 365, cc 247–8.
7. Commonwealth War Graves Commission annual report, 2011–12; www.cwgc.org/learning-and-resources/publications/annual-report.aspx.
8. Several 'posthumous' VCs were erroneously given in the Second World War, only for the recipient later to emerge from captivity. Temporary Major Herbert Wallace Le Patourel of the Hampshire Regiment had his Cross gazetted on 9 March 1943, for conspicuous gallantry in leading a party of four volunteers against machine-gun posts at Tebourba, in Tunisia, on 3 December 1942. His sister received a letter from the War Office two weeks before the *London Gazette* announcement, saying the Red Cross advised that he was a prisoner. 'The announcement of the posthumous award of the V.C. is very confusing, but I have just been ringing the War Office to explain that my brother is a prisoner' (*The Times*, 10 March 1943). Le Patourel later returned to active duties in Europe in 1944, achieving the rank of brigadier.
9. The British soldiers killed were members of the 4th Battalion, Cheshire Regiment, the Royal Artillery, and the 2nd Battalion, Royal Warwickshire Regiment. The last was the regiment Bernard Montgomery had joined upon graduating from Sandhurst in 1908. The last survivor of the massacre at Wormhout, Bert Evans, died in November 2013, aged ninety-two.
10. *Broad Arrow*, 23 August 1879.
11. Stephen Brooks (ed.), *Montgomery and the Battle of Normandy* (Army Records Society, 2008), p. 103.
12. Major R. Clark, 'Medals, Decorations and Anomalies', *British Army Review*, August 1969.

13. Sir Martin Lindsay, 'Gallantry Awards', *British Army Review*, 59, August 1978, pp. 30–2.
14. Ibid.
15. Ibid.
16. Annand was not, however, the first to appear in the *London Gazette*. That distinction goes to Lieutenant Harold Ervine-Andrews, East Lancashire Regiment, who escaped capture at Dunkirk, and Lance Corporal Harry Nicholls, who did not. Their VCs were gazetted on 31 July 1940. Both survived the war. Annand died on Christmas Eve 2004, aged ninety.
17. Oddly enough, neither of the two VCs which went to members of the Royal Tank Regiment were for firing a tank gun. Lieutenant Colonel Henry Foote got his for actions between 27 May and 15 June 1942, including leading his battalion, the 7th Royal Tank Regiment, in action while seated on the outside of the tank. Captain Philip Gardner, of the 4th Royal Tank Regiment, got his for rescuing an armoured-car officer who had his legs blown off at Tobruk on 23 November 1941.
18. Charlton's VC was not gazetted until 2 May 1946, almost a year after his act. Why the delay? Some sources suggest his recommendation and eventual citation depended largely on evidence given by the German attackers, as there were no senior British officers present. The difficulty of getting at the truth of individual cases is revealed by Charlton's VC: his citation states that his tank was blown up during the counterattack, whereas some sources suggest it had already stopped because of an electrical failure, which would have been embarrassing in a citation. The citation makes no mention of Charlton being ordered to remove the Browning and help defend the infantry; it states that he performed his courageous act 'entirely on his own initiative'. It all depends on the write-up and the political usefulness of making the award. www.london-gazette.co.uk/issues/37551/supplements/2119.
19. Seamen can be very superstitious; some worried that *Thrasher* might be an unlucky submarine. She was commissioned on the thirteenth day of May 1941; sank two ships on a thirteenth day of 1942; and by the time she was depth-charged off Crete had completed thirteen patrols. She

survived the war and was scrapped in 1947. *The Listener*, 14 January 1943, p. 41.

20. www.london-gazette.co.uk/issues/35591/supplements/2548.

21. In later life Gould reflected that the VC was an albatross around his neck. Made redundant from his job as a personnel manager in May 1965, he said: 'people in top management seem to shy away from me. I think it might be because they are afraid that a man with such a record could show too much embarrassing initiative. If it is the VC which is frightening people away from me, I wish they would forget it. Those days are over.' *Daily Telegraph*, 7 December 2001.

22. Although some make every effort to elevate the George Cross to the status of the VC, the fact remains that it is second in precedence and widely regarded as the civilian 'equivalent'. Brigadier Sir John Smyth won his own VC in June 1915 for leading a party of ten Indian troops under fire to ferry ninety-six bombs to a forward position (eight of the Indian soldiers were killed, none was awarded a decoration). When he was asked to form a VC association in 1956, he gladly did so. The first meeting was held on 27 June 1956. But including GC holders in the (renamed) Victoria Cross and George Cross Association was clearly an afterthought; GC holders were not formally admitted to full membership until May 1961. See Brigadier Sir John Smyth, *The Story of the George Cross* (Frederick Muller, 1963), pp. 181–2.

23. Brooks (ed.), op. cit., pp. 192, 206. Harry Crerar was GOC (General Officer Commanding), First Canadian Army in north-west Europe in 1944.

24. Quoted in Hugh Halliday, *Valour Reconsidered* (Robin Brass Studio, Toronto, 2006), pp. 208–9.

25. www.london-gazette.co.uk/issues/36030/supplements/2361.

26. Nettleton was later killed in action, on 13 July 1943.

27. Leo McKinstry, *Lancaster: The Second World War's Greatest Bomber* (John Murray, 2009), pp. 87–9.

28. www.london-gazette.co.uk/issues/35539/supplements/1851.

29. www.london-gazette.co.uk/issues/36693/supplements/4175.

30. Lachhiman Gurung survived the war and died in 2010, aged ninety-two.

31. Upham died at the age of eighty-six in November 1994.

32. *Daily Telegraph*, obituary, 23 November 1994.

33. *The Times*, 15 October 1941, p. 5. The other VC mentioned was that of Sergeant Alfred Hulme of the 23rd Battalion, New Zealand Army. He survived the war.

34. Upham's three daughters sold his medals in November 2006 to the Imperial War Museum for an undisclosed sum. As New Zealand legislation bans the export of historic items, the museum agreed to their permanent loan to the QEII Army Memorial Museum at Waiouru in New Zealand, where they were on display until a well-planned theft of a total of ninety-six medals, including nine VCs, on 2 December 2007. On 17 December 2007, the Commissioner of Police offered a reward of up to NZ$300,000 for information leading to recovery of the medals and Lord Ashcroft and Tom Sturgess, a New Zealand businessman, funded the reward. In January 2008 Christopher Comeskey, an Auckland lawyer, approached the police offering a deal under which the medals would be returned in exchange for the reward. The Commissioner and Mr Comeskey struck a deal and the medals were returned in February 2008. The police paid in excess of NZ$200,000 under the agreement. The police eventually arrested James Kapa and Ronald Van Wakeren and charged them with burglary. They both pleaded guilty. Upham was a tough no-nonsense man who frankly loathed Germans. He denounced Britain's membership of the Common Market and said in 1971 that 'your politicians have made money their god, but what they are buying is disaster', adding, 'they'll cheat you yet, those Germans'. He took up farming back in New Zealand after the war, but declined £10,000 raised by public donation to help him buy a farm, instead using the money to establish the Charles Upham Scholarship Fund to send the sons of ex-servicemen to university.

35. *Daily Telegraph*, 28 September 2000.

36. See *Courage and Service* for the following, a CD available from Service Publications, www.servicepub.com.

37. Projector, Infantry, Anti Tank; an unreliable weapon that was effective against tanks only over a very short distance of around 100 yards.

38. Earlier in the war Byce had won the Military Medal. His father, also named Charlie, had won the DCM in the First World War, along with the Médaille Militaire.

39. Richard Reid, *For Valour: Australians and the Victoria Cross* (Australia Post, 2000), p. 29.

40. *The Times*, 24 March 1944. Derrick was killed in action during the landing at Tarakan, an island off the coast of Borneo, on 23 May 1945. Once again, note the 'inspirational' element in his citation.

41. Martin Gilbert, *Churchill: A Life* (William Heinemann, 1991), p. 730.

42. *The Times*, 18 December 1945, p. 4. The others that he would personally bestow were: GC, Knights Grand Cross, Knights Commanders, Knights Bachelor, Companions and Commanders of Orders, DSO, DCM, Conspicuous Gallantry Medal (Naval and Air), Albert Medal, George Medal, Police and Fire Services Medal for Gallantry, and Edward Medal.

CHAPTER 7   The Integrity of the System

1. Spencer Fitz-Gibbon, *Not Mentioned in Despatches* (Lutterworth Press, 2001 edn), p. xiii.

2. C. W. McMoran [Lord Moran], *The Anatomy of Courage* (Constable & Robinson, 2007 edn), p. xxv.

3. There were also three living holders of the VC for Australia and one for the New Zealand VC.

4. http://news.bbc.co.uk/1/hi/northern_ireland/4625376.stm.

5. Richard Vinen, 'The Victoria Cross', *History Today*, vol. 56, issue 12, 2006.

6. General George S. Patton, *War As I Knew It* (Bantam Books, 1980), p. 376.

7. Ibid., pp. 341–2.

8. Foote's VC was not gazetted until 14 February 1946, when he was liberated. www.london-gazette.co.uk/issues/37466/supplements/941.

9. www.telegraph.co.uk/news/uknews/defence/6201670/Royal-Marine-to-sell-Conspicuous-Gallantry-Cross-won-in-Iraq.html. Thomas's CGC was sold at auction for £88,000 on 18 September 2009.

10. And the existence of the George Cross renders absurd attempts to

finely grade courage; the case of Corporal Mark William Wright, 3rd Battalion, Parachute Regiment, killed in action in Helmand province, Afghanistan, in September 2009, highlights the problem. Wright was awarded a posthumous GC after needlessly dying of wounds after he entered a minefield trying to save the life of another injured soldier. A subsequent military inquiry judged that Wright could have survived if the Chinook helicopter sent to his rescue had possessed a lifting winch; all such winches were back in the UK at the time, having a fault checked.

11. William I. Miller, *The Mystery of Courage* (Harvard University Press, 2000), p. 12.

12. J. O. Urmson, 'Saints and Heroes', in *Moral Concepts*, ed. Joel Feinberg (Oxford University Press, 1969), pp. 60–73.

13. Rudyard Kipling, 'Winning the Victoria Cross', www.telelib.com/authors/ K/KiplingRudyard/prose/LandandSea/victoriacross.html – originally published in the *Windsor Magazine*, June 1897.

14. Michael Ashcroft, 'A Century and a Half of Conspicuous Bravery', *The Spectator*, 22 April 2006.

15. This committee relates to, but is distinct from, the Committee on the Grant of Honours, Decorations and Medals, which is a permanent standing committee that considers general questions relating to honours and decorations, reviews the scale of awards (civil and military), and considers new awards and changes in conditions of existing awards.

16. NA WO 98/10. 'Examination of the Standards of Australian Citations for the Award of the Victoria Cross': no date but probably 1970, written by an unnamed lieutenant colonel.

17. www.london-gazette.co.uk/issues/44198/supplements/13567. Wheatley's citation states that he was told Swanton was dying by a medical assistant.

18. Can suicide be courageous? It's a grey area for the VC. The history of the Cross is of course littered with acts that turned out, loosely, to be 'suicidal' and for which a VC was awarded. Wheatley's act made 'the Palace' – and senior officers – uncomfortable about giving him a VC.

But at least one overt suicide gained the Cross. Corporal Sefanaia Sukanaivalu of the 3rd Battalion, Fijian Infantry, gained his on 23 June 1944 at Mawaraka in the Solomon Islands. Under fire, he crawled forward to rescue wounded men of his platoon. He then returned to get another man and on the way back to his own lines he was seriously wounded. Several attempts were made to try to rescue him; each failed. He called out to his would-be rescuers not to try to fetch him. His citation reads: 'Realising that his men would not withdraw as long as they could see that he was still alive... Corporal Sukanaivalu, well aware of the consequences, raised himself up in front of the Japanese machine gun and was riddled with bullets.' www.london-gazette.co.uk/issues/36774/supplements/5016.

19. Ian McNeill, *To Long Tan: The Australian Army and the Vietnam War, 1950–1966* (Allen & Unwin, 1993), p. 48.

20. *British Army Review*, no. 101, August 1992.

21. Political considerations intrude on all aspects of the VC. In 2005 Gordon Brown, then Chancellor of the Exchequer, vetoed a new design for a fifty-pence piece commemorating the creation of the VC. The original design, by the sculptor Clive Duncan, depicted a soldier carrying a wounded comrade, with the cross-hair of an enemy sniper's rifle focused on his back. Brown decided it was inappropriately gloomy. The designer reportedly wanted to spurn histrionics and 'to do justice to the cold reality of combat' (*Daily Telegraph*, 21 June 2005).

22. www.london-gazette.co.uk/issues/44925/supplements/8873.

23. As of November 2013 only two VCs – both posthumous – had been awarded for the Afghanistan War, remarkably few considering the length of the campaign and the numbers of armed forces personnel. Lance Corporal James Ashworth, 1st Battalion, Grenadier Guards, was killed on 13 June 2012 in a close-combat action; he was gazetted VC on 22 March 2013. Corporal Bryan Budd, 3rd Battalion, Parachute Regiment, was killed in action on 20 August 2006 and gazetted 14 December 2006. Wounded, Budd independently pressed on with an assault; subsequently (and after his VC had been gazetted) a coroner

ruled that Budd had probably been killed by a NATO bullet, caught in cross-fire.

24. *The Independent*, 24 July 2008.

25. Private William McFadzean's posthumous Somme VC in 1916 was for an act remarkably similar to Croucher's.

26. *Daily Telegraph*, 19 March 2010.

27. The need for this perverse interpretation exists only because the GC exists. The most outstanding example of this bizarre judgement in the post-1945 period is that of Captain Robert Nairac who, on 13 February 1979, was gazetted with a posthumous GC for 'exceptional courage and acts of the greatest heroism in circumstances of extreme peril... [He] showed devotion to duty and personal courage second to none.' Nairac was with the SAS, in civilian clothing, when he was taken prisoner by the IRA, tortured and killed. Who would honestly argue that Nairac was not in the presence of the enemy? www.london-gazette.co.uk/issues/47769/supplements/1991.

28. NA WO 373/188/247. This shows that Illingsworth's original VC recommendation was downgraded to 'Distinguished Service Medal' (an error: no such medal existed) by the 'Special Honours Committee'.

29. Jones's widow spoke to the *Observer* in March 2002 and said: 'If anybody does anything heroic or good, the British look for reasons to denigrate them. It seems to be inevitable and it's a great shame that we have this sort of national psyche. Why don't we cheer for things that are good?'

30. www.telegraph.co.uk/news/uknews/1486650/A-Falklands-hero-and-the-VC-that-never-was.html.

31. www.london-gazette.co.uk/issues/49134/supplements/12845.

32. The case of Flying Officer Lloyd Allen Trigg of RAF 200 Squadron set the precedent. In command of a Liberator bomber, Trigg attacked the surfaced U-boat 468 in the Atlantic on 11 August 1943. The U-boat's anti-aircraft guns hit the Liberator and set it on fire. Nevertheless it circled for another (and this time successful) depth-charge run, before crashing 300 yards behind the submarine, with no survivors. The U-boat commander, Oberleutnant Klemens Schamong, was captured, and on

his high praise for the pilot's courage, Trigg was granted a posthumous VC on 2 November 1943, the citation mentioning his 'grim determination and high courage'.

33. John Geddes, *Spearhead Assault* (Century, 2007), pp. 209–10.

34. Fitz-Gibbon, op. cit., p. 20.

35. Geddes, op. cit., pp. 211–12. Abols rose to the rank of captain in the Parachute Regiment; for his action at Goose Green he was awarded the Distinguished Conduct Medal.

36. The 2012 Holmes review of military medals acknowledged that there is a problem with the lack of transparency in the way decisions about military decorations are arrived at:

> the current system of decision-making is vulnerable to the charge of being a 'black box' operation, where those outside have no knowledge of what is being decided or why, and have no access to it; and where the rules and principles underlying the decisions, while frequently referred to, have never been properly codified or promulgated.

37. *The Spectator*, 7 May 2005.

38. According to the *New York Times*, 29 July 2012, in 2012 the US Air Force had 1,300 'pilots' controlling drones in Afghanistan, Pakistan, Somalia and Yemen, operating from at least thirteen bases across the US. The Pentagon estimates that by 2015 the US Air Force will need more than 2,000 drone pilots operating twenty-four hours a day.

39. Since 1991 Australia, New Zealand and Canada have had their own versions of the VC, the Australia and New Zealand VC design being identical to the original. The Canadian design is slightly different: it is a bronze cross suspended from a crimson ribbon bearing a lion and crown insignia, a fleur-de-lis has been added, and the English motto 'For Valour' has been changed to the Latin 'Pro Valore'. The first Australian VC was awarded on 16 January 2009 to Trooper Mark Donaldson for the rescue of a coalition forces interpreter from heavy fire in Afghanistan. Speaking in 2010, Robert Macklin, author of *Bravest*, a book about Australian medal winners, said: 'in a battlefield like Afghanistan, it is sometimes almost impossible to pick out the most deserving soldier

for a gallantry award. Indeed, in the action where Mark Donaldson won his VC, at least two other SAS troopers deserved decorations for bravery which have yet to be awarded. It is probably time to review the system.'

40. Nicola T, twenty-three, from Croydon, commented from the chilly climes of p. 3 in the same edition that she was 'awestruck' by the bravery of Private Johnson Beharry.

41. *Daily Telegraph*, 23 September 2006.

42. John Winton, 'The High Price of Valour', *Illustrated London News*, 29 September 1979, p. 51.

43. Lieutenant General H. J. Stannus, *My Reasons for Leaving the British Army* (William Ridgway, 1881), p. 106.

44. Ethics and the senior ranks of the military are not what they used to be. Formerly a retired general might eke out a living from his pension while tending his garden and slowly writing his memoirs. Today's generals prefer to shift to a more lucrative career in the private sector. The Advisory Committee on Business Appointments (Acoba) vets on behalf of the government all applications by senior military personnel and civil servants for jobs in the private sector. Since 1996, senior officers and MoD officials have taken 3,500 jobs in arms companies (as of the end of 2012); over that time not a single application was vetoed.

45. The current 'quota' in the 1961 warrant stipulates one commissioned officer, one NCO and one other rank (or their RN and RAF equivalent) if the unit does not exceed 100; twice that for units greater than 100 but lower than 200; above 200, the number of Crosses 'shall be the subject of special consideration'.

46. There is no evidence of a formal ballot at Gallipoli, but Major General Hunter Weston, commanding the 29th Division (which included the Lancashire Fusiliers' battalion), in recommending the VCs, implied that informal soundings had occurred. He said: 'Where all did so marvellously it is difficult to discriminate, but the opinion of the battalion is that Bromley and Willis are the officers, and Stubbs, Richards, Grimshaw and Keneally are the NCOs and men to whom perhaps the greatest credit is due.' Crook, op. cit., p. 109.

47. NA WO 32/3443.

48. www.gov.uk/government/publications/military-medals-review-report-by-sir-john-holmes.

49. Rudyard Kipling, 'Winning the Victoria Cross', first published simultaneously in *Youth's Companion* and the *Windsor Magazine* in June 1897; updated and republished in 1924 as *Land and Sea Tales for Scouts and Scoutmasters*.

Index

Aberdeen, Earl of (George
    Hamilton-Gordon) 49
  administration of 40, 43, 58
Aberdeen Journal 54, 64
Abols, Corporal David 'Pig'
    nomination for VC 237, 245
Abyssinia 66
Adams, Reverend James William
    95–7
  citation for VC (1881) 93–4, 96
Addiscombe Military Seminary 78
Afghanistan 112, 233
  Helmand Province 25, 232
  Operation Enduring Freedom
    (2001–14) 13, 25, 28, 231–2, 241,
    244
  casualties of 241–2
  GCs awarded for actions during
    232
  VCs awarded for actions during
    242
  Operation Herrick (2002–14)
    241

Aitken, Max 117
Albania 239
Albert, Prince 4, 9, 14, 24, 32–3, 54,
    65, 67, 216, 244
  role in development of VC 40–2,
    44, 59
Albert Medal 129, 138
  establishment of (1866) 83
  extension of (1877) 103
  posthumous awarding of 198
Alexandra of Kent, Princess
  family of 19
Alison, Major General Sir Archibald
  Alison Committee 6–7
Anglo Egyptian War (1882) 66
Anglo-Zulu War (1879) 99–101
  Battle of Isandlwana (1879) 27,
    102
  Battle of Rorke's Drift (1879) 20,
    27, 99, 101
  casualties of 99, 101
  VCs awarded for actions during
    20, 27–8

Annad, Lieutenant Richard
    awarded VC 194–5
Appelboom, Squadron Leader K. J. 21
Argentina
    military of 234–5
Ashcroft, Lord Michael 27, 224
    Victoria Cross Heroes 19
Ashworth, Lance Corporal James
    posthumous awarding of VC
        (2013) 16
Atticus 170
Australia 8
    Canberra 229
        Australian War Memorial 17
    military of 15, 218
    26th Australian Brigade 211
Australian Army Training Team 15
    Vietnam (AATTV) 226–7, 230
    Sydney 17
Australian Imperial Force (AIF) 147
Australian National University
    faculty of 9

Baden-Powell, Robert 120
Badsell, Andrew
    eligibility for VC 216
Bagehot, Walter 37–8
Ball, Albert 123
    death of (1917) 118, 123–4
Bankes, Cornet
    posthumous award of VC 75
Barnard, General 72
Bauward, Major A. C. 108
Beale, Lieutenant Colonel Percy 74

Beharry, Private Johnson 221
    awarding of VC (2013) 16, 27, 220,
        223, 242
Belgium
    Flanders 17, 126, 130–1, 155
    River, Dyle 194
    Ypres 139
Bengal Civil Service
    personnel of 72
    VCs awarded to 94–5
Bengal Ecclesiastical Service 93
Bhagat, Second Lieutenant
        Premindra Singh
    awarded VC 206
    recommended for MC (1940)
        206
Bishop, William 'Billy' Avery 117, 119
    gazetted with VC (1917) 116–17,
        218
Black & White 105–6
Blair, Tony 221
Bleicher, Hugo 174
Bonaparte, Napoleon 241
Brade, Sir Reginald
    Permanent Under-Secretary of
        State for War 140
Brett, Lieutenant Colonel 81
British Army Review 229–30
British Broadcasting Corporation
        (BBC) 204
    Antiques Roadshow 19
British Empire 191
British Expeditionary Force (BEF)
        118

personnel of 14, 52, 126, 132
British military xvii, 8, 13, 36, 41, 53,
  85–6, 146–7, 163, 179
  1st Cheshire Regiment 130
  1st Royal Irish Regiment 128
  10th Foot 74
  14th Batteries 108
  14th Hussars 100
  14th Royal Irish Rifles 138
  2nd New Zealand Expeditionary
    Force 208
  20th Battalion 207
  2nd Rifles Battle Group 233
  20th Hussars 87
  21st Lancers 19
  24th Regiment 83, 99–100
  42nd Royal Highlanders 75
  44th Foot 63
  46th Regiment 50
  54th Foot 81
  57th Regiment 33
  60th Regiment 103
  66th Batteries 108
  7th Hussars 75
  90th Light Infantry 54
  Army Nursing Service 158–9
  Auxiliary Territorial Service
    (ATS) 164–5
  Bengal Army
    Meerut Division 88
  British Indian army 86, 89, 98
    1st Battalion
    Burma Rifles 177
    1st Punjab Cavalry 87

19th Hyderabad Regiment 177
104th Bengal Fusiliers 150
4th Punjab Rifles 75
Coldstream Guards 34
Corp of Indian Engineers 206
Dublin Fusiliers 104
Durham Light Infantry 104
  2nd Battalion 194
First Aid Nursing Yeomanry
  (FANY) 158, 165, 169, 178
Fusilier Guards 34
Gordon Highlanders 104
  1st Battalion 193
Gurkhas 152–4
  8th Rifles 206–7
Irish Guards 209
  1st Battalion 208–9
King's Royal Rifle Corps 108
Queen Alexandra's Imperial
  Military Nursing Service
  (QAIMNS) 162
Parachute Regiment 220, 234, 237
  2nd Battalion 237
Rifle Brigade
  1st Battalion 82
Rifles, The
  1st Battalion 25
Royal Army Medical Corps 26,
  157
Royal Artillery
  Territorial Reserve 209
Royal Berkshire Regiment 34
Royal Field Artillery 134
  7th Battery 109

Royal Horse Artillery 93
Q Battery 112
U Battery 112
Royal Irish Fusiliers 133
Royal Irish Regiment 216
    1st Battalion 97
Royal Logistic Corps
Explosive Ordnance Disposal
    Regiment 233
Royal Marines 232
    Reserve 232
Royal Scot Fusiliers 193
Royal Welch Fusiliers
2nd Battalion 130
service of women in 149, 155,
    180–2
Special Air Service (SAS) 220,
    236, 238
Welsh Guards 147
Women's Army Auxiliary Corps
    (WAAC) 149
    creation of (1917) 155
Women's Royal Army Corps
    (WRAC) 181
Broad Arrow 192
Broadwood, Brigadier General
    Robert George 112
Brodrick, William
    Under-Secretary of State for War
    109
Bromhead, Lieutenant Gonville 101
Bronze Stars 239
Brooke, Field Marshal Sir Alan 201
Brown, Father G. 95

Brown, William 20
Brownlow, Field Marshal Sir Charles
    115
Buckmaster, Colonel Maurice
    Head of SOE F Section 171–2
Budd, Corporal Bryan
    posthumous awarding of VC
    (2006) 16
Budgen, Patrick Joseph
    awarded VC 147–8
Buller, General Sir Redvers Henry
    108–10
Burke's Peerage 153
Burma 96, 177, 207
    Mewado 178
    Rangoon 178
Byce, Acting Sergeant Charles
        Henry
    awarded DCM 211
    citation for VC 209–11
Byrne, Private Thomas
    acquisition and sale of duplicate
        VC by family of 19

Callwell, Colonel Charles 66
Cameron, Lieutenant Donald 199
    awarded VC 200
Cameronians Regimental Museum
    18
Campbell, Lieutenant General Sir
    Colin 70, 72, 74, 78–80, 245–6
Canada 81–2, 118–19
    military of
    1st Army 211

Lake Superior Regiment (Motor) 209–11
  1st Canadian Division 201
  2nd Canadian Infantry Division 200
  Royal Hamilton Light Infantry 219
Canning, Lord Charles John
  Governor-General of India 76
Cardigan, Lord (George Brudenell-Bruce) 62
Cardwell, Edward
  Colonial Secretary 84
Carve Her Name With Pride (1956) 173
Cather, Lieutenant Geoffrey St George Shillington
  death of 132–3
Catholicism 95
Chamberlain, Crawford 87–8
Chard, Lieutenant John Rouse Merriot 101
Charlotte of Wales, Prince 36
Charlton, Guardsman Edward
  awarded VC 195
Chatfield, Lord
  Admiral of the Fleet 160
Chelmsford, Lord 99, 101
Cheshire, Group Captain Leonard
  awarded VC 205–6
Cheshire Observer, The 62
Chicken, George Bell 72
China 66
Christian Victor, Prince 113
Christianity 67

Church of England
  ministers of 95
Churchill, Peter 173–4
Churchill, Winston 105, 117, 127, 146–7, 163, 168–9, 179, 186, 189–90, 203, 212
  First Sea Lord 135
  military career of 67, 103–6
  River War, The 106
  Secretary of State for War
  signing of extended VC warrant (1920) 145, 158
  signing of GC warrant (1940) 195
Clark, Major R. 23
Clay, Lieutenant Colonel H. Clay 127
Clery, Major Francis 101
Clinton, Bill 239
Coghill, Lieutenant Nevill Josiah Aylmer 99
  posthumous awarding of VC 101–2
Colliss, Gunner James
  recommended for VC (1880) 93
Committee on Co-ordination etc. of Warrants Relating to the V.C. (1918) 142–4
  findings of 159
  members of 143, 145–6
Committee on Honours, Decorations and Medals in Time of War 161, 223
Commonwealth xiii, xvi, 3
  military forces of 8, 13, 147, 227, 241

Congreve, Captain Walter Norris 108
  recommended for VC 109–10
Conservative Party (Tories/Tory
  Party) 134
  members of 168, 170, 179
Conspicuous Gallantry Cross (CGC)
  26, 219
  awarding to women 180
  eligibility standards of 220–1
  establishment of (1993) 22
  posthumous awarding of 220
Conspicuous Gallantry Medal
  (CGM) 200
  establishment of (1854) 39
Coppard, George 121–2
Cornwell, Alice 120, 139
Cornwell, John ('Jack') Travers
  awarded VC 120–1, 218, 223
Courtney, William 63–4
Crerar, General Harry
  Commander of 1st Canadian
    Army 211
Crimean War (1853–6) xiii, 25, 37, 39,
    45, 48–9, 55, 59, 69, 99, 113, 244
  Battle of Alma (1854) 35, 48
  Battle of Balaclava (1854) 45, 54
  Battle of Inkermann (1854) 35, 48
  belligerents of 25, 46–8, 91
  casualties of 35–6, 38, 48–50, 242
  Siege of Sevastopol (1854–5) 12,
    33, 35, 48
  VCs awarded for actions during
    13–14, 25, 33–4, 45–7, 64, 71, 73,
    91, 242

Critchley, Alexander 179
Croix de Guerre
  perceived cheapening of 16, 23
  women awarded 167
Crook, Michael 76
Croucher, Lieutenant-Corporal
    Matthew
  awarded GC (2008) 231–2
Cruickshank, John
  awarded VC (1944) 215
Cunningham Admiral Sir Andrew
  Commander-in-Chief of
    Mediterranean Fleet 198
Curtis, Henry 33

Daily Sketch 170
Dallas, George Frederick 50
Dalton, Hugh
  Secretary at War 163
Dare, Acting Major Norman Fielden
    134
Daubeney, Lieutenant Colonel
  self-nomination for VC 47
Davies, Lieutenant General Sir
    Francis 141–2
  Military Secretary at War Office
    141
De-la-Noy, Michael
  Honours System, The 243
Democratic Republic of Vietnam
    (North Vietnam) 226
  Vietcong 226
Dempsey, Private Dennis
  claim placed for VC 74

Derrick, Sergeant Thomas 211–12
  awarded DCM 211
Desanges, Louis
  Victoria Cross Gallery 62
Dicey, A. V. 46
Distinguished Conduct Medal
  (DCM) 14, 128, 137–8, 157, 211,
  230, 234, 245
  establishment of (1854) 39
  posthumous awarding of 234–5
Distinguished Flying Cross (DFC)
  203, 215
  awarded to women 179
Distinguished Service Cross (DSC)
  128, 135, 166
  women awarded 166
Distinguished Service Medal (DSM)
  128
Distinguished Service Order (DSO)
  13–14, 22–3, 128–9, 135, 146,
  167, 178, 193, 198, 200, 203
  ban on posthumous awarding of
  194
  eligibility standards for 133
Distinguished Warfare Medal
  establishment of (2013) 239–40
Divane, Private J. 103
East India Company
  Bengal Establishment 95
  personnel of 76, 78
  soldiers of 13, 68
Eden, Anthony 170, 173
Edward, Prince (Duke of Kent)
  death of 59

family of 58–9
Edward VII, King 134
  family of 38
  ruling on posthumous awarding
  of VC (1907) 5, 75, 102, 128
Egypt 66
  Cairo 212
Elizabeth II, Queen 19
Elliott, Lieutenant W. G. R. 130
Elliston, Captain George Sampson
  189
Elton, Lieutenant Colonel F. C.
  awarded VC (1855) 91
Engels, Friedrich 49
Eton College 78
Everett, Admiral Sir Allen Frederic
  141–3, 145, 159, 183
  Naval Secretary 245
Examiner 89

Falklands Islands
  Darwin Settlement 234
  Goose Green 236–8
  Goose Settlement 234
  Mount Longdon 238
Falklands War (1982)
  casualties of 242
  MCs awarded for actions during
  236, 238
  VCs awarded for actions during
  234–5
Fieldhouse, Admiral John
  Commander of Falklands Task
  Force 235

First Anglo-Afghan War (1839–42)
87
First World War (1914–18) 5, 25, 76,
103, 116, 119, 122, 124, 127, 139,
149, 156, 172, 198, 221, 237
Battle of Arras (1917) 117
Battle of Jutland (1916) 120
Battle of the Somme (1916) 117,
131–2, 138
belligerents of 13, 17, 158
casualties of 14, 127–8, 132–3,
139–40, 191
Croix de Guerre awarded for
actions during 16
Gallipoli Campaign (1915–16) 17,
126, 245
Iron Crosses awarded for actions
during 16
MCs awarded for actions during
134
MMs awarded for actions during
158
Médailles Militaires awarded for
actions during 16
participation of women in
149–50
Treaty of Versailles (1919) 192
VCs awarded for actions during
13, 116, 120–1, 123–4, 128,
132–3, 138–9, 143–4, 191
Western Front 121, 127
Zeebrugge Raid (1918) 43, 147,
245
Fitz-Gibbon, Spencer 10

Foot, M. R. D. 163
Foote, Reverend John Weir
awarded VC 219
Ford Motor Company 172
France 16, 38, 48, 116, 134, 136, 143,
165–7, 175, 188–9, 204
Marseilles 167
Occupied (1940–4) 169, 179
Paris 48
Saint-Jorioz 174
Tomb of the Unknown Warrior
124
Fraser, George Macdonald
Flashman in the Great Game (1975)
77
Fraser, Sir William 92–3, 98
Frederick, Prince (Duke of York and
Albany)
appointed as Commander-in-
Chief of Army (1795) 57–8
French, General Sir John 126
French, Sir John 130
Fry, Willy 116

Gammage, Prof Bill 9
Gardner, Captain Allen 100
Garnett, Flight Sergeant Jack
awarded DFC 215
Geddes, John 237–8
Geneva Conventions 164–5
George, Prince (Duke of
Cambridge) 88–9
George Cross (GC) 169, 171, 173,
178, 182–3, 190, 195, 197, 231

common view of 197
eligibility standards of 232–3
establishment of (1940) 159, 161,
  195
posthumous 170–1, 176–7, 233
George III, King
  appointment of Prince Frederick
    as Commander-in-Chief of
    Army (1795) 57–8
George IV, King 35, 55
George Medal (GM) 195
  awarded to women 168
  establishment of (1940) 159–61
George V, King 118, 120, 131, 134–5,
  139, 145–6, 158, 219–20
George VI, King 159, 161, 192, 212–13
  establishment of GC and GM
    (1940) 159–61, 195
Germany 16, 38, 134, 192, 204
  Bavaria
    Augsburg 204
  Düsseldorf 188
  Hamburg 195
  Hochwald Forest 209–10
  Schweinfurt 187
Gibson, Wing Commander Guy
  awarded VC 203–4
Glasgow Herald 76
Godfrey, John
  family of 35
Goodman, Flight Lieutenant
  Michelle
  awarded DFC (2008) 179
Gorst, Sir John Eldon 153

Gough, Lord Henry 87
Gould, Petty Officer Tommy 198–9
  awarded VC 196–7
Graham, Colonel 142–3, 245
Grant, Lieutenant Charles 154
Graphic, The 99–100
Greece
  Crete 196, 207
Grey, Sir George
  Governor General of New
    Zealand 84
Griffiths, Private W. 103
Grimwood, Ethel 152, 154, 180
  debates regarding issuing of VC
    to 150–1, 153–5
  family of 150
Grimwood, Frank St Clair 151
  family of 150
Grimshaw, Sergeant John
  raised to VC 245
Gubbins, Brigadier Colin 174
  Head of SOE 172
Gunn, Herbert 170–1
Gurung, Lachhiman
  awarded VC 206–7
Guy, Lieutenant General Sir Roland
  235

Hagel, Chuck
  US Defense Secretary 240
Haig, Field Marshal Sir Douglas 118,
  143, 147, 156
  view of 'civilized war' 131–2
Haldane, Captain James 104–6

Hall, Virginia
  awarded DSC 166
  service in SOE F Section 166
Hambly, Leading Seaman Cyril
  posthumous awarding of Albert
    Medal 198
Hamilton, Captain Gavin John 245
  awarded MC 236
Hamilton, General Sir Ian 49, 107,
    126
Harding, Israel
  gazetted VC (1882) 98
Hardinge, Henry 58, 92–3, 98
  Commander-in-Chief of Army
    92
Harris, Elizabeth Desborough
  family of 150
Harris, Lieutenant Colonel Webber
    Desborough
  family of 150
Harris, Sir Arthur 'Bomber'
  RAF Marshal 171
  Commander-in-Chief of RAF
    Bomber Command 203
Hartley, Edmund Barron
  sale of VC awarded to 18
Hastings, Macdonald
  family of 11
  Men of Glory (1959) 11–12
Hastings, Sir Max
  family of 11
Havelock, Brigadier General Henry
  death of 70
  family of 70

Havelock, Lieutenant Henry 84
    Marsham
  family of 70
Hayward, J. B. 20
Heaphy, Charles 92
  recommendation for VC 83–5
Henty-Creer, Lieutenant Henty
    199–200
Hero of the Soviet Union 16, 182
Hitch, F. 20
Hitler, Adolf
  'Commando Order' (1942) 165
Hollingsworth, Sergeant Jon
  posthumous awarding of CGC
    220–1
Holmes, Sir John 247
Horsford, General Sir Alfred
  Military Secretary 89

Illingsworth, Private Stephen 238,
    245
  posthumous awarding of DCM
    234–5
Illustrated London News 139
Imperial War Museum 27
  Lord Ashcroft Gallery 19
India 66, 80, 87, 112
  Agra 88
  Allahabad 70
  Amritsar 78
  British Raj (1858–1947) 89
  Calcutta 78, 95, 150–2, 154
  Delhi 28, 72, 78
  Delhi Durbar (1877) 95

government of 151
Indian Mutiny (1857–8) 13–14, 18
    28–9, 67–70, 73–5, 78, 84, 96,
    132, 147
    Sarah Sands incident 80, 82
    VCs awarded for actions during
    71–6, 78, 94–5, 147
Kandahar 79, 93
Lucknow 18, 28, 70, 72–4, 78
Manipur 151, 154
    Imphal 150
Simla 88
Indian Naval Brigade 72–3
Iran
    Tehran 212
Iraq
    Baghdad 239
    Basra 179, 20
    Mosul 216
    Operation Iraqi Freedom (2003–
    11) 26–7, 220, 238–40
    Bronze Stars awarded for actions
    during 239
    CGCs awarded for actions during
    220
    Silver Stars awarded for actions
    during 239
    VCs awarded for actions during 27
Iron Cross 137
    perceived cheapening of 16, 23
Italy 134

Jackson, Flight Sergeant Norman
    187–8

gazetting of VC (1945) 188–9
    sale of VC awarded to 18
Japan
    Imperial (1868–1947) 177
        Kempei Tai 162
Jepson, Selwyn 164, 174
Jones, Lieutenant Colonel Herbert
    237
    death of 237–8
    posthumous awarding of VC 234,
    245

Kabul Field Force 95
Kavanagh, Thomas Henry 72, 77
    Assistant Commissioner in Oudh
    73, 76
    How I Won the Victoria Cross (1860)
    76
Keane, Lieutenant Colonel Bob
    Keane 211
Keane, Private John 63
Keeble, Major Chris 237
Keegan, Sir John 15–16, 220
Kenneally, John
    awarded VC (1943) 208–9
    desertion 208–9
Khan, Noor Inayat
    posthumous awarding of GC
    (1949) 171
Kipling, Rudyard 79, 112, 224,
Kitchener, Sir Horatio Herbert
    106–7, 135–6
    death of 158
    role in development of MC 136

Secretary of State for War 155–6
view of VCs 131–2
Knight Grand Cross 56
Korean War (1950–3) 13
  VCs awarded for actions during
  227
Kosovo War (1998–9)
  NATO bombing of Yugoslavia
  (Operation Allied Force) (1999)
  239

Labour Party
  members of 194
Laos 230
Laurie, Lieutenant-General John
  Wimburn 109
Lawrence, Sir John 88
Lawson, Jack
  Secretary of State for War 194
Le Matin 172
Légion d'Honneur 167
Leopold I of Belgium, King 36
Liberal Party
  members of 40, 129
Libya
  Tripoli 198
Limbu, Rambadahadur
  awarded VC 220
Lindsay, Sir Martin 125
  military career of 193–4
Little Andaman Island incident
  (1867)
  VCs awarded for actions during
  82–3

Liverpool Mercury 44
Lloyd George, David
  administration of 117
Lloyd's Weekly Newspaper 52
London Gazette xiii, 10, 34, 73–4, 81,
  83, 96, 110, 134, 137, 157, 167,
  171, 198, 219, 229, 233, 236
Long, Colonel Chris 108
Lucas, Charles 232
Lugard, Sir Edward 81
Lyndhurst, Lord (John Copley)
  48–9

MacArthur, General Douglas 212
Mackenzie, Lieutenant Hugh 197
Magennis, Leading Seaman James
  price history of VC awarded to
  18–19
Mahdist War (1881–99) 66, 106, 131
  Battle of Omdurman (1898) 19,
  104
  casualties of 107–8
Major, John
  reform of honours system (1993)
  22–3
Malaya 162
Mangles, Ross Lowis 72
  Assistant Magistrate at Patna 73
Mansfield, Sir William
  Commander-in-Chief of British
  Military in India 87
Manson, Reverend J. 95
Marx, Karl 49
Mary, Queen 146

Mauritius
  Port Louis 79
McCandlish, Major General John
  Director of Personnel Admini-
    stration at War Office 181
McCarthy, Corporal James
  death of (1918) 128
McDonald, Christopher 217
  eligibility for VC 216
McDonnell, William Fraser 72
McDowell, George Patrick
  posthumous awarding of Albert
    Medal 198
McFadzean, Billy 143
  posthumous awarding of VC to
    138–9
McKay, Sergeant Ian
  death of 238
  posthumous awarding of VC 234
McNaughton, Lieutenant General
    Andrew
  GOC of First Canadian Army
    200
McNeill, Sir John 51
McWheeny, Sergeant William
  awarded VC 63
Medal of Honor 19, 124, 166
  establishment of (1862) 16
Médailles Militaires 16
  establishment of (1852) 38
Melvill, Lieutenant Teignmouth
    99–100
  posthumous awarding of VC
    101–2

Mentioned in Dispatches (MiD) 8,
    39, 128–9, 193, 200, 206
Michel, Colonel 81
Military Covenant
  concept of xvi
Military Cross (MC) 125, 128–9,
    133–4, 136, 146, 179, 189, 206,
    236, 238
  awarded to women 25–6, 180
  citations for 26, 133–4
  establishment of (1916) 13, 136
  development of 136–7
  extension to all ranks (1993) 22
Military General Service Medal
    (MGSM) 55
Military Medal (MM) 125, 137
  abolition of (1993) 22
  establishment of (1916) 13, 157
  issuing to women 158
Miller, William I. 24, 123, 222
Moncel, Brigadier R. E. 211
Montgomery, General Bernard
    192–3, 200–2
de Montmorency, Captain Raymond
  awarded VC (1898) 104
More, Colonel 143–4
Morris-Jones, Henry 190
Morning Post 104

Napier, Lord 89
  Viceroy of India 87
Napoleon III
  establishment of Médailles
    Militaires (1852) 38

Napoleonic Wars (1803–15) 55
  Battle of Waterloo (1815) 45, 55,
    208
National Archive 21, 176
National Film Board of Canada
  Kid Who Couldn't Miss, The 119
National Service Act (1941) 161
Nesbitt, Kate 27
  awarded MC (2009) 25–6
Netherlands 188
Nettleton, John 204–5
  awarded VC 204
New Guinea
  Sattelberg 211–12
New York Post 166
New York Times 61
New Zealand 66, 85
  General Assembly 84–5
  indigenous population of 84
  River, Mangapiko 84
New Zealand Company (NZC)
  establishment of (1837) 84
New Zealand Wars (1845–72) 66
Newcastle, Duke of (Henry Pelham-
    Clinton)
  role in development of VC 42–3
  Secretary of State for War and the
    Colonies 41–3, 58, 113
Nicholson, James
  awarded VC 202–3
Nightingale, Florence 48, 153
Nile, River 103
non-commissioned officers (NCOs)
    28, 137

VCs awarded to 138
Norris, Michelle
  awarded MC (2006) 26
Norris, Sergeant J.W. 188
North Atlantic Treaty Organization
  (NATO) 239
Norway 199
Narvik 185

Ogilvy, Sir Angus 19
O'Hea, Private Timothy 83
  awarded VC 82
Order of the Bath 35, 39–40, 42, 56,
  61
  Knight Grand Cross (CGB) 96
Order of the British Empire 140
Order of the Garter 61
Order of the Thistle 61
Ottoman Empire
  Moldavia 48
  Sublime Porte 47–8
  Wallachia 48
Outram, Major General Sir James 70

Paine, Major General Sir Godfrey 144
Palestine
  Ain Kanish 128
Palmer, Rear Admiral Norman Craig
  140
Palmer, Roundell Cecil Palmer
  169–70
Palmerston, Lord (Henry John
    Temple)
  administration of 44

death of 85
Panetta, Leon
  role in establishment of
    Distinguished Warfare Medal
    (2013) 239–40
Panmure, Lord (Fox Maule-Ramsay)
  33, 44–5, 75
  Secretary of State for War 32, 44,
    54–5, 73
  view of VC 35
Patton, General George 123, 218, 239
Peel, Captain 73
Peel, General Jonathan
  role in extension of VC eligibility
    81
  Secretary of State for War 80
Pennington, Edward 81–2
Phipps-Hornby, Major Edund 112–13
Pile, General Sir Frederick
  Commander of Air Defence in
    Britain 164
Place, Lieutenant Godfrey 199
  awarded VC 200
Plowman, Max 130–1
Pollard, Alfred Oliver 121, 127
  awarded VC 120–1, 123, 223
  Fire-Eater: The Memoirs of V.C.
    121
Ponsonby, Sir Frederick 38, 134–7,
  142–4, 245
  Acting Private Secretary to
    Queen Victoria 113
  Keeper of the Privy Purse 136
Presbyterians 95

Probyn, General Sir Dighton
  MacNaughton
  awarded VC 147–8
Profumo, John
  Secretary of State for War 186
  signing of revised warrant for VC
    (1961) 186
Punch 53
Purple Heart
  eligibility standards of 239

Quinton, James Wallace 153–4
  Chief Commissioner in Assam
    151

Raby, Commander Henry James
  awarded VC 33
Raglan, Lord 52, 54–5
Reed, Captain Hamilton Lyster
  recommended for VC 109–10
Reed, General 72
Reid, Flight Lieutenant William
  awarded VC (1943) 188
  military service of 188–9
Reeve, Henry 53
Religious Tract Society
  Boy's Own Paper 11–12
Rennie, William
  sale of medal set of 18
Republic of Ireland 209
  Dublin 89
Republic of Vietnam (South
  Vietnam) 226
  Kon Tum Province 230

Quang Ngai Province
  Tra Bong Valley 227–8
Resistance Medal 167
Reynolds's Newspaper 99
Richards, Frank
  Old Soldiers Never Die (1933) 25, 130
von Richtofen, Baron Manfred 118
Roberts, First Lieutenant Peter
  198–9
  awarded VC 196–7
Roberts, Frederick 78–9
  death of 108, 110
  family of 108
  gazetted for VC (1900) 110,
  112–13, 184
Roberts, General 93, 95–6
Roberts, Lady 111–12
Roberts, Lord 107
  family of 108
Roosevelt, Franklin D. 212
Royal Air Force (RAF) 165, 171,
  181–2, 186, 202, 225
  249 Squadron 203
  44 (Rhodesia) Squadron 204
  97 Squadron 205
  Bomber Command 187, 202–4
  Coastal Command 202, 215
  Medical Service 146
  RAF Shipdham 188
  VCs awarded to personnel of
  203–6
  Volunteer Reserve 18
  Women's Auxiliary Air Force
  (WAAF) 165, 169

Royal Army Corps 189
Royal Australian Naval Reserve 8
  HMAS *Armidale* 8
Royal Flying Corps (RFC) 117–18,
  123
  60 Squadron 117, 119
  85 Squadron 118
Royal Navy 39, 120, 135, 143, 165,
  202, 225, 245
  HMS *Chester* 120
  HMS *Hampshire* 158
  HMS *Hardy* 185–6
  HMS *Hecla* 34, 232
  HMS *Kandahar* 198
  HMS *Pargust* 245
  Mediterranean Fleet 198
  Royal Naval Volunteer Reserve
  (RNVR) 199
  Thrasher 196–8
Royal Red Cross 153
Royal Victory Hospital 64
Rudellat, Yvonne
  service in SOE F Section 166
Ruggles-Brise, General 144
Russell, Lord John
  Secretary of State for Foreign
  Affairs 40
Russell, William Howard 45
Russian Empire 48, 134

Sandhurst, Lord
  Under-Secretary of State at War
  Office 129
Sansom, Odette 172–3

awarded GC (1946) 173–5
  objections to 173
  media depictions of 173
Sardinia 48
Saturday Review 76
Schmid, Sergeant Olaf
  death of (2009) 233
  gazetted posthumous GC 233
Schofield, Captain Harry Norton 108
Scobell, Captain George Treweeke
  support for establishment of
    'Order of Merit' (1854) 40, 50
Scot, Major A.J.L. (Scott) 117
Seagrim, Hugh Paul 177–8
  awarded DSO 178
  awarded GC 177
Second Anglo-Afghan War (1878–
    80) 93, 112
  Battle of Kandahar (1880) 96
  Battle of Killa Kazi (1879) 95–6
Second Anglo-Sikh War (1848–9) 87
  Battle of Gujrat (1849) 87
Second Opium War (1856–60) 66
Second World War (1939–45) 4,
    8, 124–5, 127, 159, 161, 177–8,
    180–1, 184, 206, 217, 225, 241
  Battle of El Alamein (1942) 208,
    211
  belligerents of 13, 162, 177
  Bergen-Belsen concentration
    camp 166
  Blitz, The (1940–1) 159–60, 164,
    183
  casualties of 191, 241–2

Colditz Prison 208
  Dachau concentration camp 171
  Dambuster Raid (1943) 203
  DCMs awarded for actions during
    211
  Dieppe Raid (1942) 165, 219
  Dunkirk Evacuation (1940) 172,
    192
  Hero of the Soviet Union
    awarded for actions during 182
  Normandy Landings (D-Day/
    Operation Neptune)(1944) 192
  Operation Source (1943) 199
  Pacific Theatre 212
  Ravensbrück concentration camp
    170, 174
  Resistance activity in 167
  service of women in 161–2, 182–3
  Tehran Conference (1943) 212
  VCs awarded for actions during
    13, 19, 171–5, 184–6, 191, 193–7,
    202–7, 212, 215, 219
Selborne, Lord
  Minister of Economic Warfare
    204
self-sacrifice 8, 12, 18
Seven Years' War (1756–63)
  Battle of Quebec (1759) 7
Sheean, Teddy
  case for retrospective awarding of
    VC 8–10
Sherwood DFC, Squadron Leader
  J.S.
  recommended for VC 205

Shout, Captain Alfred John
medals awarded to 17
Silver Stars 239
Simonds, Lieutenant General Guy
201, 211
directive on military honours and
awards (1943) 201–2, 207, 209
GOC of 2nd Canadian Infantry
Division 200
Simpson, Lieutenant 152
Simpson, Warrant Officer Ray
awarded DCM 230
recommended for VC (1967) 230
Sinclair, Sir Archibald
Secretary of State for Air 169
Singapore 162
Skene, Lieutenant Colonel Charles
151–2
Smith, F. E. 117
Smith-Dorrien, General Sir Horace
14
Smyth, John
President of VC Association 21
Sotheby's
VCs sold at 18
South Africa 104, 107, 113, 135
Bloemfontein 112
Cape Town 111
Colenso 104
Estcourt 104–5
Ladysmith 104
Natal 99, 102
Pretoria 113
South African War (Second Anglo-

Boer War) (1899–1902) 103,
108–9, 111, 113–14, 132, 198
Battle of Colenso (1899) 108, 110,
184
Battle of Spion Kop (1900) 111
Black Week (1899) 108
casualties of 109–10
VCs awarded for actions during
142–3, 184, 245
South Georgia 236
Southborough, Lord 146
Soviet Union (USSR) 16, 182
Red Army 182
Special Honours Committee 234
Special Operations Executive (SOE)
163, 169–70, 172, 175
arguments over eligibility of
personnel for VC receipt 7,
169–72
F Section 165–6, 171, 174
service of women in 163–7, 183
Spectator 224
Spence, Private Edward
posthumous awarding of VC 75–6
Stalin, Josef 212
Stamfordham, Lord
Private Secretary to George V 145
Stanlack, Private William
awarded VC 34
Stannus, Lieutenant General Henry
James 87–9, 98, 223
criticisms of VC 86–7, 90–1, 93–4,
97–8
Curiosities of the Victoria Cross 93

My Reasons for Leaving the British Army 89
Stewart, Donald 88
St Helier, Lady Mary 117
Stirling, Major 70
Stokes, Kerry 17
Sudan 66
Sun, The 242
Sunday Pictorial 205
Swanton, Warrant Officer 228
Swift, Jonathan
    Gulliver's Travels 247
Switzerland 156
Sydenham, Lord 129
Sylvester, Henry Thomas 27
    awarded VC 25–6
Szabo, Violette
    campaign for posthumous
      awarding of VC to 170–2, 175,
      183
    death of 176
    posthumous awarding of GC 170,
      176–7
    service in SOE 170, 175–6

Taliban 25, 232
Taylor, Edward 20
Taylor, Elizabeth
    family of 35
Taylor, John 33
    death of 35
    family of 35
Tenko (TV Series) 163
Territorial Army 130–1

Thangal 151–2, 154
Thatcher, Margaret 234–5
Third Anglo-Burmese War (1885)
    96
Third Reich (1933–45) 11, 171, 173,
    186
    Abwehr 174
    Gestapo 162, 165, 167, 174–5
    Luftwaffe 159
    Schutzstaffel (SS) 167, 192
    Waffen-SS
      Liebstandarte Adolf Hitler
      regiment 192
Thomas, Lance-Corporal Justin
    awarded CGC 220–1
Thompson, Private Alexander 75
Thomson, Lieutenant Colonel
    Robert
    Commander of 2nd Rifles Battle
      Group 233
Tikendrajit 151–2, 154
Times, The 20, 32–3, 45, 50, 52–3, 56,
    60, 63, 72, 77, 84, 111, 114, 120,
    153–4, 157, 208, 212
Tinsley's Magazine 61
Toomey, T.E.
    Victoria Cross and How Won (1889)
    97–8
Trant, Lieutenant General Sir
    Richard
    Land Deputy Commander in
      Falklands 235
Trenchard, Air Marshal Sir Hugh
    118, 147

Trinity College, Dublin 95
Tulloch, Colonel Alex 51
Tunisia
   Tunis 209
Turkey 48, 166
Turner, Margot
   death of (1993) 162
   media depictions of 163
   military career of 162–3

United Kingdom (UK) 3, 233
   Air Ministry 144
   Colonial Office 141
   Foreign Office 171, 227
   government of 124
   Lanarkshire
      Hamilton 18
   London 19–20, 31, 48, 51–2, 80–1,
      86, 95, 113, 117, 120, 127, 130,
      150, 155, 166–7, 172, 174, 183,
      212, 227, 229
   military budget of 185
   Ministry of Defence (MoD) 182,
      220–2, 227, 229–31, 243
      Examination of the Standards of
      Australian Citations for the Award of
      the Victoria Cross 15
      Women in the Armed Forces (2002)
      181
   Northern Ireland 19
      Belfast 139
   Office of Public Information 118
   Parliament 56–7, 69, 128
      House of Commons 22–3,
         39–40, 50–1, 58, 80, 109, 153,
         169, 186, 189
      House of Lords 40, 42, 48, 129
   Poor Law 51
   Royal Military Academy
      Sandhurst 78, 103, 177
   Secret Intelligence Service (SIS/
      MI6) 161
   Southampton 203
   Treasury 20–1, 50, 174
   War Office 4, 35, 51, 68–70, 74,
      81–2, 84, 95–6, 112–13, 118, 127,
      129, 140–1, 156, 181, 225
   Westminster Abbey
      Tomb of the Unknown Soldier
      124
   Whitehall 10, 29, 86, 180
United States of America (USA) 180
   Air Force (USAF) 238–9
      use of drone technology 239–40
   Arlington Cemetery
      Tomb of the Unknown Soldier
      124, 183
   Central Intelligence Agency (CIA)
      166
   Civil War (1861–5) 16
   Office of Strategic Services (OSS)
      166
   service of women in military of
      180
Upham, Captain Charles
   awarded bar for VC 207–8
   awarded second VC (1942) 208
Urmson, J.O. 222

Vause, Stephen 179
VC Association
  personnel of 21
VC Register 34
  names removed from 17
Vichy France (1940–4) 166
Victoria, Queen xvii, 9, 14–15, 24,
    32–4, 36, 44–6, 49, 52, 57, 64–5,
    67, 69, 73, 96, 111–13, 134, 216,
    244
  accession of (1837) 57
  death of (1901) 66, 96, 113
  family of 36, 38, 58–9
Victoria Cross (VC) xiv–xvii, 3–4, 7,
    9–11, 14–15, 20–2, 26, 29–30,
    32–9, 41, 43, 46, 56, 62–5, 67–9,
    71–3, 75–6, 78, 80–3, 97–8,
    103, 106–8, 116, 119–21, 123–5,
    128–30, 132–3, 135–7, 140–4,
    146–9, 156–7, 160, 168–9, 172,
    178–9, 185–8, 191–2, 194–7,
    200–7, 212–14, 217–19, 224, 229,
    231–4, 240, 242–4
  bars 70–1, 134, 137–8, 146, 198,
    204, 207
  citations for 10, 28
  criticisms of 85–6, 90–4, 97–8,
    111, 196
  duplicate 17, 19
  eligibility standards 15, 17–18,
    21–4, 35, 84, 94, 103, 114–15,
    189, 207, 209, 215–17, 221–2,
    225, 232–3, 235–8
  control over 69–70

  extensions (1858) 81
  inconsistencies in 25–8, 82, 91–2
  establishment of/warrant issued
    (1856) 5, 9–10, 16, 46, 59, 66,
    68, 84, 91, 94, 102–3, 113, 126,
    140–1, 158, 181, 189, 217, 245
  development of 40–4, 59–61, 113,
    146
  revised warrant (1920) 146, 158,
    163, 185, 190
  revised warrant (1961) 186,
    215–16, 221–3, 226, 245
  first investiture (1857) 64–5
  for Australia 8–9
  holders of xiii
  issues regarding awarding of to
    women 168–9, 172, 178–9
  monetary value of 17–19
  pensions associated with 39–40
  posthumous awarding of 5–6,
    15–16, 75–6, 101–2, 112, 128–30,
    138–9, 166, 183, 188–9, 215, 227,
    234–5, 245
  pre-gazetting 109
  quota systems for 191–3, 224–6,
    245
  retrospective 6, 8
  social view of 60–2
  terms for awarding of xiv–xv, 8,
    14–15
Vietnam War (1955–75)
  belligerents of 15, 226, 228
  DCMs awarded for actions
    during 230

VCs awarded for actions during
227, 229–30

Wake, Nancy
death of (2011) 167–8
service in SOE 167
Walsh, Private Andrew 82
application for awarding of VC
81–2
Walters, Sergeant George
awarded VC 34
War of the Austrian Succession
(1740–8)
Battle of Dettingen (1743) 7
Warburton-Lee, Captain Bernard
awarded VC 185–6
death of 186
Ward, Dame Irene 169–70, 178
lobbying activity of 170–2, 175, 183
objection to awarding of GC to
Odette Samson 173
Warren, Lieutenant General Sir
Charles 111
Wellington, Duke of (Arthur
Wellesley) 55, 58, 92
Wheatley, Warrant Officer Kevin
posthumous awarding of VC
227–9
Whitmore, Lieutenant General Sir
Edmund Augustus 96
Military Secretary 95
Wilkinson, John 23
Wilson, Major General Archdale 72
Wilson, Woodrow 185

Windsor Castle
Royal Archives 44
Witherington, Pearl 166–7
Wolseley, General Sir Garnet 102
Wood, Lieutenant Henry Evelyn 101,
106
awarded VC 73
women 149–50, 161–3, 165–9
awarding of Croix de Guerre to
167
awarding of DFC to 179
awarding of DSC to 166
awarding of GCM 180
awarding of GM to 168
awarding of MC to 25–6, 180
awarding of MM to 158
issues regarding awarding of VC
to 168–9, 172, 178–9
military service of 149, 155, 180–2
service in SOE 163–7, 183
Wotherspoon, Lieutenant Colonel
G. D. 211

'X', Lieutenant Colonel 225, 230,
233–4, 236–7

Yeo-Thomas, Wing Commander
Forest 177
citation for GC (1946) 171
Yugoslavia
NATO bombing of (1999) 239

Zululand 101
Zulus 99, 132

About the Author

Gary Mead was a journalist for the *Financial Times* for ten years and has worked for the BBC and Granada TV. He is the author of *The Doughboys: America and the First World War* (2000) and *The Good Soldier* (2007).